OXFORD IN INDIA READINGS
Debates in Indian History and Society

GENERAL EDITORS
- Sabyasachi Bhattacharya
- B.D. Chattopadhyaya
- Richard M. Eaton

India and the World Economy
1850–1950

Contents

General Editors' Preface

The DEBATES IN INDIAN HISTORY AND SOCIETY series is an exploration in the discourse of history to focus upon the diversity of interpretations. The series is intended to address widely debated issues in South Asian history (including contemporary history) through volumes edited by experts in the concerned area of study. The editor of each such volume is asked by the General Editors to select writings by various scholars focusing upon a debated theme and to write an introductory essay. The approach encourages the interrogation of history, as distinct from the common tendency to present history as a collection of 'given' facts. It brings to the reader the research base upon which scholars have founded their interpretative framework. And it opens up to the students bridge-heads into the terrain of research.

This volume, the second in the series, reflects the agenda outlined above. Dr G. Balachandran, in editing this collection of essays, evidently bore in mind the objective of focusing upon the diversity of interpretations—and the implicit debate on the ideological premises of interpretations—in the literature on India's historical role in the global economy from the mid-nineteenth century. In order to sharpen the focus on the issues debated, the editor has fore-grounded the 'revisionist' critique that developed in recent times in response to the Nationalist economists' paradigm. This discursive strategy has opened up many questions which merit attention. Did Dadabhai Naoroji

and R. C. Dutt's emphasis on Indo-British economic relations, to
the exclusion of India's commercial links with Asia and Africa
and other parts of the world, engender a lopsided appreciation
of this country's global trade relationships? How does the pattern
of colonial India's external account liabilities, including the 'drain
theory' of the nationalists, look like in the light of the scrutiny of
recent day economic historians? What were the implications of
colonial India's external liability translated into domestic liabilities
for the country's population and did that promote an 'internal
drain', i.e. transfer of incomes from the peasant households to
the trading intermediaries, from the rural hinterland to the
colonial metropolises? Given the priority accorded by the colonial
government to the discharge of India's external account
obligations, have the revisionist critics of the nationalist thesis
underestimated the importance of India's subordinate political
position and exclusion from participation in policy making? These
and other questions posed in this volume invite new research
and at the same time the book offers a summing up of the
present state of historical knowledge in an area of study which
is beginning to receive a lot of attention in this 'era of
globalization.'

Tables and Figures

Figures

1

Introduction

G. Balachandran

For a subject that was so central to the formative impulses of its economic nationalism, India's historical engagement with the international economy has attracted relatively little scholarly attention in the last few decades. Several reasons may be held to account for this neglect: the canonical status of the 'nationalist economists' who wrote on the subject, in particular Dadabhai Naoroji and R. C. Dutt; the tightening of India's external economic controls since the 1950s; and the complicit evolution of disciplinary regimes in both mainstream economics and history. Thanks to this neglect, what passes for 'common sense' about India's recent past as a trading and commercial nation is based on highly reductionist and ahistorical readings (absorbed mainly through text-books produced by the National and State Councils of Educational Research and Training) of Naoroji and Dutt.

This common sense, oddly though it may sit with some current fashions, is not intrinsically 'wrong' (or 'right'). It is nevertheless instructive to tease its principal constitutive elements out into the open and widen the perspectives with which to address them. India's early economic nationalists possessed an extensive awareness of the wider world as it was forming around them in the closing decades of the nineteenth century. But their sights were unwaveringly trained on the British Empire and on India's imperial economic relationships. Whether this was merely a discursive strategy or reflected the influence of contemporary liberal economic and political beliefs in Britain must remain a matter of debate. Yet it is essential to note the resulting neglect of the wider web of the colony's external relationships in favour of a bilateral framework that focussed attention on economic relations with a late-Victorian Britain likewise disengaged from its evolving commercial and financial links with the rest of the world.

India's economic links with the rest of Asia and Africa received only cursory attention in this framework which also oversimplified the significance of economic and financial links with its principal colony for the international trading and financial system that Britain sought to shape and preside. Restoring India to regional and international networks of flows of goods, services, capital, labour, and entrepreneurship is essential for at least four reasons: to enrich our understanding of the international economy of the period; to better understand India's multiple locations and balancing roles in the world economy; to recuperate the agency of traders, bankers, and other entrepreneurs, and workers from the subcontinent in the making of this economy; and not least, to belatedly complement in meaningful ways the pioneering insights of its economic nationalists about India's historical role in the world economy.

India as a Colonial Economy

India, in the parlance of neo-classical economics, was a small, open economy during the period of its history with which this volume is concerned. India was 'small' in the sense that its external trade accounted for a small proportion (about 2 to 3 per cent) of total world trade. It was, as such, a 'price-taker', that is, demand and supply conditions in India had little influence over the international price level, both overall and in respect of most of the goods that comprised its trading-basket. It was open in the sense that except during short periods (briefly during World War I, at the height of the Depression in 1931, and during World War II) there were no controls over its external transactions on the current and capital accounts.

However, in contrast to most colonial and underdeveloped economies of the period, foreign trade accounted for a relatively small proportion (15–17 per cent) of India's estimated national income.[1] Besides, its exports, though comprising mainly of raw materials and agricultural products, were also rather more diversified.

Nevertheless its external sector had a disproportionately large influence on the Indian economy and the livelihoods of its people. Even if they did not necessarily represent it in these terms, until the late 1910s India was imagined as a 'small, open economy' by successive generations of economic officials.[2] Doing so predisposed Indian policy-makers to adopt a passive macro-economic stance even with respect to such targets as prices (of which the colonial state compiled aggregative series that were beginning to be used, among others, by emerging nationalist groups to fashion their 'technology' of resistance) and pro-cyclical behaviour that intensified the impact of external influences on the Indian economy.[3] Although peacetime experiments in macroeconomic management are of later origin, few non-industrial countries in the nineteenth and twentieth centuries pursued their commitment to preserving an open economy (including allowing destabilizing short-term capital movements to take place without let or hindrance) and discharging external obligations with the same tenacity and consistency as colonial India. This, more than the intrinsic exposure of its economy to foreign trade, explains why India was always a passive victim of trade and economic shocks originating overseas.

It is useful at this stage to separate our discussion of two aspects of this tenacious openness—short-term capital movements and the discharge of *current* account obligations. The latter has attracted a certain amount of attention in the context of discussions of the 'drain', and we will return to this subject shortly. But the importance of the former has been less well recognized even when it has not been conflated or confounded with the latter.

The principal component of short-term capital movements to (and from) India was banking or trading capital. This consisted primarily of the funds that flowed to India to finance trade during each busy season (running roughly from October to April) when interest rates tended to rise, and returned to London at the end of the season. In addition, asset and liquidity management decisions by European-owned and managed banks that mobilized deposits in India and kept a large portion of them as reserves in London might also lead to substantial movements of short-term funds. Though short-term seasonal inflows helped finance trade, they also accentuated India's economic and institutional weaknesses and its vulnerability to external pressures in several directions. These included the persistent under-development of the Indian banking system and promoting the centralization of Indian banking resources in London. While the latter helped better London's position as an international financial centre, both factors reinforced India's dependence on overseas short-term capital and exchange banks to finance trade. These flows, needless to stress, were extremely sensitive to global trading conditions and helped transit them directly to the Indian producer.[4] India's dependence on London-based banks for financing trade also disabled it from imposing controls on destabilizing short-term capital *outflows* because of the risk of endangering *future inflows*.

Finally, the effects of variations in these flows were not confined to the Indian producer of exportables. It remains an open question whether and how far exchange banks' pre-emption of trade financing, which was the safest yet most profitable segment of banking in India, discouraged the development of commercial banking by raising the overall risk-profile of commercial banks' assets.[5] But in the virtual absence of commercial banking, India's monetary system comprised almost wholly of currency and coin until the 1920s. Even this underdeveloped monetary system was virtually inelastic in that currency expansion was determined by the inflow of funds to finance trade.[6] Consequently, trading shocks that affected the quantum (or direction) of short-term capital inflows immediately exerted a severe monetary and macroeconomic impact on the colony.

The second aspect of India's openness was its tenacious discharge of external current account obligations. There are two issues here, viz. the 'quality' of these obligations and the effects on the economy of servicing them. In assessing the latter we may distinguish between secular (or long-term) effects and short-term effects (including the aggravated effects of the transfer in the presence of economic or financial instability). Besides, since tracing these effects also involves establishing the mediating processes, it may be useful to speculate on the impact of the transfer process, overall, on the institutional features of the colonial Indian economy.

The quality of colonial India's external current account liabilities has been the subject of passionate debate. The views of economic nationalists such as Dadabhai Naoroji and R. C. Dutt on the subject are well-known, and representative reflections on these views are included (or excerpted) in this volume.

It is useful, however, to bear in mind here that assessments of the quality of these obligations can often turn on their context, as the examples below illustrate:

- According to a widely-shared consensus, the military 'services' Britain charged to India were excessive and unjustified. But Davis and Huttenback argue on the basis of a comparative counterfactual analysis that even here India did not quite pay its way.[7]

- Whether Indian payments to Britain for insurance and shipping services should be reckoned as part of the 'drain' can be debated. Though damaging to sovereignty, dependence on a single power for such services may be justified on efficiency grounds. On the other hand, as is well known, British shipping and insurance firms colluded to fix freight and premiums. British shipping firms also followed discriminating pricing and initiated aggressive price wars to deter competition. Besides, though India's development experience of the last five decades might suggest otherwise, given some time horizon it may not be impossible, in principle, to reconcile sovereignty with efficiency.

- The notorious railway guarantees would have appeared less offensive, and not peculiarly colonial, to a student who first came across them in the early 1990s (when the Indian government offered extravagant sovereign guarantees and counter-guarantees on rates of return to attract foreign investments into power and infrastructure projects or in the spring of 2001 when some of these guarantees came back to haunt the government) than to someone in the 1970s when India was a closed economy with little exposure to foreign direct investment or international capital markets.

- Naoroji and Dutt believed the employment of European civil servants and professionals represented a 'moral and material drain' from India. On the other hand, for Alfred Marshall, the liberal economist, the drain ran in the other direction as Britain sacrificed its best and brightest young men for lifelong service in a distant colony:

  > Nations do not make presents to one another. They . . . borrow and . . . lend, and the dislocations between . . . exports and . . . imports, which are continually attracting attention, seem to me to be all due either to a change in the relations of borrowing and lending or to a change in the character of the services and goods rendered. For instance we export to India every year a great number of prime young men. If their value were capitalized, as it would be if they were slaves, it would be several thousands of pounds apiece. We bring them back afterwards, if they come back at all, more or less shrivelled and worn out. Those are vast unreckoned exports. India complains that she sends us a tribute of goods for which we have given no return. We have given a return for many of them in the shape of men in the prime of life, who, on the whole, I think are very cheap for the purpose.[8]

- Finally, present-day liberal or 'Little Englander' critics of Britain's nineteenth century imperial project (such as Patrick O'Brien) argue, in contrast to nationalist Indian critics of the same project, that the Empire was a loss-making proposition for the metropolitan country.[9]

The relativity inherent in any assessment of the quality of current account obligations underlines the critical importance of the principle of sovereignty (and its denial) in judgements about colonial India's transfers of current incomes to Britain. This point was not lost among others on Naoroji who told the Herschell Committee that though Brazil (an independent country) and Australia (a self-governing dominion) paid 'large sums to foreigners' every year, these obligations had their 'people's consent'. India, by contrast, was 'helpless and voiceless in all burdens put upon her'.[10]

The processes by which India's current account transfers impinged on the domestic economy have not been investigated in equal detail outside the rather neglected literature on 'forced commercialization'. It seems apparent, *a priori*, that annual transfers of the order of 1 to 2 per cent of estimated national income (or some 15–25 per cent of estimated domestic capital formation) could not have taken place year after year without exerting a depressing effect on growth.[11] Of equal significance is the manner in which these transfers were effected. The economic literature on unilateral transfers identifies two mechanisms, operating via terms of trade and incomes. To put the matter rather starkly, as a country's external liability translates into a domestic liability for its population, the latter has to sell (that is, export) more of what it produces or consumes/invests a smaller proportion of income in order to meet the liability. The former mechanism depresses export prices and the terms of trade, while the latter depresses incomes and growth to finance the external transfer.

If we assume India was a small country in the sense explained above, we may rule out the former mechanism operating to depress the *world* prices of Indian exports. We may conjecture, therefore, that India's overseas transfers were financed through income adjustments. On the other hand, domestic markets probably worked less well than world markets during this period, so that it is not unlikely that the compulsion on Indian economic agents (let us for the present assume these were peasant households facing fixed revenue obligations that were the domestic counterpart of India's external obligations) to sell their output (to traders) to finance their obligations would have depressed the prices they received for it. Given parametric world prices (and a fixed exchange rate), this would have meant a transfer of incomes from peasant households to traders and other market intermediaries.[12] The resulting 'internal drain', as R. C. Dutt was among the first to emphasize, too would have had a depressive effect on domestic incomes and consumption by more than the actual extent of the initial transfer.

We may complicate this story by introducing non-peasant households in India—let us say wage-workers in agriculture whose services are the (internationally) non-traded good, and who consume the exportable good, the latter in this case being the food sold by peasant households (their employers) and exported by trading companies. In this situation, while wages (being the price of the non-traded good) may be expected to fall relative to that of the traded good (food) and workers would experience a decline in real incomes, the distribution overall of the economic impact of the fiscal burden between traders, peasants, and wage-workers would also depend on the relative imperfections of the two (that is, food and labour) markets.[13] We may further complicate these scenarios by distinguishing between various kinds of revenue settlements, tenurial and institutional relations in agriculture, competition in the market for manufactures, etc. These and similar scenarios, featuring more realistic institutional features, form the staple of the literature on 'forced commercialization' in the presence of what was essentially a regressive tax regime.[14]

It may be plausibly argued that this tax regime, the economic and social structure (characterized by a thick layering of rentier intermediaries) that arose due to the colonial state's overriding concern to collect revenues cheaply and 'efficiently', the distributional consequences thereof (of which the greater intensity of famines was an indicator), and the demand and supply conditions flowing therefrom distorted the structure of incentives in the economy, and thus depressed the secular rate and pattern of investment and the rate and quality of economic growth.[15]

These hypotheses await investigation. We must consider, in addition, the effect on the economy and its institutions of the priority accorded by colonial authorities to the discharge of India's current account obligations.

India's external current account obligations were no more or less inflexible, in principle, than the current account obligations of other non-industrial countries, many of which defaulted, some repeatedly, on their overseas loans and lived to borrow another day.[16] But several factors—notably (a) Britain's fear of the contagion effects of an Indian default and its determination to ensure that 'debtors' fulfilled their 'contracts'; (b) the colony's subordinate political position; and (c) the exclusion of representative Indians from policy-making, especially in the sphere of 'high finance' which was dominated by London institutions such as the Bank of England, the Treasury, and the India Office, and by expatriate officials of the Government of India accountable to London—converged to ensure that India's ability to meet external obligations became the most important goal of public policy in the colony and the sole test of its economic health.[17]

Depressive enough when international trade, prices, and incomes, and Indian agricultural output were buoyant, the priority accorded to servicing external obligations could greatly accentuate the impact on incomes and consumption in India of a shock affecting its trade. Consider as an example of such a shock an exogenous decline in the world price of the Indian exportable good. This would mean, other things remaining the same, India having to export more to finance a given sterling liability and the Indian producer having to sell a larger proportion of output to meet the corresponding tax obligation. This may force the producer to depress (often essential) consumption, or in more severe instances such as during the inter-war Depression when there were large distress sales of gold from rural India, compel him to liquidate accumulated savings from the past.[18] With public revenues also suffering in the slump, the presence of fixed external obligations dictated pro-cyclical policies, such as cuts in other expenditures and tax increases, that intensified the impact of the original shock.[19]

Our discussion of the domestic economic impact of India's external obligations has so far proceeded without any reference to the monetary and banking systems through which these 'real' internal and external transfer processes were mediated. From the early 1860s, when something like a uniform currency system had been brought into existence in British India, official currency and banking policy was strongly motivated towards financing Indian trade and the transfers referred to above.

Although local marketing networks stayed largely in place, by the latter half of the nineteenth century the business of moving India's produce to overseas markets had passed into the hands of European trading houses.[20] At various times, depending on the availability of these media and the relative profitability of employing them, trading houses and their bankers moved funds to India in the form of either precious metal (gold and silver) or through the 'council bills' mechanism, which is discussed in greater detail below.

The ascendancy of these trading houses and the banks that financed them was by no means natural or predestined, and the processes by which it came about remain to be studied. It is also likely to have had wide-ranging consequences for the structure of production and the trading orientation of the Indian economy. While these remain mostly unresearched, our ignorance of the regional aspects of the subcontinent's trade after about the middle of the nineteenth century remains profound. Be that as it may, let us merely note here that Indian bankers were closely involved in financing the East India Company and that they and Indian traders were active in the China trade and cultivated extensive business links with East Africa, the Persian Gulf, Persia and Central Asia, and South-east Asia. But their relatively decentralized operations were not amenable to control and regulation by a colonial state interested not merely in ensuring the financing of Indian exports (and the creation of the export surplus, which Indian bankers could be relied upon to do), but also in ensuring that the surplus was smoothly remitted to London to settle India's obligations there.[21]

It is not easy to generalize about the changes in the structure of production and trading orientation referred to above, once we move beyond the Gangetic delta. There are well-known dangers, besides, in attributing the entirety of these changes to the impact of colonialism. But it seems plausible that at least in some sectors of agricultural production, colonialism and commercialization, and consequently changes in cropping patterns, came together.[22] Likewise, not all new trade with Europe represented diversion, whether of goods from traditional markets or of the resources employed in producing them. There were well developed local, regional, and Asian trade networks in the middle of the nineteenth century;[23] and as P. Harnetty, K. Specker, and K. Sugihara, among others, have argued, these networks received a stimulus in the closing decades of the nineteenth century from several unfolding processes in India and South-east Asia that may be separable in principle from colonial efforts to restructure external trade.[24] On the other hand, it seems quite plausible to hypothesize that the changes associated with greater colonial penetration of the Indian economy, in particular the institution of the colonial fiscal apparatus and the newer mediatory regimes in trade and banking referred to above, not to mention railways which were 'proverbially' believed to 'make trade', may have compelled retrenchment in some sectors of the Indian economy and the redirection of their resources towards production for Western markets.[25] (These factors would also have affected the patterns of specialization, trade, and production of regions which had earlier had a relatively more autonomous trading orientation, and subordinated their economies to those of the major ports trading with the industrial West.)

As discussed below, an important development during the last quarter of the nineteenth century was the depreciation of silver, and with that, of the rupee and other Asian currencies. This may have had a direct positive effect on growth in this region. Some expansion in regional trade would have also taken place alongside and as a result of this growth. Besides, currency depreciation would have encouraged import substitution locally within India and in the regional economy of silver-using Asia, of products that were earlier imported from Europe. This, too, would have boosted regional trade and growth.[26] Changes in relative prices due to currency depreciation would have also increased the 'profitability' of producing for European markets relative to that of producing 'non-traded' goods. One may classify under this influence at least some part of the acreage shifts from 'coarse' cereals, that were typically consumed locally, to 'finer' cereals such as wheat which India began to export in the closing decades of the nineteenth century.[27]

It also remains moot whether trade with industrializing Europe was intrinsically more dynamic than that with traditional spheres of Indian external commerce, or whether the latter's relative eclipse was aided by the newer institutional developments in international trade and finance that were spreading to Asia under colonial auspices. However, what is clear is that the entry of newer intermediaries led to a 'duality' in the market for credit, with one market looking out towards trading houses and the London-based banks financing them, and the other towards smaller traders and 'traditional' bankers specializing in financing domestic trade, overland trade to Persia and Central Asia, and some part of India's seaborne trade, mainly with Ceylon, South-east Asia, the Persian Gulf, and East Africa. We are accustomed to regarding indigenous bankers financing local and regional trade as niche players mainly because the bulk of their activities lay outside the official line of vision which focussed almost wholly, at least until the 1931 Banking Enquiry Committee, on institutions and transactions that could most reliably secure the imperial financial interest in India. Yet this market was by far the larger of the two.[28] However, it was populated by a large number of relatively small operators, with low overheads and community-based networks of information, credit appraisal, and remittance, far more adept at developing new markets and businesses than at resisting the predatory entry into these markets, after these had become sufficiently well established, of large, well-funded exchange banks backed directly or indirectly by the colonial authorities.[29]

How this dual market would have evolved, had it been left to itself, must again remain a subject for speculation. As it happened, however, the colonial authorities struck a decisive blow against indigenous banking by closing India's mints to free coinage of silver in 1893 and establishing a gold exchange standard (c. 1900) in which sales of Council Bills to an exclusive group of London-based exchange banks, rather than free movements of metal, increasingly provided the resources for monetary expansion.[30] These measures signalled a further measure of centralization, now of resources for *monetary* expansion whose availability became inflexibly tied to the Council Bills mechanism and, in turn, to monetary conditions in London.[31] Indigenous bankers could no longer augment their resources by importing silver for coinage and were forced now to seek avenues of growth through accommodation with European-owned and operated banks in India for whom many of them became intermediaries.[32] It would be surprising, indeed, if these processes had not led to a measure of disintermediation in the financial sector of the Indian economy and thus to reduced efficiency in the use of its financial resources.

Although Presidency Banks (and after 1920 the Imperial Bank) helped promote commercial banking in colonial India to some extent, these European-owned and run institutions were largely confined to the major ports and urban centres and operated at some remove from the *bazaar*. In the words of one scholar, 'joint-stock banks remained a thin veneer on the credit structure'.[33] The emergence of modern, indigenously-owned and managed banks was also a slow process, made all the more uncertain by British bankers' fear of competition, the prejudice of colonial officials, and the tendency of the early Indian commercial banks to indulge in speculation.[34] Besides, the expansion of the banking system, which became more noticeable from the 1930s, was entirely demand-driven.[35]

As pointed out above, it is impossible to say for certain whether and to what extent the quality of its external current account obligations would have been superior had India been a sovereign country rather than a colony. But as our discussion thus far suggests, it may plausibly be argued that the colonial relationship was an important factor in creating a dependent and distorted financial system in India and in promoting public policies that privileged the discharge of these obligations and the freedom of capital movements over other functions and priorities.

Bringing the World Back into the Empire

India's colonial relationship with Britain was undoubtedly a major determinant of the principal structural and institutional features of its economy. But important as this bilateral relationship was, it represented only one aspect of colonial India's engagement with the world economy. On the other hand, if Britain comprised India's world for historians of the colony's trade and finance, recent historians of the international economy before World War II and Britain's external economic relations during this period have tended to shut the Empire out of their conceptions of Britain's world.[36]

By bringing new methods and perspectives to bear on historical analysis, historians of the modern world economy have undoubtedly helped enhance our understanding of the functioning of the world economy, and indirectly also of imperial economic arrangements. But at a gratuitously high price: because historians of the Empire prefer assuming simple textbook versions of the world economy to exploring its construction, they often end up reproducing accounts of an elegant past of the world economy that derive from the perspectives, concerns, and methods of international economic history and reinforce the foundations of the underlying models better than they reflect the actual, and very messy, diversity of historical evidence and experiences.

It is almost a starting premise of international economic historians that Victorian Britain's greater or lesser pre-eminence in the world economy was an obvious result of the levels of its economic and institutional efficiency. This premise has tended to blind scholars to the political and social processes, both at home and overseas, that enabled Britain to play a leading role in the emerging world economy, the relatively brief duration of its ascendancy, the inherent fragility of the British position in the face of growing domestic opposition and external challenge to its international role, and the trials Britain endured domestically and externally (including *vis-à-vis* its imperial possessions) to achieve or preserve it.[37] Although far less justified even on the face of it, and despite the Empire's evident importance to the restorationist agenda Britain pursued in the inter-war period, modern historians have also fought shy of integrating the Empire into studies of Britain's external relationships during this period. They prefer instead to posit an artificial conflict between a policy that advocated closer ties with the Empire and one that counselled disengagement from the latter to pursue a more 'international' role, and to argue a resolution of the conflict that, depending on whether one is talking about the 1920s, the Depression years, or the post-war era, always involved sacrificing one or the other.[38]

There were undoubtedly differences of opinion in inter-war Britain over whether the Empire should be the 'site' upon which to craft the recovery of the metropolitan economy, or whether it should merely be an instrument for the greater purpose of restoring Britain's former pre-eminence. (Those who pressed the latter course put into circulation, sometimes for strategic reasons but often because they knew little better, images and descriptions of Britain's effortless pre-eminence in the past, that continue to shape modern readings of the nineteenth century world economy and Britain's role within it.[39]) But such differences were not peculiar to inter-war Britain. They also cropped up with unfailing regularity in the last quarter of the nineteenth century and in the 1900s, not to mention during the First World War, and reflected the seeming contradiction between Britain's reality as a great imperial power and its self-image as a champion of free trade and a liberal world economy.[40] In practice, imperialism and liberal internationalism were not mutually exclusive strategies but fluid, rhetorical positions broadly reflecting interests as well, across which compromises were possible, and indeed necessary, to sustain Britain's ambiguous role in the world. There is no basis, in particular, for the suspicions of imperial ideologues that British internationalists sought to turn their backs on India and the Empire—for instance Montagu Norman, governor of the Bank of England and the high priest of inter-war British financial internationalism, was at least as concerned about India as he was about cementing ties with the United States—and suggestions to the contrary largely reflect readings through reified categories of a past evoked by post-war British debates over its future in Europe and the role of the sterling.[41]

Interpreting imperialism and liberal internationalism as rival, even if not exclusive, strategies blinds us to the many synergies that bound Britain's imperial and international economic interests and arrangements together well beyond the decolonization process that set in after World War II.[42] Exceptionally, historians have explored intra-imperial relationships between Britain and two or more constituent parts of the Empire. Some interesting insights have also been developed about how these intra-imperial relationships, underwritten by bank and shipping and insurance companies, subserved broader imperial interests.[43] But relatively little effort has gone into mapping imperial relationships on to Britain's global economic and financial relationships and investigating the extent to which the two sets of relationships drew strength from each other.

Consider, for instance, the gold standard which is widely regarded as the centrepiece of *liberal* international trade and payments arrangements as these emerged or functioned between 1870 and 1940. The association between the gold standard and the liberal world economy is debatable.[44] Be that as it may, the gold standard is important for our purposes because it is functionally inseparable from the multilateral payments system, of which India as S. B. Saul underlined four decades ago was the key protagonist because its surpluses with the rest of the world helped Britain offset its deficits with this region and run a current account surplus that it could use to lend abroad, and the regime of (short-term) capital flows that came into existence in the last quarter of the nineteenth century and operated with reasonable efficiency until World War I.[45]

Besides, sterling's stability and role in the pre-war gold standard centred on London was also due, in other respects too, to Britain's ability to draw upon the resources of India and the rest of its Empire. The gold standard and the multilateral trading system functioned fitfully between the wars. Britain itself emerged from the war with its economy in tatters, yet harbouring ambitions of global financial leadership it was no longer equipped to undertake on its own, and which its preferred partner, the United States, was mostly loathe to indulge. With both its domestic and external economic policies generating intense controversy and conflict at home, Britain utilized its control (albeit declining, since 'self-governing' dominions such as Australia and South Africa began to pursue more independent policies) over the Empire's resources to reconcile its global ambitions with a darker domestic reality dominated by severe unemployment and price disequilibrium.

After its hopes of reconstructing the pre-war world economic order had to be abandoned in the late 1920s, Britain began to consolidate imperial economic arrangements, among other reasons in order to (a) promote its own recovery, (b) prevent constituent parts of the Empire from breaking away to pursue economic policies that ignored London's financial interests, (c) strengthen its own position for the eventuality of trade and financial conflicts intensifying as a result of the Depression, and (d) keep in functioning order a sub-global economic arrangement under its control to give itself a major say in any future efforts to restore global multilateral trade.

Therefore, not only are simple associations between liberal trading arrangements and the gold standard quickly belied by the latter's functioning, especially from the early years of the twentieth century, they also ignore the complex arrangements involving finance and power that sustained the pre-war gold standard and Britain's international *financial* position in a greater measure than was warranted by its declining *economic* leadership in the world economy. Though these arrangements became more transparent (and less effective) in the inter-war period as conflicts between Britain's domestic and external objectives intensified, they had already been crafted into place towards the end of the nineteenth century to enable Britain to ride out domestic challenges to its international role and external challenges to the pre-eminence of its financial interests in the world economy.

This is not the place to attempt a comprehensive review of the Empire's contribution to Victorian Britain's pre-eminence in the international financial system of the period.[46] In what follows an attempt is made to locate India more centrally in the web of international economic and financial relations emanating from London from the latter part of the nineteenth century.

India, Empire, and the World

Though Britain largely stuck to the gold standard after 1717, even making a bruising return to it at the end of the Napoleonic wars, careful observers at mid-century might have regarded silver as the more probable basis of a future international monetary system. The gold standard's rather fortuitous career as a *global* system was inaugurated by the new German empire's move to adopt a gold currency in 1871. Thereafter, as silver prices began to tumble, many more countries abandoned it for gold in the next two decades.

The seductive appeal of the association between a liberal world economy and the gold standard conveys an air of inevitability about this movement. But as some recent research suggests, the world went on the gold standard rather unwillingly from the 1870s, at least partly for fear of the domestic effects of greater financial integration. Besides, we now know that far from abating, interest in silver and bimetallism received a fillip in the course of the long slump that the industrial West experienced in the mid-1880s. The resulting monetary controversies raised a fascinating array of political, economic, and social debates in several countries. These controversies and debates not only necessitated the staging of several international conferences relating to silver, their resolutions were also far more crucial to the subsequent course of Western capitalist development and the international economy than is often recognized. (Incidentally, American monetary controversies of this period gave birth to that memorable children's classic, Frank L.Baum's *The Wonderful Wizard of Oz*.)[47]

Of particular relevance to this essay, political and economic developments in the United States, Britain, India, and western Europe interacted with one another, with developments and policies in one country determining the range of possibilities and alliances, as well as the relative bargaining strengths of their constituents, in others. Apart from being too narrowly focussed to capture the contingent processes that unfolded especially in the 1880s and 1890s, research on silver-related monetary controversies has generally concentrated on countries with a major direct interest in the metal (such as the United States) on the assumption that Britain escaped these late nineteenth-century controversies because of its long association with the gold standard. But as some other studies have shown, the bimetallic campaign gained rapid strength from the 1880s even in Britain in the background of its economic slump and Indian currency problems, and if allowed to grow unchecked, was feared capable of undermining the pound sterling's link with the yellow metal. Financial opinion in the City of London was by no means unanimous on the superiority of gold. But supporters of the gold standard represented the more influential segment of this opinion, and they feared grievous damage to their interests, both directly and indirectly if sterling's position was thereby undermined, of either a switch to silver or the adoption of a bimetallic standard.[48]

India's late nineteenth-century currency problems are discussed in some of the essays in this volume. It is sufficient to note here that thanks to falling silver prices, the Indian rupee fell steadily through the 1870s and 1880s. Its value was also affected by the India Office financing the Indian government's annual liabilities in London through large sales of council bills (that is, increased supply of rupees). As the two effects fed on each other, India became a sink for the world's silver and the virtual buyer of last resort of the falling metal. The depreciating rupee benefited Indian manufacturers and exporters, but hurt Lancashire cotton manufacturers, English wheat farmers, and English civil servants in India. Currency depreciation also caused serious budgetary problems for the Indian government because it pushed up the rupee cost of servicing its external obligations.

In 1893 the Indian government decided to end the free coinage of silver and thus sever the rupee's link with the white metal. This, and the US government's suspension of silver purchases under the Sherman Act, intensified the slide in silver prices and caused English manufacturers to fear losing other markets in the east. For the next four years, the future of Indian currency became a handy lever in the hands of British campaigners for a bimetallic standard, who hoped thereby to restore the international competitiveness of Britain's declining industries.

Broadly speaking, two views were in vigorous contention in Britain on this question. The demand to stabilize the price of silver through an international bimetallic agreement came, as noted above, from industrial and agricultural interests facing increasing competitive pressure in domestic and overseas markets. On the other hand, financial, banking, and other rentier interests, citing the sanctity of existing contracts and threats to London's international financial role, opposed changing existing currency arrangements.[49] This debate raged for several years in the press and Parliament, and was ventilated through Royal Commissions investigating industrial and agricultural conditions (1886 and 1894) and by the Gold and Silver Commission (1888).[50] By 1895 the campaign for a bimetallic sterling had become so powerful that British supporters of the gold standard set up a Gold Standard Defence Association to combat it. They also stepped up their advocacy of a gold standard for India, less because they were convinced of the intrinsic advantages of the system for the colony and more in the knowledge that it would cripple the bimetallist cause in Britain.[51]

Thus as late as the 1890s the gold standard was not a foregone conclusion even in Britain, let alone elsewhere. Against this background, India's adoption of the gold standard not only held important implications for the colony, it also represented a pivotal moment for Britain's political economy. In particular, this decisive blow against bimetallism forced agricultural and industrial interests to advocate a more defensive and divisive policy, viz. protection, that effectively forced the working class out of the producers' coalition in Britain, and advanced the City's efforts to sponsor the financial integration of the world economy and cement London's primacy as an international financial market.

Plans for an Indian gold standard failed to make headway in the 1880s because world gold output, which had fallen from 7 to 5 million fine ounces in the preceding three decades, was thought to be inadequate to support gold currency in a large country well known for its appetite for precious metals. World gold output rose threefold after 1885 to reach nearly 16 million ounces by 1899 and, together with the United States' emergence as an exporter of capital, fuelled fears of global inflation. Not only did an Indian gold standard begin to appear more affordable, it might also now offer a possible defence against the dangers of global inflation.[52] But almost immediately after India was put on a gold standard, confidence in Britain's financial future suffered a sharp setback as a result of the South African war.

In the lively debate that has raged on the causes of this war, Hobsbawm's view that 'whatever the ideology, the motive for the Boer War was gold' represents something of a consensus.[53] But the South African war was a financial disaster for Britain in the near term—it led to higher public expenditure and public debt, created acute monetary stringency, stimulated external borrowing for the first time since the Seven Years' War, and in Kathleen Burk's view, inaugurated and foreshadowed the eventual shift of financial power from Britain to the United States.[54] As trade suffered, Britain's current account surplus halved from £55.5 million to about £28 million between the first and second halves of the 1890s. Under these conditions, as de Cecco's essay in this volume argues, an Indian gold standard was a luxury Britain could not afford. Plans to open a gold mint in India were indefinitely postponed and the colony's gold standard reserve was transferred to London and used to steady the prices of British government stock. By the end of 1902, all but £0.25 million of a total gold standard reserve of £3.75 million was held in the form of sterling securities.[55]

The South African war was the first of several shocks that the international financial system suffered before World War I, and although world trade and capital flows expanded rapidly, the decade preceding the war saw a 'frenzied quest for gold' that reflected both a process of 'monetary rearmament' and the ongoing restructuring of international trading relations.[56] The latter trend was more remorseless and enduring, and is usefully illustrated by the rise in official US gold stocks from about £140 million in 1899 to more than £290 million eleven years later.[57] Since London was the world's principal gold market and the Bank of England the reserve buyer and seller of the metal in the system, this early scramble for gold inevitably affected monetary conditions in London, intensified its dependence on timely gold flows from smaller centres to ease short-term strains, and caused uncertainty for British trade and industry whose representatives also began to protest the frequent use of the London bank rate to attract short-term capital from abroad. Thanks to these conjunctural and structural features of the pre-1914 world economy, Britain was greatly hampered in its ability, whether alone or together with the other major financial centres, to regulate the functioning of the international monetary system.

The recent setbacks suffered by supporters of imperialism and protection did not signal the end of the Empire as a feature of practical policy in Britain in the early 1900s, since liberal internationalists within the British financial establishment had always been aware of the Empire's potential as a vehicle for furthering their global aspirations.[58] As Britain's international economic and financial position grew less assured and began to threaten greater domestic costs, they became increasingly attracted to the advantages of forging closer financial and monetary links with the colonies. Through a combination of financing, shipping, insurance, and banking arrangements, not to mention political pressure, Britain had already ensured that South Africa and Australia marketed their gold in London and were tied to the pound sterling. The time had now arrived to draw India firmly into this matrix.

As a key protagonist of the multilateral payments system centred on London, India's allegiance was critical to Britain's position in the international financial system. As India's trade surplus tripled on the back of expanding world trade, from about £19 million in 1897–8 to £57 million on the eve of the war, Britain found it necessary to finance this surplus without allowing a corresponding increase in gold outflows to the colony. This was mainly achieved through the council bills mechanism that substituted sterling remittances for gold shipments to finance Indian trade.[59] Apart from the direct effect of higher inflows or lower outflows of gold, council bill operations helped steady interest rates in London further because their proceeds were immediately lent by the Secretary of State to City finance houses, or placed at the Bank of England. With its surpluses also being invested in British government securities, India emerged within a few years of the South African war as the largest official holder of these securities, accounting in 1913 for nearly a third of total official holdings of sterling paper. These loans and investments, as many contemporaries acknowledged, eased monetary conditions in London and helped stabilize the market for both sterling and British government securities.[60] Moreover, with India so closely tied to the London market, the greater responsiveness of Indian (and other colonial) funds to movements in the London bank rate also made the latter a more effective instrument than it might have been otherwise.[61]

Britain's desire to centralize gold stocks and thwart flows to India also affected its currency policies in other parts of the Empire. For instance, the currency system of the Straits Settlements was reorganized in 1908 and its gold reserves moved to London from Singapore in order to make them less susceptible to pressures from the Indian gold market.[62]

Regulating India's demand for gold assumed even greater importance for Britain during the inter-war period because of its daunting domestic and external economic crises. The overvalued sterling's hopes of a stable return to the gold standard at a time of high domestic unemployment (and social tension) depended on an expansionary world economy promoted by greater US overseas lending. But Indian gold demand, which tended to rise in a boom and moderate it, was feared to come in the way. Therefore Britain intensified earlier efforts to reduce the use of gold in the colony's monetary system.[63] Secondly, it strove to regulate India's counter-cyclical role in the world economy, that is, thwart the colony's absorption of gold during the expansionary years of the inter-war period. And when India began to export the yellow metal on a large scale in the depressed 1930s, policy focussed upon encouraging gold exports. These exports enabled India to run a current account surplus, discharge a part of its foreign debt, and lend abroad. Given the conditions of the world economy and Britain's external liquidity position, Indian gold exports functioned as a critical counter-cyclical variable during the Depression, and contemporaries welcomed them as a powerful expansionary influence globally and on the British economy.[64]

The neglect of the Empire and of India's wider locations in the international economy in the six or seven decades preceding World War II have helped promote a Eurocentric history of the world economy in which its central institutions, such as the gold standard, are believed to have emerged spontaneously to meet the needs of the contemporary world economy. Disregard for India's wider financial role in this economy and Britain's inter-war efforts to regulate it have also helped perpetuate the neglect of a crucial aspect of metropolitan efforts at domestic and global financial reconstruction. These efforts have largely been discussed in relation to domestic conflicts, inter-war monetary reform proposals, Eastern and Central European stabilization, and financial relations with the United States.[65] There is some recognition, too, of Britain's keenness to retain South Africa and Australia's financial allegiance to London and to the pound sterling.[66] But the only effect this literature seems to have had on historians of British India has been to confirm the belief that its control over India conferred no economic or financial benefits to an inter-war Britain that, as a result, largely focussed its energies outside the Empire. Consequently, India's involuntary role in advancing Britain's efforts to regain its financial pre-eminence, and its contribution to the stability and functioning of the world economy and its recovery in the Depression, evoke little or no discussion in their histories.[67] Restoring India and the Empire to the intricate web of relations that constituted the nineteenth- and early twentieth-century international economy is thus essential not only for its own sake, but also to achieve a more rounded understanding of this economy as well as of modern colonialism.

Other Globalisms: Labour and Enterprise

Modern international economic history is almost wholly concerned with the worldwide movement of goods and factors, and with the global economic and financial structures that were made and unmade by these flows or which facilitated (sometimes hindered) them. As remarked upon earlier, these structures are also assumed to develop spontaneously in response to economic opportunity. In turn, they conveyed information and generated incentives that rational economic agents exploited for their own and greater gains.

This may be a useful approximation of the real world for the purposes of certain types of economic theories. But it is flawed on at least five counts as a serviceable framework for understanding the past. First, as already noted above in the context of the gold standard, in focussing on structure it says little about how this structure came into being. Second, it makes most forms of successful human agency predictable, unexceptional, and trivial. Third, it is not interested in 'failed' actions (which are defined residually and in some respects arbitrarily) except when the scale of failure matches the global scale on which 'success' is judged, and encourages the exclusion of large swathes of economic activity that do not fit into dominant historical conceptions of the making of the modern world economy. (Thus almost the only 'global' migrations international economic historians are interested in are European migrations to America.) Fourth, it therefore creates a distinct and distantiated *haute* sphere of international economic activity to which other rungs of economic activity either do not relate, or do so passively. Lastly, as a result, it ignores or oversimplifies the links between the international economic system and regional and local economic and social processes, and reinforces the distance separating international economic history from regional or local economic and social histories.

Consider in this light certain aspects of India's participation in the nineteenth-century world economy that are rarely regarded in that light, for example, the movement of labour and entrepreneurship from India to other parts of the world, near and distant. The quantitative impact of these movements for the world economy may not have been significant in the aggregate as the latter is conventionally understood and estimated, but these movements were nevertheless extremely important for individual regions and sectors of this economy.

It is well known that India emerged as an important exporter of labour in the nineteenth century. It was an important source of indentured workers for the plantation economies of the Caribbean, Indian Ocean and Pacific islands, and South and South-east Asia, and for the building of railways, mainly in Africa. In addition, relatively small groups of workers, especially from the Punjab and the north-west, migrated at various times to work on farms in Australia, Canada, Latin America, and the United States.

Relatively little is known about the latter movements.[68] We have, however, a better awareness of the role and importance of Indian plantation workers, and many aspects of their recruitment, transport, deployment, and disciplining.[69] There is also an intriguing possibility, foreshadowed in some studies but which still awaits detailed investigation, that these movements formed part of a global and distantiated accumulation process in which the demand for labour arising from the growth of a capitalist economy in one part of the globe was met by the growth of wage labour in another part, half a world or more away.[70] The migration of workers on indenture was as important, and to those who suffered it, as wrenching (in some cases liberating) an experience as 'deindustrialization' for the artisan. It was also perhaps more crucial than we suppose in creating the broad patterns of nineteenth century specialization that are generally assumed to be the product of historically given differences in 'factor endowments' between various regions of the world economy. Hopefully, the current interest in Indian diaspora studies will extend to researching the role of these subaltern agents in the creation of the nineteenth century world economy.

Though indentured labour is the best known instance of Indian workers migrating to the frontiers of an emerging capitalist world economy, of equal significance was the employment of Indian workers in international merchant shipping. Already a well-established presence on East India Company and other vessels by the late-eighteenth century, their employment rose steadily in the latter part of the nineteenth century after the large-scale adoption of steam. Wages of Indian maritime workers were about a fifth to a quarter of British wages. Unlike British seamen they were not yet unionized nor as prone, despite low wages and long hours of work, to the demoralization that reportedly drove British sailors to drunkenness and insubordination. The number of Indian workers employed on international merchant vessels grew rapidly from the 1880s[71] This was particularly true of British shipping which employed 24,000 'lascars and other Asiatic seamen' (who represented some 10 per cent of all those employed on British vessels) in 1891 and 52,000 (17.5 per cent) in 1914.[72] By 1937 Indian workers accounted for a quarter of the employment on British vessels, and this proportion remained largely unchanged in 1952.[73]

These numbers refer to a point in time. However, since Indian seamen entered into short-term agreements and spent considerable amounts of time on land between voyages, the above figures represent only a fraction of the total number of ocean-going seamen in India. Besides a majority employed on British merchant vessels, Indian seamen were also a substantial presence in German, Italian, American, and Norwegian shipping. According to one estimate, India's maritime labour force numbered 235,000 in 1935.[74] But even this estimate excludes the vastly larger labour force employed on tens of thousands of 'coasting' and sea-going 'native' vessels that bustled around the region's sea-lanes, carrying freight and passengers between various Asian and African ports in the Indian Ocean. What is clear, nevertheless, is that seafaring in international waters was an important occupation in the subcontinent, not only in the coastal regions of Bengal and western India whence the vast majority of crews came, but also in the Punjab and the north-western provinces which rather unexpectedly sent out thousands of men to work below decks as engine room crews on international vessels.

Reference was made above to Indian Ocean trade. It seems clear, as Sugihara's essay cited earlier suggests, that certain economic links within maritime Asia were re-articulated rather than replaced by the pressures and opportunities created by the expansion of the world economy in the nineteenth century. These processes led to a considerable export of entrepreneurship from India. (Even in the maritime context it was often not clear where entrepreneurship ended and wage-labour began because many participants owned a share of the vessels on which they worked and had a right to a corresponding share of the profits.)

The role played by Nattukottai Chettiar bankers in the economies of South-east Asia was referred to above, and is well known. The expansion of the trading world of Sindhi merchants against the backdrop of the nineteenth century world economy has also been the subject of a recent study by Claude Markovits. It is clear from these accounts that while the nineteenth century integration of regional economies into a putative world economy weakened or displaced some agents, such as most famously the bankers to the East India Company in Bengal, smaller agents from less exposed centres were less adversely affected. Some of them even discovered new market niches and business openings in the interstices between the local and the global economies that afforded them the possibility of starting a new business or expanding or diversifying an existing one. Thus, for example, in Markovits's account of Sindhi traders, the expansion of British power in Asia enabled Shikaripuri bankers to expand their trading and money-lending activities into Central Asia, while the growth of maritime transport and tourism opened new avenues for traders from Hyderabad who, in a matter of decades, established trading emporia and networks that girded the globe from Kobe to Panama.[75]

It is easy to lose sight of these and other participants because they are normally relegated to the margins of grand narratives about international economic integration. But in ignoring them we turn a blind eye to an important part of the processes by which this integration was experienced or executed in several regions and spheres of the world economy. Not to mention the risk of obscuring our historical understanding of contemporary phenomena such as the migration and settlement of overseas South Asian working class, entrepreneurial, and professional communities in several parts of the world.

Issues and Debates

In reading rather like a survey of the issues, more than of the literature, and a conspectus for future research on India's regional and continental economic relations during the colonial period, this essay reflects the current state of historical research in this area. Such being the case we can only rue our failure so far, with some exceptions, to meaningfully assimilate insights and perspectives from the research reported in recent years in such areas as domestic and inter-regional trade, agriculture, banking, money and currency, and labour, to their wider context of an open economy. The external sector of the Indian economy remains as a result, to all intents and purposes, a historical black box, our knowledge of which is limited by the fading light still filtering through apertures made a century or more ago.

We may identify three such apertures, two of them only a small distance apart, that reveal three broad aspects of India's relations with the nineteenth and twentieth century world economy. The first is, of course, the so-called 'drain'. K. N. Chaudhuri's polemical, and self-consciously 'economistic' essay questions the very concept, whilst presenting a useful (partial euilibrium) survey of India's nineteenth-century external economy from a global, welfare-maximizing perspective that, given the imperial context, seems just as odd now as it musthave done in the 1960s. Though most visibly associated with the liberal Dadabhai Naoroji, the drain is in reality a hybrid concept deriving from a (not unjustified, yet contestable) mercantilist perception of the nineteenth century world economy. The resulting relativity is reflected in estimates of the drain that have formed an important focus of recent and earlier debates. Reproduced or excerpted in this volume are two broadly representative essays on the drain by John McLane and Sunanda Sen.

The second aspect featured here concerns India's experience as an open economy. Amiya Bagchi's paper discusses the structural impact on this colonial economy of its integration with an unstable late nineteenth-century world economy. Global economic instability also provides the setting for Omkar Goswami's essay as it attempts to uncover in close and fascinating detail the chronological and the deep and lasting structural impact of the Great Depression on a major constituent of this open economy, viz. the peasant jute economy (and society) of east and north Bengal.

B. R. Tomlinson's paper deals with India's currency crisis in the inter-war Depression. Though addressing a general crisis, his essay is structured by the bilateral imperial relationship about which its arguments and conclusions however raise rather large questions. By contrast, Marcello de Cecco's essay brings to the economic historiography of colonial India a perspective deriving from a wider and deeper understanding of the *world* economy, in particular its emerging financial architecture and interrelationships. It relates to the third aspect of nineteenth century India's external economic links with the world economy that greatly exercised contemporaries, viz. Britain's perceived 'manipulation' of the colony's currency. As de Cecco, shows, these arrangements were put in place from the 1890s to integrate India financially with the world economy whilst minimizing its capacity to destabilize Britain's external, especially short-term, finances. Thus the rationale for these arrangements was provided by Britain's *global*, rather than merely imperial, interests and projects. In a similar perspective, G. Balachandran's essay locates Indian policies and experiences during the Depression in the wider context of India's counter-cyclical role in the *world* economy and uncovers metropolitan efforts to regulate this role as a means of easing the severe economic and financial crises that Britain faced during the inter-war years. Reframing the problem in this manner helps shed an entirely new light on some familiar features of the Depression, such as for example, India's large exports of gold that have only been addressed bilaterally in the literature. It also draws attention to the possibility and importance of using sources and materials—for example, in this instance records of the US Treasury, State Department, and the Federal Reserve Bank of New York—that one does not normally associate with *imperial* or *colonial* economic and financial history.

Understanding the Empire thus demands keeping the wider world always in the picture. In ignoring this truism, modern economic historians of the Empire do a greater disservice to themselves than merely impoverishing their own research. More seriously, they encourage the disregard of the converse truism, that to understand our world and its making it is essential to also understand the making and working of modern empires. Keeping the latter truth in mind has never been more important than today, when it is fast becoming common for international economic historians, in particular, to regard the memories, histories, and legacies of modern empires as unprepossessing, if unfortunate and sometimes disconcerting, furrows in sands that have not been swept by the liberal tides of globalization.

Notes

1. K. N. Chaudhuri, 1982, 'Foreign Trade and Balance of Payments c. 1757–1947', in Dharma Kumar and Meghnad Desai, eds, *Cambridge Economic History of India*, vol. 2 (Cambridge: Cambridge University Press) (hereafter CEHI II), p. 804.

2. This reflected the influence upon officials of a kind of liberal economic theorizing that was still relatively recent (and not yet well-established) even in Britain, let alone elsewhere. See J. Maloney, 1985, *Marshall, Orthodoxy and the Professionalization of Economics* (Cambridge: Cambridge University Press).

3. The 1904–08 inflationary episode coincided with the early stirring of nationalist politics, notably in Bengal, and is discussed in S. Ambirajan, 1984, *Political Economy and Monetary Management: India, 1860–1914* (Madras: Affiliated East-West Press), pp. 166–7.

4. D. E. Moggridge and E. Johnson, eds, 1971, *The Collected Writings of John Maynard Keynes*, vol. 1, *Indian Currency and Finance* (London: Macmillan for the Royal Economic Society) (hereafter *JMK I*), pp. 151–6; on the vulnerability of these funds and of the Indian financial system generally to a crisis in London, see pp. 149–51.

5. *JMK I*, p. 147: 'Indian exchange banking is no business for speculative and enterprising outsiders, and the large profits which it earns are protected by established and not easily assailable advantages.'

6. Chaudhuri, 'Foreign Trade', p. 805; R. W. Goldsmith, 1983, *The Financial Development of India, 1860–1977* (Delhi: Oxford University Press), p. 9; A. G. Chandavarkar, 1982, 'Money and Credit, 1858–1947', in *CEHI II*, p. 774; *JMK I*, p. 40.

7. L. E. Davis and R. A. Huttenback, 1986, *Mammon and Pursuit of Empire: The Political Economy of British Imperialism, 1860–1912* (Cambridge: Cambridge University Press), pp. 160–2; for critiques, see Paul Kennedy, 1989, 'The Costs and Benefits of British Imperialism 1846–1914', *Past and Present* (no. 125), pp. 186–92; G. Balachandran, 1990, 'Imperialism: The Auditors' Report', *Indian Economic and Social History Review*, pp. 234–5, vol. 27, no. 2; A. Offer, 1993, 'The British Empire, 1870–1914: A Waste of Money?', *Economic History Review*, vol. 46, no. 2, pp. 222–36.

8. Indian Currency Committee (Fowler Committee), 1899, *Minutes of Evidence*, Part II, Cmd 9037 (London: HMSO [His/Her Majesty's Stationery Office]), q. 11818; note also that it was common until quite recently to refer to the outflow of educated professionals from India as a 'brain *drain*'.

9. Patrick O'Brien, 1988, 'Costs and Benefits of the Empire', *Past and Present*, no. 120, pp. 163–200. Strange alliances can fructify across these positions: one of O'Brien's arguments for why Britain would have continued to enjoy prosperous trade with India even without the Empire is derived from a nationalist view that the eighteenth century was not, as apologists for the Empire believed, a period of strife and decline in India but one

of dynamism and expansion. Citing Bipan Chandra, 1984, *Communalism in Modern India* (Delhi: Vikas), O'Brien also invokes the 'plausible and carefully researched antithesis' that 'Muslim separatism and violent communalism' were fostered by Britain's 'divide and rule policy', 1989, 'Reply', *Past and Present*, pp. 192–4. Nationalist historians deploy similar arguments to deny the integrative effect of colonial rule or to emphasize its retarding effect on the Indian economy while also stressing that Britain made money from the colony: see Balachandran, 1990, 'Imperialism', p. 235. For a less optimistic estimate of Britain's trading losses in the absence of the Empire, see M. Edelstein, 1981, 'Foreign Investment and Empire, 1860–1914', in D. N. McCloskey and R. Floud, eds, *The Economic History of Britain since 1700*, vol. 2 (Cambridge: Cambridge University Press).

10. Indian Currency Committee (Herschell Committee), 1983, *Minutes of Evidence*, Cmd 7060-II (London: HMSO) qq. 2346–53. Naoroji added that unlike Australia, India had also to pay for 'European directions and service'. Naoroji's argument privileging sovereignty should not surprise us, for he was a liberal who found India's lack of autonomy to take decisions on matters that affected its economic well-being more offensive than any loss of autonomy arising from its membership of an open international economy.

11. The precise extent of this loss would depend on the counterfactuals used, including the alternative political state assumed, its stability, government policy on transfers, trade, and other macro- and sectoral economic policies, access to the international capital market, etc. For an argument stressing the impact of these transfers on growth, see Utsa Patnaik, 1984, 'Transfer of Tribute and the Balance of Payments in the *CEHI*', *Social Scientist*, vol. 12, no. 139, pp. 49–55.

12. This is consistent with the point made by A. K. Bagchi's essay in this volume (Chapter 5) that movements in the external terms of trade may tell us nothing about producers' gains and losses from trade in the presence of domestic market imperfections. Note also that a rupee depreciation would have increased the rupee earnings of agents engaged in the export trade, but may not have translated into higher prices for producers if the domestic (export) product market was uncompetitive.

13. According to the Indian government's Director General of Statistics, J. E. O'Conor, in the 1880s and 1890s, even skilled

workers suffered a decline in real wages despite being in short supply in the major urban centres and particularly in Bombay— Fowler Committee, 1899, *Minutes of Evidence,* Part I, qq. 887–96.

14. See, for instance, Utsa Patnaik, 1999, *The Long Transition: Essays on Political Economy* (Delhi: Tulika), chs 8 and 10 and the references cited therein; for an application of this argument, see A. K. Bagchi's essay in this volume (Chapter 5).

15. Following Michael Adas, 1988, 'Market Demand versus Imperial Control: Colonial Contradictions and the Origins of Agrarian Protest in South and Southeast Asia', in E. Burke III, ed., *Global Crisis and Social Movements: Artisans, Peasants, Populists, and the World Economy* (Boulder, Co.: Western Press), pp. 89–116, one may dispute the revenue efficiency gains arising from employing intermediaries. But such gains may exist both when 'efficiency' is understood broadly as derivative of a social structure that yields up surpluses without resistance, as well as narrowly in relation to the cost of revenue collection.

16. Countries that defaulted in the 1930s, for instance, did better both in the Depression and over the next three decades than those that discharged their obligations punctiliously. See A. O'Connell, 1984, 'Argentina into the Depression: Problems of an Open Economy', in R. Thorp, ed., *Latin America in the 1930s: The Role of the Periphery in the World Crisis* (London: Macmillan); E. Jorgensen and J. S. Sachs, 1989, 'Default and Renegotiation of Latin American Foreign Bonds in the Interwar Period', in B. Eichengreen and P. H. Lindert, eds, *The International Debt Crisis in Historical Perspective* (Cambridge, Mass.: MIT Press), pp. 57–68. As studies of nineteenth century international financial markets show, defaults were also frequent and widespread in this period. See for example, C. Marichal, 1986, *A Century of Debt Crisis in Latin America: From Independence to the Great Depression* (Princeton: Princeton University Press).

17. This was so even in the inter-war Depression when many other non-industrial countries repudiated their external commitments to focus on domestic recovery. On Britain's economic priorities in Depression-hit India, see G. Balachandran, 'The Depression' in this volume (Chapter 9).

18. On gold sales in the Depression, see Balachandran, 'The Depression' in this volume (Chapter 9); according to a former Government of India official, David Barbour, gold ornaments

were melted down in India for export in the 1880s as well. See Fowler Committee, 1899, *Minutes of Evidence*, Part I, q. 1060.

19. For example, see D. Rothermund, 1981, 'The Great Depression and British Financial Policy in India, 1929–34', *Indian Economic and Social History Review*, vol. 18, no. 1, pp. 1–17. On the impact of this external shock on a peasant economy, see O. Goswami's essay in this volume (Chapter 6).

20. On the ascendancy of European trading houses and banks, see R. Ray, 1992, 'Introduction', in R. Ray, ed., *Entrepreneurship and Industry in India, 1800–1947* (Delhi: Oxford University Press), pp. 13–30; for a closely researched account of the markets of the Patna–Saran region of Bihar, see Anand Yang, 1998, *Bazaar India: Markets, Society, and the Colonial State in Gangetic Bihar* (Berkeley: University of California Press); the arrival of firms such as Ralli Brothers is discussed on p. 250. Also see Government of India, Indian Central Banking Enquiry Committee (hereafter CBEC), 1931, *Majority Report*, vol. 1, part 1 (Calcutta: Government of India, Department of State and Public Institutions), ch. 13 and pp. 319–20; and S. R. Ralli's answers to the Fowler Committee, 1899, *Minutes of Evidence*, Part I.

21. The majority report of the 1931 Banking Enquiry Committee blamed the 'downfall' of indigenous bankers on technological factors, but also noted that the East India Company promoted the development of 'credit institutions of the western type' to meet 'administrative requirements' and finance trade: CBEC, 1931, *Majority Report*, vol. 1, part 1, p. 14. This view was faithfully echoed by the 1971 Banking Commission's *Report of the Study Group on Indigenous Banking* (Bombay: Government of India, 1972), p. 13.

D. W. Rudner, 1995, *Caste and Capitalism in Colonial India: The Nattukottai Chettiars* (Delhi: Munshiram Manoharlal), p. 69 points out that the Chettiars' shift to South-east Asia was hastened by their displacement from the 'investment and exchange market throughout greater British India'. But the British occupation of East Africa opened new opportunities for Indian traders and money changers; likewise its post-World War I occupation of Iraq and other parts of West Asia. On East Africa, see R. M. Maxon, 1989, 'The Kenya Currency Crisis, 1919–21 and the Imperial Dilemma', *Journal of Imperial and Commonwealth History*, vol. 17, no. 3, pp. 323–48; W. Mwangi, 2001, 'Of coins and Conquest: The East African Currency Board, the Rupee Crisis, and the Problems of Colonisation in the East African Protectorate', *Comparative Studies in Society and History*, vol. 43, no. 4, pp. 763–87; and on West Asia, G. Balachandran, 1998, *The Reserve Bank of India, 1951–1967* (Delhi: Oxford University Press), pp. 628–9, 690–2.

22. Even if, as Michael Adas suggests, commercialization may have been a double-edged weapon that in the longer run also undermined colonial control and stimulated agrarian protest: 'Market Demand versus Imperial Control', pp. 108–10.

23. For an interesting but neglected mid-nineteenth century perspective on India's coastal and regional trade derived using shipping data, see A. C. Staples, 1970, 'Indian Maritime Transport in 1840', *Indian Economic and Social History Review*, vol. 7, no. 1, pp. 61–90.

24. P. Harnetty, 1991, 'Deindustrialization Revisited: The Handloom Weavers of the Central Provinces of India, c. 1800–1947', *Modern Asian Studies*, vol. 25, no. 3, pp. 455–510; K. Specker, 1989, 'Madras Handlooms in the Nineteenth Century', *Indian Economic and Social History Review*, vol. 26, no. 2, pp. 131–66; and K. Sugihara, 1986, 'Patterns of Asia's Integration into the World Economy, 1880–1913', in W. Fischer, R. M. McInnis and J. Schneider, eds, *The Emergence of the World Economy, 1500–1914* (Wiesbaden: Franz Steiner Verlag), pp. 714–21. Note that for Sugihara, Japanese industrialization seems to drive Asia's 'autonomous' growth.

25. 'It has, in fact, become proverbial now in India that "railways make trade"'—J. E. O'Conor's statement to the Fowler Committee, 1899, *Minutes of Evidence*, Part I, q. 1382.

26. On the effect of silver depreciation on Asian growth in the late nineteenth century, see J. B. Nugent, 1973, 'Exchange-Rate Movements and Economic Development in the Late Nineteenth Century', *Journal of Political Economy*, vol. 81, no. 5, pp. 1110–35; also Sugihara, 1986, 'Patterns of Asia's Integration', pp. 718–20.

27. The extent to which higher relative rupee prices for India's exportables translated into higher rupee incomes for their producers would have depended, as noted above, on how local markets operated. For instance, currency depreciation may change the relative prices facing producers by increasing exportables' prices, lowering those of non-traded goods, or both. Thus producers could be induced to grow exportables even if

monopsonistic traders held the latter's prices steady while managing to bid down prices of non-traded goods. Indian agricultural product market conditions have been debated in the context of commercialization. David Washbrook's arguments stressing monopsonistic market conditions in Madras Presidency have, for example, been challenged by Bruce Robert. See David Washbrook, 'Economic Development and Social Stratification in Rural Madras: The Dry Region 1878–1929', in Clive Dewey and A. G. Hopkins, eds, *The Imperial Impact: Studies in the Economic History of Africa and India* (London: Athlone Press for the Institute of Commonwealth Studies, 1978), pp. 68–82 and Bruce Robert, 1983, 'Economic Change and Agrarian Organization in "Dry" South India, 1890–1940', *Modern Asian Studies*, vol. 17, no. 1, pp. 59–78.

Alfred Marshall (Fowler Committee, 1899, *Minutes of Evidence*, Part II, qq. 11771–2) cited the greater volatility in the prices of jowar (a 'non-traded' good) than of tradeable goods to argue that trade (and presumably the depreciation of the rupee) had not led to a rise in domestic prices. While Marshall's argument may be valid in a static sense, the reported price variations may also have resulted from prolonged dislocations in production, marketing, and processing that often accompany major shifts in production and trade.

28. For instance, the all-India rural credit survey estimated in the early 1950s that over 90 per cent of the total lending to agriculture was 'non-institutional credit': Balachandran, 1998, *Reserve Bank of India*, p. 235.

29. Apart from L. C. Jain's classic study, other more recent accounts of indigenous trading and banking communities and their operations include Rudner, 1995, *Caste and Capitalism*, pp. 67–88; W. S. Weerasooria, 1973, *The Nattukottai Chettiar Merchant Bankers in Ceylon* (Dehiwala: Tisara Prakasakayo); T. A. Timberg, 1978, *The Marwaris: From Traders to Industrialists* (New Delhi: Vikas); R. Brown, 1994, *Capital and Entrepreneurship in South-East Asia* (London: Macmillan); C. Dobbin, 1996, *Asia's Entrepreneurial Minorities: Conjoint Communities in the Making of the World Economy, 1570–1940* (London: Curzon), chs 4, 5 and 6; and C. Markovits, 2000, *The Global World of Asian Merchants, 1750–1947: Traders of Sind from Bukhara to Panama* (Cambridge: Cambridge University Press). The exalted position occupied by exchange banks in the colonial economy was a source of bitter

resentment among Indian businessmen and bankers: CBEC, *Minority Report*, vol. 1, part 2, chs 11–15; and 1931, *Majority Report*, pp. 355–67. However, as Brown, Markovits, and Rudner point out, the immediate impact of the arrival of Western banks could be mixed, especially where indigenous bankers became their intermediaries.

30. On the currency impact on trade of the closure of mints in 1893, see Fowler Committee, 1899 *Minutes of Evidence*, Part I, S. R. Ralli's answers to qq. 6053–8, 6073–86, 6178–82, and 6233–46.

31. On the council bills mechanism and exchange banks' remittance operations, see *JMK I*, pp. 145–9.

32. See Weerasooria, 1973, *Nattukottai Chettiars*, ch. 2, for a detailed discussion of these bankers in the role of intermediaries for exchange banks.

33. A. K. Bagchi, 1985, 'Anglo-Indian Banking in British India: From the Paper Pound to the Gold Standard', in A. N. Porter and R. F. Holland, eds, *Money, Finance and Empire, 1790–1960* (London: Frank Cass), p. 98; more generally, pp. 98–101.

34. S. K. Muranjan, 1948, *Modern Banking in India* (second edition, Bombay: Kamla Publishing House), chs 6, 7, and 9; Chandavarkar, 1982, 'Money and Credit', pp. 779–82; CBEC, 1931, *Majority Report*, p. 312; also *JMK I*, pp. 156–9, 162–4.

35. Even the Imperial Bank, which was set up to help deepen India's financial sector, followed an expansion strategy based on responding to revealed demand rather than exploring and developing latent business potential. For some evidence of this attitude from the late-1940s, see Balachandran, 1998, *Reserve Bank of India*, pp. 322–3.

36. See, for example, Barry Eichengreen, 1992, *Golden Fetters: The Gold Standard and the Great Depression* (New York: Oxford University Press).

37. For a discussion of domestic opposition to Britain's international role before World War I, see P. J. Cain and A. G. Hopkins, 1993, *British Imperialism: Innovation and Expansion, 1688–1914* (London: Longman), ch. 7. There is an extensive literature on this for the inter-war years. In particular, see the essays by W. A. Brown Jr., L. J. Hume, and R. S. Sayers in S. S. Pollard, ed., 1970, *The Gold Standard and Employment Policies between the Wars* (London: Methuen); G. Ingham, 1984, *Capitalism Divided? The City and Industry in British Social Development* (London:

Macmillan); and R. W. D. Boyce, 1987, *British Capitalism at the Crossroads, 1919–1932: A Study in Politics, Economics and International Relations* (Cambridge: Cambridge University Press). For an interpretative survey, see P. J. Cain and A. G. Hopkins' 1993, *British Imperialism: Crisis and Deconstruction, 1914–1990* (London: Longman), pp. 49–58 and 69–70.

38. See Cain and Hopkins, 1993, *British Imperialism: Crisis and Deconstruction*, chs 2–5 for a critique.

39. A good example of this is the report of the Cunliffe Committee on the restoration of the gold standard after World War I. Walter Cunliffe was the wartime governor of the Bank of England. See the *Interim Report* (1918) and *Final Report* (1919) of the Committee on Currency and Foreign Exchanges after the War; also M. J. Flanders, 1990, *International Monetary Economics 1870–1960: Between the Classical and New Classical* (Cambridge: Cambridge University Press), p. 83; more generally see pp. 67–83. R. S. Sayers, 1976, *The Bank of England, 1891–1914*, vol. 1 (Cambridge: Cambridge University Press), pp. 110–11, suggests that the Committee's report was limited by the experience of its officials which was largely confined to the immediate pre-war period.

40. The paradox is perhaps less apparent in the late-nineteenth or early twentieth centuries than earlier because of the convulsions British liberals had meanwhile undergone over Ireland and the Empire.

41. On Norman's preoccupation with inter-war India, see G. Balachandran, 1996, *John Bullion's Empire: Britain's Gold Problem and India between the Wars* (London: Curzon), pp. 178–82, 200–211. On post-war British debates over sterling and decolonization, see G. Krozewski, 2001, *Money and the End of Empire: British International Economic Policy and the Colonies, 1947–58* (New York: Palgrave).

42. On the later period, see G. Krozewski, 1993, 'Sterling, the "Minor" Territories and the End of Formal Empire, 1939–1958', *Economic History Review*, vol. 46, no. 2, pp. 239–65, and on the earlier period, Balachandran, 1996, *John Bullion's Empire*, ch. 8.

43. For example, see Andrew Pope, 1993, 'The Imperial Matrix: Britain and the Australia-India Gold Trade, 1898–1919', Unpublished Ph.D. Thesis (Perth, W. A.: Curtin University); idem., 'Precious Metal Flows in the Indian Ocean in the Colonial Period: Australian Gold to India, 1866–1914', in John McGuire, Patrick Bertola, and Peter Reeves, eds, 2001, *Evolution of the World*

Economy, Precious Metals, and India (New Delhi: Oxford University Press), and idem., 1996, 'Australian Gold and the Finance of India's Exports during World War I: A Case Study of Imperial Control and Coordination', *Indian Economic and Social History Review*, vol. 33, no. 2, pp. 115–31. For a discussion of agreements between the Bank of England and British shipping companies concerning the movement of South African gold, see Russell Ally, 1994, *Gold and Empire: The Bank of England and South Africa's Gold Producers, 1886–1926* (Johannesburg: Witwatersrand University Press), p. 51; also W. A. Brown Jr., 1929, *England and the new Gold Standard* (New Haven: Yale University Press), pp. 39–40. There has also been some discussion of London's control over South African gold flows enhancing confidence in the pound sterling: see Eichengreen, 1992, *Golden Fetters*, pp. 42–8; J. J. Van-Helten, 1982, 'Empire and High Finance: South Africa and the International Gold Standard', *Journal of African History*, vol. 23, no. 4, 1982, pp. 529–48.

44. G. Balachandran, 2000, 'Power and Money in International Relations: The Gold Standard, 1890–1926', mimeo.

45. S. B. Saul, 1960, *Studies in British Overseas Trade, 1870–1914* (Liverpool: Liverpool University Press), pp. 56–63.

46. For a preliminary review, see Balachandran, 'Power and Money'.

47. For a recent account that emphasizes the spontaneous bandwagon effect of Germany's move to gold, see B. J. Eichengreen and H. James, 'Monetary and Financial Reforms in Two Eras of Globalization (and In Between)', in Michael D. Bordo, Alan Taylor, and Jeffrey G. Williamson, eds, *Globalization in Historical Perspective* (forthcoming). For a sample of the literature that discusses *The Wizard of Oz* as an allegory on contemporary monetary controversies in the US, see G. Ritter, 1997, *Goldbugs and Greenbacks: The Antimonopoly Tradition and the Politics of Finance in America, 1865–1896* (New York: Cambridge University Press), pp. 19–25 and 288–90.

48. E. H. H. Green, 1988, 'Rentiers vs Producers? The Political Economy of the Bimetallic Controversy', *English Historical Review*, vol. 103, no. 408, pp. 588–612.

49. Green, 1988, 'Rentiers vs Producers?'; the sharpness of these battle-lines has been debated: A. C. Howe, 1990, 'Bimetallism, c. 1880–1898: A Controversy Reopened' and Green, 'The Bimetallic Controversy', both in *English Historical Review*,

vol. 105, no. 415, pp. 387–8 and 676–7 respectively; also M. J. Daunton, 1989, 'Gentlemanly Capitalists and British Industry, 1820–1914', *Past and Present*, no. 122, pp. 132–42, 150–1; and M. J. Daunton, 1992, 'Financial Elites and British Society, 1880–1950', in Y. Cassis, ed., *Finance and Financiers in European History, 1880–1960* (Cambridge: Cambridge University Press), pp. 139–40.

50. P. L. Cottrell, 1992, 'Silver, Gold, and the International Monetary Order, 1851–1896' in S. N. Broadberry and N. F. R. Crafts, eds, *Britain in the World Economy, 1870–1939* (Cambridge: Cambridge University Press), pp. 234–9.

51. Green, 1988, 'Rentiers vs Producers', pp. 605–07.

52. For the Bank of England's figures of gold output, see Ally, 1994, *Gold and Empire*, app. I, p. 144; Sayers, 1976, *Bank of England*, vol. 1, p. 51.

53. Hobsbawm, 1987, *Age of Empire*, 1875–1914 (London: Weidenfeld and Nicolson), p. 66. This view goes back to J. A. Hobson, 1900, *The War in South Africa: Its Causes and Effects* (London: Nisbet). For some recent studies, see R. V. Turrell, 1987, '"Finance . . . the Governor of the Imperial Engine": Hobson and the Case of Rothschild and Rhodes', *City and Empire*, Institute of Commonwealth Studies, mimeo (London), vol. 2, pp. 87–90; S. Marks and S. Trapido, 1979, 'Lord Milner and the South African State', *History Workshop*, vol. 8, no. 1, pp. 50–80; Ally, 1994, *Gold and Empire*, pp. 25–8; I. Phimister, 1993, 'Unscrambling the Scramble for Southern Africa: The Jameson Raid and the South African War Revisited', *South African Historical Journal*, no. 28, pp. 203–30; and the survey in Cain and Hopkins, 1993, *British Imperialism: Innovation and Expansion*, pp. 376–81.

54. Kathleen Burk, 1992, 'Money and Power: The Shift from Great Britain to the United States', in Y. Cassis, ed., *Finance and Financiers in European History*, pp. 359–60; Cain and Hopkins, 1993, *British Imperialism: Innovation and Expansion*, p. 452; Sayers, 1976, *Bank of England*, vol. 1, pp. 51–2.

55. *Royal Commission on Indian Finance and Currency* (Chamberlain Commission) (Cd 7070, London), 1913, app. III, pp. 96–7.

56. M. de Cecco, 1974, *Money and Empire: The International Gold Standard, 1890–1914* (Oxford, Blackwell), p. 124.

57. Chamberlain Commission, 1913, *Interim Report*, app. XXX.

58. This may explain why the attitude of early twentieth century liberal economic theorists (such as Keynes) to the Empire's political status was marked by a rectitude better suited to an earlier era; see in this connection, U. B. Mehta, 1999, *Liberalism and Empire: India in British Liberal Thought* (Delhi: Oxford University Press), pp. 5–8; 67–8.

59. The Secretary of State for India sold council bills in London against sterling for redemption in rupees in India. At first this system was meant to save the Indian government the costs of shipping gold from India to meet its liabilities in London and was used only to a limited extent. But as Britain's external position deteriorated, council bill sales became a major means of financing the colony's trade and were used to displace gold shipments from London. From the early 1900s, other remittance instruments (called intermediates and telegraphic transfers) were also used, whenever required, to compete with gold shipments to India from Egypt and Australia. By centralizing in London gold stocks that would otherwise have flowed to India, this mechanism helped stabilize monetary conditions in Britain. India nevertheless remained a large importer of gold because the shortage of banking facilities and the instability of silver made it the preferred store of value, and markets were quicker than London officials to spot arbitrage opportunities. *JMK I* (pp. 72–87 and 145–9) remains the best exposition of the council bills mechanism.

60. P. H. Lindert, 1969, *Key Currencies and Gold, 1900–1930* (Princeton: Princeton University Press), pp. 18–22; L. S. Pressnell, 1981, 'Sterling System and Financial Crises before 1914', in C. P. Kindleberger and J. P. Lafargue, eds, 1981, *Financial Crises: Theory, History, and Policy* (Cambridge: Cambridge University Press). For a contemporary view, see *JMK XV*, pp. 89–90. For a more detailed analysis , see de Cecco's essay in this volume (Chapter 7).

61. For example, see the *Statist*, 14 June 1913; and the prominent London banker, Felix Schuster's evidence to the Chamberlain Commission. Also see *JMK XV: Activities, 1905–1914: India and Cambridge* (London), 1971, pp. 89–90.

62. W. E. Nelson, 1987, 'The Gold Standard in Mauritius and the Straits Settlements between 1850–1914', *Journal of Imperial and Commonwealth History*, vol. 16, no. 1, pp. 68–9. The effects of this reorganization on the region's trade with India has not been

investigated. In contrast, when Mauritius faced similar pressures in 1876, Britain encouraged the colony to demonetize sterling and join the rupee area because at this time, Britain felt secure about its own financial position (p. 53).

63. G. Balachandran, 1996, 'Gold, Silver, and India in Anglo-American Monetary Relations: 1925–1933', *International History Review*, vol. 18, no. 3, pp. 573–90.

64. See Balachandran's essay in this volume (Chapter 9); for a wider discussion, see Balachandran, 1996, *John Bullion's Empire*, chs 1–2 and 4–5.

65. Sayers, 1976, *Bank of England*, vol. 1, pp. 133–210; D. E. Moggridge, 1969, *The Return to Gold, 1925: The Formulation of Policy and its Critics* (Cambridge: Cambridge University Press), and Moggridge, 1982, 'The Gold Standard and National Financial Policies, 1913–39', in *CEHI* VIII; S. K. Howson, 1975, *Domestic Monetary Management in Britain, 1919–1939*(Cambridge: Cambridge University Press); R. H. Meyer, 1976, *Bankers' Diplomacy: Monetary Stabilization in the 1920s* (New York: Columbia University Press); S. V. O. Clarke, 1967, *Central Bank Cooperation, 1924–1931* (New York: Federal Reserve Bank of New York); S. V. O. Clarke, 1973, *The Reconstruction of the International Monetary System: The Attempts of 1922 and 1933* (Princeton: Princeton University Press); M. J. Hogan, 1977, *Informal Entente: The Private Structure of Cooperation in Anglo-American Economic Diplomacy, 1918–1928* (Columbia: University of Missouri Press); F. C. Costigliola, 1977, 'Anglo-American Financial Rivalry in the 1920s', *Journal of Economic History*, vol. 37, no. 4, pp. 911–34; A. Orde, 1990, *British Policy and European Reconstruction after the First World War* (New York: Cambridge University Press); D. P. Silverman, 1982, *Reconstructing Europe after the Great War* (Cambridge, Mass.: Harvard University Press); and Boyce, 1987, *British Capitalism*.

66. B. R. Dalgaard, 1981, *South Africa's Impact on Britain's Return to Gold, 1925* (New York: Arno Press); L. S. Pressnell, 1978, '1925: The Burden of the Sterling', *Economic History Review*, vol. 31, no. 1, pp. 67–88; and Ally, 1994, *Gold and Empire*.

67. For example, see B. R. Tomlinson, 1979, *The Political Economy of the Raj, 1914–1947: The Economics of Decolonization in India* (London: Macmillan); and J. Gallagher and A. Seal, 1981, 'Britain and India between the Wars', *Modern Asian Studies*, vol. 15, no. 3, pp. 387–414.

68. For example, see Vijay Prashad, 2000, *The Karma of Brown Folk* (Minneapolis: University of Minnesota Press), pp. 71–2. Australian and Canadian immigration restrictions were at least partly a response to fears of an influx from South Asia.

69. H. Tinker, 1974, *A New System of Slavery: The Export of Indian Labour Overseas, 1830–1920* (London: Oxford University Press for the Institute of Race Relations) remains an acknowledged classic. Also see M. Carter, 1992, *Servants, Sirdars, and Settlers: Indians in Mauritius, 1834–1947* (Delhi: Oxford University Press) and the essays on Indian indentured labour in the special number on 'Plantations, Proletarians, and Peasants in Colonial Asia' in the *Journal of Peasant Studies*, vol. 19, nos 3/4 (1992); for an accessible introduction to indentured labour migration to the Caribbean that also focusses on issues of identity, in regard to which there has been much recent research, see M. Kale, 1996, 'Projecting Identities: Empire and Indentured Labour Migration from India to Trinidad and British Guiana, 1836–1885', in P. van der Veer, ed., *Nation and Migration: The Politics of Space in the South Asian Diaspora* (Philadelphia: University of Philadelphia Press).

70. C. Bates and M. Carter, 1993, 'Tribal Migration in India and Beyond', in Gyan Prakash, ed., *The World of the Rural Labourer in Colonial India* (Delhi: Oxford University Press); for early discussions between Trinidad planters and Calcutta traders in the 1830s about the possibility of exporting indentured workers from India to the Caribbean to replace slave labour, see Kale, 1996, 'Projecting Identities'.

71. For a general account of the recruitment and employment of Indian maritime workers in international merchant shipping during the nineteenth and twentieth centuries, see G. Balachandran, 1997, 'Recruitment and Control of Indian Seamen, Calcutta, 1880–1935'. *International Journal of Maritime History*, vol. 9, no. 1, pp. 1–18.

72. C. Dixon, 1980, 'Lascars: The Forgotten Seamen', in R. Ommer and G. Panting, eds, *The Working Men who Got Wet* (St. Johns: Newfoundland Maritime History Group), p. 281. For an attempt to argue the location of North African seafarers in an 'Indian Ocean world economy', see J. J. Ewald, 2000, 'Crossers of the Sea: Slaves, Freedmen and other Migrants in the Northwestern Indian Ocean, c. 1750–1914', *American Historical Review*, vol. 105, no. 1, pp. 69–91.

73. *Daily Herald,* 24 May 1939; Ronald Hope, 1990, *A New History of British Shipping* (London: John Murray), pp. 383, 392.

74. Dinkar Desai, 1940, *Maritime Labour in India* (Bombay: Servants of India Society), p. 20.

75. C. Markovits, 2000, *The Global World of Indian Merchants, 1750–1947: Traders of Sind from Bukhara to Panama* (Cambridge: Cambridge University Press), ch. 6.

2

India's International Economy in the Nineteenth Century: A Historical Survey[*]

K. N. Chaudhuri

Introduction: Problems of General Approach and Methodology

This chapter stems from a dissatisfaction with the present state of historical writings on India's international economy in the nineteenth century. While the task of reducing the mass of literature available on the subject to a coherent and meaningful survey is a difficult and perhaps not very fruitful exercise, it is rather easier to understand why such writings on Indian economic history in general and trade history in particular have remained confused and often internally contradictory.

There are three fundamental reasons. In the first place, Indian historians have been excessively concerned with qualitative evidence as opposed to quantitative and empirical observation of data. Secondly, the selective method of presenting evidence, as implied by the above point, has been inspired by a corresponding preoccupation with welfare postulates in the place

[*] Previously published in *Modern Asian Studies,* II, 1 (1968), pp. 31–50. A version of this chapter was read at the xxvIIth International Congress of Orientalists, Ann Arbor, Michigan, in August 1967.

of a positive approach. Instead of asking how does the existence of a drain of wealth affect India's balance of payments and national income, Indian historians have traditionally inquired how does the drain impoverish the Indian people. Finally, the general reluctance to apply the tools of economic analysis in the study of India's economic history has inevitably resulted in a confusion of the main issues involved in matters of both interpretation and methodology. It is difficult to understand how otherwise respected historians in the field of Indian studies could have shown such a surprising degree of lack of understanding involving the simplest terminology of international trade theory.

Apart from this, the most serious methodological failure can be ascribed to the general readiness to accept the concept of a particular problem which has gained wide currency at the popular level and the tendency to work forward from a position so established without examining carefully whether such concepts have any real validity or relevance to the economy in question. An example of this can be found in the attitude adopted by the so-called nationalist historians towards the entire subject of India's foreign trade. This trade, it was vaguely felt, was nothing but an instrument in the hands of the imperial power for the economic exploitation of India and therefore intuitively considered to be harmful to the true interests of the nation. R. C. Dutt, for instance, dramatically stated that 'The richest country on earth stoops to levy this annual contribution from the poorest . . . . The contribution does not benefit British commerce and trade, while it drains the life-blood of India in a continuos flow'.[1] But even he realized that a country which derived a large proportion of its total national income from foreign trade was in a different position from the one which was not fundamentally dependent on exports and imports to maintain its standard of living.[2] However, Dutt chose not to draw the obvious conclusion: the necessity of estimating the role of foreign trade in India's national economy. Such an investigation might have led to the awkward conclusion that by the end of the nineteenth century, the total value of India's external trade was perhaps only a very small percentage of her total national income.

The importance of international trade to the economy of Britain was obviously a strong determinant of the attitude of the British economists towards trade; the Indian natioalist historians unconsciously absorbed this preoccupation, which provided them with a unique opportunity to build up a political case against British rule in India, without the trouble of inquiring first whether such an approach was really relevant to the Indian situation. Thus, a major weakness in our understanding of the part played by international trade in India's economy has stemmed from a neglect of the dynamic changes which occurred along the given functional relationships of this trade during the nineteenth century as a whole.

It was generally recognized that in the first three decades of the century, certain structural changes took place in India's international economy as a result of her political and commercial connection with Great Britain. But the usual tendency has been to treat these changes as once-for-all and then to proceed estimating their effects on India taking the whole of the nineteenth century as a homogeneous time period. It does not need much elaboration to point out that this type of static approach is likely to result in a seriously distorted view of the actual course of Indian economic development. The purpose of this chapter is to review briefly some of the established notions of India's nineteenth century external economy and suggest some possible alternative lines of investigation.

At the centre of all discussion regarding structural changes in India's overseas trade has been the controversy surrounding the famous theory of an economic drain from India. Almost equally important, but conducted at a lesser analytical depth, was the question associated with the effects of competitive imports on India's international specialization pattern. The third and final point that gave rise to much public debate in the closing years of the century concerned the effects of foreign trade on India's domestic economy operating through monetary factors and the price level. For the sake of convenience we shall take the second point first and then go on to a discussion of the drain theory and the currency controversy.

Competitive Imports

The contemporary views regarding the effects of the rising volume of imports in India's foreign trade covered practically all the major aspects of the theory of international trade. More specifically such discussions were concerned with (i) the pure theory, that is the question as to what factors determined the composition and volume of traded goods; (ii) commercial policy in terms of 'welfare' economics; and (iii) the wider question of the relationship between trade and domestic employment and income.

In order to understand the significance of the contemporary preoccupation with the problem, it is necessary to say a few words about the nature of India's foreign trade during the pre-British or pre-Industrial Revolution period. Traditionally, the main characteristic of trade between India and Europe was a one-way flow of goods. India exported much more than she imported leading to a corresponding reverse flow of treasure to correct the imbalance. There were complexities introduced through monetary fluctuations which led to bimetallic movements of treasure to and from India but such factors did not fundamentally change the general picture. The classical explanation of this unbalanced structure of trade was to emphasize the rigidity of consumer tastes with its assumption of very low price elasticity of demand which inhibited the growth of imported goods from Europe. It is conceivable, however, that the imbalance was due to a wide disparity in the structure of prices and the costs of production in Europe and Asia.[3] By the early nineteenth century, technological revolution in Britain, with sharply decreasing costs and rising productivity, had radically changed the potential relationship underlying the trade between India and Europe. The manufacturing industries in Europe were now in a position, for the first time in their history, to overcome the barrier imposed by the disparity in the levels of prices. The result could be seen in the rapid substitution of British cotton goods in the international market for India's export products followed by a rising flood of imports into India itself.

Between 1828 and 1840, for example, the value of cotton piece-goods exported from India fell by 48 per cent while the imports of cotton yarn and cotton goods increased by 80 and 55 per cent respectively.[4] The rate of expansion in imports which followed the opening of Indian trade to private European traders in 1814 proved much faster than the corresponding increase in exports from India.[5] Thus an increasing proportion of total export earnings was being currently spent on imports. Since Britain supplied between 65 and 70 per cent of the total value of imports, it is reasonable to conclude that manufactured goods came to play an increasingly dominant role in the composition of India's imports.

One must, however, note that although most of these were products of advanced industrial technology, some categories of imports—such as iron and steel and cotton yarn—had a different role from the finished consumer goods. The effect of these two imports would obviously be what is known as the import multiplier, or in other words they would serve as inputs to Indian domestic industries leading to some employment and income generation, assuming that the decreased cost of the inputs offsets the contracting effect of the substitution of foreign imports for the domestically-produced raw and semi-finished industrial material.[6] The imports of machinery, tools, and implements, in so far as they raised the efficiency of production, must also be distinguished from other goods. However, these were more complex aspects of the question to which contemporary observers paid little attention. Their main concern lay in gauging the effects of those imports which directly competed with Indian domestic products.

The crude view of the competitive effect of cheap imported textiles from Britain was that it led to the complete destruction of the Indian handloom weavers. The famous quotation given by Marx that the bones of the Indian weavers bleached the plains of India was only one example of the general run of sentiment. In 1840, for example, in the questions formulated by the Parliamentary Committee appointed to consider the trading relations between India and Britain, it was automatically assumed that the competitive position of the British cotton industry had led to a drastic reduction in the size of the Indian domestic industry. But opinion differed whether such an effect was good or bad. Charles Trevelyan and Montgomery Martin took the view that institutional rigidities such as caste and occupational structure had prevented the displaced handloom weavers from turning to alternative employment, while Andrew Sym stated that they were absorbed by agriculture.[7] John Crawfurd, in his sketch of the Indian economy in 1837, thought that the law of comparative costs justified India's increasing specialization in agricultural products.[8]

These reassuring appeals to theory did not entirely satisfy public conscience, and in the 1880s there was much public unease in India that the effect of a policy of partial free trade had been to restrict employment opportunities. Such views were reflected in the well-known observation of the Famine Commission of 1880 that one of the chief causes of poverty in India was to be found in the fact that agriculture formed almost the sole occupation of the mass of the population.[9] Modern writers have made much of the suggestion that the construction of railways in India in the second half of the century accentuated the decline of handicrafts by extending the market for imported goods and destroyed employment opportunities by economizing the use of labour.[10]

In the absence of detailed empirical studies, it is difficult to make precise statements about the effects of competitive imports. We may, however, distinguish two different types of problems posed by the increasing level of imports into India during the nineteenth century. One relates to the problem of aggregate effect and the other to the relative real wages earned by the various factors of production. Professor Kindleberger has put forward the general proposition that imports can stimulate or retard economic growth, depending on the capacity of a particular economy to transform itself and make the best use of its resources. In an underdeveloped economy, however, where the factors employed in import-competing industries already operate at a subsistence level, the effect of an inability to move into other occupations may be to destroy them altogether through the competition of imports. The general effect then is to encourage an unbalanced growth of the economy through its reliance on agriculture, which ultimately leads to trade acting as a depressor through the operation of diminishing marginal returns and deterioration in the terms of trade. On the other hand, if rising imports are a function of increasing exports, income, and saving, they might lead to various secondary effects which encourage economic growth.[11]

Obviously, the case of India cannot be explained merely by one or two simplified models. In the first place, it is by no means clear what the precise degree of contraction was in the textile industry. The general expansion in India's economy in the nineteenth century brought about by the construction of railways and the extension of agriculture, together with the rapid development of cotton mills in the 1870s and 1880s, might actually have increased the size of the textile industry proportionately from what it had been in pre-British days. Secondly, a rising secular trend in the volume of imports can be scarcely maintained if the contraction in the income of the factors engaged previously in the import-competing industries is equal to the increment brought about by expanding exports. One must assume either that some effective transformation took place or that the degree of contraction was not quite as severe as it was taken to be. While no one denies that in the short-run, the imports of cheaper machine-made textiles must have produced a painful dislocation, it is difficult to imagine in view of the size of the Indian textile industry at a later time that some sort of adjustment did not take place in either direction to offset the initial reduction in the level of non-agricultural employment.

It may be argued that this was precisely what the nationalist historians were objecting to, namely, the so-called ruralization of India and its inhibiting effects, since agriculture was subject to diminishing marginal returns while industrial expansion was capable of constant returns to scale.[12] The answer to this objection must depend on formulating the right kind of 'deductive-hypothetical' questions, or in other words estimating what would have happened in the absence of competitive imports. Even admitting that the initial effects of the imports were detrimental to the welfare of labour engaged in Indian handicrafts, it must be remembered that labour was already the more abundant factor and was probably earning a lesser share of real wages relative to other factors. It has been theoretically demonstrated that the effect of trade is to lower the return to the more scarce factor and in this light it may be interesting to investigate the impact of competitive imports in capital rather than labour in India.[13] There was at least one nineteenth-century observer who thought that the increase in trade and competition brought about by the opening of roads and the construction of railroads had lowered the rates of profits and therefore return to capital.[14] It is hypothetically possible to argue that the competition created by trade lowered the interest rates in India in at least that sector of the capital market which had been previously financing the production of handicrafts, and to relate the effect of such changes to the establishment of the machine textile industry in the subcontinent in the mid-nineteenth century. In this case the role of competitive imports would fit one of Kindleberger's models where imports stimulate economic growth by inducing technological innovations.[15]

One final word may be added on the commercial policy adopted by the British government in India. A modern British economic historian has condemned this policy as being utterly selfish and the group-reaction from the Indian side has also been to deplore universally the destructive influence of partial free trade on one sector of the Indian economy. We do not propose to go into this question in detail, but it is worth noting here that the effect of the adoption of a particular commercial policy is not always the same for all countries. For example, the response of the various European countries to the supply of cheap imported wheat was different in each case. In England the policy of free trade led to the destruction of agriculture. In Germany and France, a protective policy was adopted and largely preserved the traditional character of agriculture, while in Denmark, the effect of cheaper cereal imports was economically the most satisfactory in the form of a switch to the more efficient and intensive dairy and animal farming.[16]

Foreign Trade and the Theory of Economic Drain

More than anything else, the concept of an economic drain was the most influential factor in shaping the attitude of Indian historians towards India's foreign trade since the latter was the obvious channel through which the drain was effected. The exponents of the drain theory can be divided into two groups, the vulgar theorists arguing simply that British rule in India was primarily exploitative and those who attempted to build up a more elaborate argument based on statistical calculations to show how the drain actually operated. In the former category were public writers such as Robert Knight, one-time editor of the *Indian Economist,* who asserted in 1869 that India's double misfortune was in being at once a poor country and a country governed by strangers whose administration was not only very costly but marked by all the evils of absenteeism.[17] Such sentiments were reflected at many levels; Major-General F. Marriot, for example, thought in 1874 that the effect of British rule in India was to make everything more costly since basically a poor country was governed by one of the richest which had no notion of public economy.[18] The real exponents of the drain, however, were not concerned with vague ideas of the exploitative character of the British government in India; they were trying to present rigorous statistical proof that foreign trade acted to depress the total national income and levels of employment in India. Thus the essence of the drain theory was to establish a causal link between the changes in the domestic economy on the one hand and foreign trade on the other by using a crude concept of 'gains from trade'. There were also other writers who were concerned less with questions of welfare and more with the positive aspects of the drain. In other words, this latter group of observers tried to isolate the effects of the drain on India's balance of payments and the mechanism of adjustment.

Historically, the discussion on the problem of drain falls into two periods. Most of the early nineteenth-century discussions were concerned with the balance of payments problems but towards the end of the century, the latter issue faded into the background and the main public concern was with the income effect of the drain. There was practically no discussion of the drain theory from Indian writers before Naoroji began his investigations in 1865. The most widely held definition of the concept of a drain was that of an export surplus in India's current account for which there was no corresponding entry on the debit side of the balance of payments whether in the form of import of merchandise, treasure, or securities. From this proposition and the statistical demonstration provided by a comparison between India's total exports and imports, the protagonists of the drain went on to show how India was impoverished by the growing export surplus year by year throughout the nineteenth century. For the sake of getting the problem of definition out of the way, we might note that India's active merchandise balance of trade was liquidated by the following offsetting items: (i) the Government of India's foreign obligations arising out of administrative charges incurred in Britain or other parts of the Empire; (ii) invisible service charges such as freight and banking; (iii) remittance of retained profits by foreign entrepreneurs and the savings of British civil servants in India; and (iv) payment of interest on foreign borrowings.

During the first half of the nineteenth century, the main edge to the whole question was provided by the problem of whether the current expansion in India's foreign trade, particularly her export earnings, was sufficient to cover the £3.5 million required by the government and some of the other payments plus a reasonable level of merchandise imports. A detailed investigation of India's foreign trade during this period shows that there was indeed matter for concern, and that the Parliamentary Committees were right to investigate thoroughly the whole process of adjustment in international balance of payments disequilibrium which in India's case was likely to be introduced through the presence of a unilateral transfer of funds.[19] The two questions most frequently put before the various witnesses were, first, whether there was likely to be any difficulty in remitting the £3.5 million on the government's account through the normal channels of trade and secondly, if the exports in any particular year fell short of the necessary sterling exchange requirements, how would trade react? Contemporary thinkers approached the questions from two directions: as an adjustment process following an autonomous disequilibrium in the balance of payments and secondly in terms of the specific factors which kept the balance of payments in current surplus. The answers given by the Indian monetary experts on the first problem were essentially the same as those developed by Ricardo and John Stuart Mill who used price discrepancies in the surplus and deficit countries operating through the fluctuations in rates of exchange, export of bullion, and the resultant fall in domestic prices in relation to those abroad to explain the mechanism of adjustment.

However, the question as to what factors kept the balance of payments in permanent surplus, as was required in the Indian case, was more difficult to answer and indeed was not attempted in theoretical terms. Instead, the Select Committee of 1840 raised the question of whether India had the necessary capacity to pay the so-called 'tribute' and whether or not such payments impoverished the country. The question was put to Horsley Palmer who was himself connected with an Indian business house and had been the governor of the Bank of England. Palmer's reply was that the power of production in India was so great and the commodities themselves so valuable that there was never likely to be any difficulty in making the required payments through the commercial products of the country. As to the second part of the question, Palmer answered that the degree of impoverishment was substantially reduced if the remittances were made in the produce of the country because 'the money levied in the shape of tax upon the population of India is re-expended in the production of India for which a demand arises in Europe and therefore, though the drain to a certain extent does exist, still it is so small as not materially to affect the prosperity of the country'.[20]

It is not difficult to see that even in the 1830s and 1840s, classical thinking on the Indian drain problem comprised two distinct components: the income effect and the monetary effects associated with a short-term disturbance in the balance of payments. It was natural in the circumstances that the latter should have received much more attention than the former, because the 1830s were a period of acute trade fluctuations in India, which produced certain immediate effects on the Indian domestic economy. The most important of these was the sudden drop in India's exports, combined with a sharp increase in the level of remittances which in 1831–2 and 1832–3 caused a net export of treasure from India. The monetary effects of the deflationary situation were observed by Charles Trevelyan, who stated that the contraction in the domestic supply of currency was such as to cause a marked fall in the prices of commodities and increase the burden of taxation to a grievous extent. But he also noted that this was essentially a short-term disturbance which was corrected by a large inflow of bullion in the years following the Depression.[21] The expansion in the value and volume of India's exports and the relative absence of any serious balance of payment crisis (1847–8 was an exception) to some extent diverted attention from the monetary aspects of India's unilateral transfer of funds and stilled some of these earlier fears.[22] The appearance of Naoroji's *Poverty of India* in 1876 reopened the discussion at a different level, which was then continued by Naoroji himself and the others right down to the First World War.

Naoroji's thinking on the theoretical issues arising out of the drain problem was extremely confused and largely coloured by political feelings. Again, he was essentially concerned with welfare analysis and adopted two crude methods to prove his case. One was to give extensive quotation from the observations of British administrators in India to show how the drain had impoverished the country, and the other was to make a rough calculation of the actual extent of the drain. By taking the total value of exports and imports of India from 1835 to 1872, he concluded that Britain had kept back £500 million for her own benefit. He admitted that certain items such as the interest payments on railway loans could not properly be considered part of the drain and therefore have to be deducted from the above sum. But even so, a substantial balance still remained unaccounted for, which explained the current financial and economic exhaustion of India. Naoroji did not stop at this point, but went on to argue that the 'normal' foreign trade of a country usually showed an import surplus which he called the profits of exports, and therefore according to his reasoning there was a secondary burden on

India through the loss of this profit on exports remitted home though an import surplus. It is quite clear that Naoroji did not distinguish between the f.o.b. (free on board) valuation of exports and c.i.f. (cost, insurance, freight) of imports and failed to take account of capital flows and invisible payments in the balance of payments account.

Further inconsistencies appeared in Naoroji's calculations as he went on elaborating the theory, which will be too tedious to go into here.[23] However, since his arguments have been described by an Indian historian as foreshadowing the concept of the investment multiplier, it is worth mentioning that he paid little attention to the income effects of exports as, for example, represented by the heavy net imports of monetary silver.[24] His reasoning on this point was that the import of bullion was necessary for purely currency purposes, that it was insignificant in per capita terms, and that anyhow most of it did not remain in British India but went to the Native Princely States.

The substance of Naoroji's argument was repeated by R. C. Dutt in more eloquent language. According to Dutt, one-fourth of the total annual revenue of India was remitted out of the country, and he concluded that

> When taxes are raised and spent in a country, the money circulates among the people, fructifies trades, industries, and agriculture and in one shape or other reaches the mass of the people. But when the taxes raised in a country are remitted out of it, the money is lost to the country for ever, it does not stimulate her trades or industries.[25]

The most able answer to these allegations of an economic impoverishment of India operating through the exports surplus was provided by Sir Theodore Morison who made a careful analysis of the various items on India's total international obligations and came to the conclusion that the only possible item which could properly be called a drain was the payment of Home Charges, all other items being payments for services or import of capital which had contributed in one way or the other to India's economic development.[26] It may be argued that this way of looking at India's international balance-sheet might reduce the total extent of the drain, but after all Naoroji and Dutt were basically objecting to the payment of the political charges which, according to the latter, constituted a serious depressor in the economy. It is obvious that the final answer to the whole controversy must depend on making some sort of estimates of the total value of India's foreign trade in her national income and determining whether the exports were a 'leading', 'balancing', or 'lagging' sector.[27] It is conceivable also that this proportion did not remain constant over the nineteenth century as a whole, and that the problem of remittances or the drain was much more critical in the first half of the century when the stimulus to overall economic development in the subcontinent was probably less than in the later period relative to the size of the outflow of funds. Some idea of the relationship between the rate of increase in Indian exports and imports and the size of the debt payments can be gathered from the modern studies of India's balance of payments. In Table 2.1 we have set out the index number of export and import values between 1898 and 1914 and shown the proportions of imports, total invisible and debt payments, and the Home Charges in the total export values which are also given as percentages of estimated agricultural output. It will be seen that though the share of exports in total value of agricultural production was rising during the period, the proportion of debt payments was falling, while the Home Charges constituted only an insignificant part of the total exports. It is also significant that the imports of merchandise tended to absorb a greater share of the export proceeds. The only conclusion one can derive from these figures is that the proportion of invisible and debt servicing charges in the current account of the balance of payments could not have been much more than 5 per cent of India's national income in this period.

While statistical computations provide the most convincing and reliable demonstration of the insignificance of the drain controversy, at least in the context of the later nineteenth-century developments, there is also another way of testing such a conclusion, namely, by looking at the problem through the use of analytical techniques recently developed in the theory of balance of payment adjustment, particularly the branch of the theory termed the 'absorption approach'. We have already referred to the classical explanation of the adjustment process to a balance of payment disequilibrium, expressed mainly in terms of the quantity theory of money. The modern counterpart of this theory is derived from the Keynesian revolution which emphasizes the role of the foreign trade multiplier which, under certain assumptions of the state of elasticities of demand, tends to bring about adjustments through fluctuations in the levels of income and employment. The 'absorption approach' is essentially an extension and refinement of the latter theory incorporating also modern monetary theories.

Table 2.1 *Index of exports, imports, and treasure; percentages of imports, invisible and debt payments, and Home Charges in the total export values; exports as percentages of total agricultural output, 1898–1914*

Year	1	2	3	4 (Per cent)	5 (Per cent)	6 (Per cent)	7 (Per cent)
1898–9	100	100	100	56	33	1.9	
1899–1900	97	103	124	59	34	1.8	
1900–01	95	112	99	61	30	1.7	13.8
1901–02	111	121	87	59	35	0.6	16.6
1902–03	115	116	151	56	30	1.6	14.7
1903–04	136	127	225	50	28	1.1	18.5
1904–05	140	144	219	55	29	1.0	19.3
1905–06	143	169	154	64	33	0.8	20.3
1906–07	157	166	370	60	22	0.9	19.4
1907–08	157	193	351	70	23	1.0	25.6
1908–09	136	179	156	75	25	1.4	18.4
1909–10	166	172	297	59	34	1.0	19.3
1910–11	186	189	310	58	27	1.0	21.8
1911–12	202	201	410	56	24	0.9	25.4
1912–13	218	230	488	60	23	0.8	27.4
1913–14	221	264	346	69	21	0.8	29.7

Column 1: Index number of export values
Column 2: Index number of import values
Column 3: Index number of net import of treasure

Contd.

Table 2.1 contd.

Column 4: Value of imports as percentage of exports
Column 5: Total invisible and debt charges as percentage of exports
Column 6: Home Charges as percentage of exports
Column 7: Value of exports as percentage of estimated agricultural output in
       India.

Sources: Y. S. Pandit, 1937, *India's Balance of Indebtedness 1898–1913* (Oxford);
K. M. Mukherji, 1963, *Levels of Economic Activity and Public Expenditure in India*
(Bombay), Table 3, column 6.

The Keynesian approach starts with the hypothesis that an increase in the level of exports leads to increasing income in the export sector of the economy without, however, providing a corresponding supply of domestically produced goods, while imports constitute a leakage from the circular flow of income by diverting expenditure away from domestic goods. It follows from this that a rise in exports without a corresponding increase in imports results in increased activity in the country with the trade surplus in a period subsequent to the initial rise, some of which will eventually be spent on imported goods.[28] In the case of a deficit or import surplus, the process operates in the reverse direction. The modern theory starts from the same premises but it extends the analysis to include the total aggregate receipts (which include exports or other foreign payments) and total disbursements (which again include imports) by the residents of the country concerned and to see how a possible deficit or surplus in the aggregate accounts can be corrected under full employment or inflationary conditions. The possible alternatives open to the policy-makers are either to reduce the domestic expenditure or to divert expenditure from domestic or foreign goods.[29]

If we now go back to the Indian situation, we can see that a 'flow' type of disturbance made it necessary to keep the balance of trade permanently in surplus. So far as the Government of India's own foreign obligations were concerned, the authorities adopted a very simple method: through budgetary policy they created surplus funds which were then placed to the credit of the foreign importers of Indian products through the government's foreign exchange operations and the transfer was thus automatically effected through exports. This was an 'expenditure reducing' operation and was the source of a major confusion in the thinking of Naoroji and Dutt. The latter considered that the entire amount of the exports, equivalent to the payment of Home Charges and financed out of taxation, was a net abstraction from the economy, whereas it is quite clear that some sort of value-added concept must be used here. In this connection, the point made by Horsely Palmer was vitally significant, since the effect of financing exports through taxation is to divert resources to the export industries and increase the income of the factors engaged in the production of export goods. If there is some spare capacity in the economy, it allows the existing level of employment to be maintained, even if it does not lead to the actual growth which might have followed an autonomous increase in exports. In the absence of spare capacity, an inflationary situation might develop, leading to rather different results and therefore this assumption is crucial to our analysis of the Indian economy. In his lectures on Naoroji, Professor B. N. Ganguli derived the following equation: $Y - T = (C + I) + (X - M)$ where Y is national income, T is tribute, C consumption, I investment, X exports, and M imports. The effect of an increase in T, according to him, is to lead to a reduction in Y, an increase in export surplus, and the squeezing of domestic consumption and investment.[30] Obviously, this is true only if we assume that the increase in T is unaccompanied by changes in Y, which under the Indian condition of expanding net export surplus (that is, the import of monetary silver) and capital import is an unrealistic assumption. In fact, it can be argued that a policy of taxation encouraging the export industries allows unutilized capacity or resources to be brought into employment and if accompanied by a rise in productivity, it may even lead to a net rise in national income.

In India's case we know that both the budgetary policy of the government and an autonomous rise in foreign demand for her exports were operating simultaneously. It is also not difficult to show that during much of the nineteenth century, there was some excess capacity in India in the form of underemployed labour and wasteland. The combination of the latter situation may seem a paradox, and indeed such a possibility is excluded under the classical theory of international trade. But Professor Hla Myint has convincingly argued that the pattern of economic development in the nineteenth century in the case of countries engaged in the production of primary commodities has been strongly influenced by a combination of underemployed labour, surplus resources, and the stimulus provided by expanding trade. This type of situation was observed by Adam Smith and led to the development of his theory of 'vent for surplus' or trade arising out of a highly 'skewed' resource base.[31] The existence of surplus labour is explained by the fact that in a subsistence economy, owing to the lack of efficient transportation, the consequent limitation of the market, and absence of specialization in production, there is little incentive to maximize potential output. The introduction of trade and the construction of social overhead capital with foreign entrepreneurial skill change the pattern of consumer tastes as well as the supply functions, often leading to an absolute and proportional increase in output. That this kind of situation was common in India was observed by Sir Thomas Munro as early as 1797 when he noted that one of the chief difficulties in raising the level of agricultural income in Salem district was due to the limitation of the markets and the high cost of transporting produce outside the district.[32]

To return to the problem of the drain, it can be argued on the basis of the preceding discussion that even if it is admitted that the existence of the unilateral transfer slowed down the rate of growth in India which might otherwise have been expected from the rate of expansion in the value of exports, it is by no means true that it acted as a net depressor in the Indian economy, as was stated in the politically irresistible language of Naoroji and Dutt. We do not of course wish to minimize the benefit to Britain provided by her expanding balance of payment surplus with India but, as Professor Saul has shown, export of capital from Britain and her growing demand for imports stimulated the general expansion in the level of world trade by acting as a 'leading' sector from which India benefited indirectly.[33]

Foreign Trade and Monetary Problems

While the questions relating to the competition of imported manufactured goods and the unilateral transfer of funds aroused the deepest emotion in India, the discussions centring upon the relationship between foreign trade and India's monetary problems were more impersonal, technical, and illuminated by little understanding. The complexity of the Indian currency system baffled observers both in India and Britain. An example of this was the famous 'silver scandal' which caused the youthful John Maynard Keynes to remark in 1912 that such misunderstandings would continue to arise in the future so long as the relations of the House of Commons to India combined in a high degree of responsibility and ignorance.[34] An exhaustive discussion of India's financial and currency problems is outside the scope of this chapter, which will therefore make only some brief concluding remarks on the monetary aspects of India's international economy.

In the nineteenth century, the money supply in India consisted of (i) copper and silver coins freely coinable at the government mints; (ii) gold mohurs of limited legal tender; (iii) paper currency backed by metallic reserves; (iv) bank deposits of the Western type; (v) native internal bills of exchange; and (vi) the credit created by Indian bankers and moneylenders. Of these, the metallic currency was naturally the most important, and since India did not produce any silver, it had to be obtained through foreign trade. In such circumstances, any instability in the Indian monetary system was likely to arise out of her international financial position and, as we have already seen, the operation of the 'gold standard' mechanism following a deterioration in her balance of payments in 1831-3 led to a severe crisis in the internal economy. The Select Committee investigating the remittance problem was clearly puzzled by the degree of dislocation and analyzed the factors responsible for the deflation as follows:

> The cause of these results is to be found principally in the great consumption of the precious metals which takes place in India. . . . It

is to be remembered too, that in India a temporary deficiency of metallic currency is not supplied, as in this country, by an issue of paper. An export of treasure is a net diminution of the circulating medium; and while the habits of the people remain what they are, and the monetary system what it is, any considerable export of treasure must produce embarrassments similar to those which have been described by Mr. Trevelyan.[35]

The absence of any financial institution in the country with some of the functions of a modern central bank clearly made the whole system highly vulnerable, since a temporary balance of payments crisis could not be corrected by appropriate monetary measures. But in actual fact, the frequency of such financial upheavals was not very great, and it was not until the final quarter of the century that the Indian currency system came under sustained pressure. As was to be expected, the origin of the disturbance was external and its effects were transmitted to India through the prolonged rise in the bimetallic ratio from the 1870s and the consequent fall in the rupee–sterling exchange rates. Since India was obliged to pay large sums fixed in terms of sterling, government finance was gravely threatened and private trade reduced to a chronic state of uncertainty. The most serious implication for India's export economy was the possibility of a deterioration in her terms of trade which the presence of the transfer problem made almost certain, although it must be realized that there was also a fall in the gold price of India's imports simultaneously with the depreciation of the exchange rate. One of the side-effects of the latter phenomena was to provide in effect partial protection to the newly established cotton and jute mills in India which might otherwise have been in serious difficulty, though here again it has been argued that at least the cotton industry was secure against the competition of cheapening foreign imports by concentrating on a very specialized section of the market.[36]

By the 1890s, the failure to secure an international agreement on bimetallism led the government to take drastic measures, and in 1893, on the recommendation of the Herschell Committee, the Indian mints were closed to free coinage and the value of the rupee divorced from the market price of silver, the sterling exchange of the rupee being arbitrarily fixed at 1*s*. 4*d*. The reasoning behind these measures was that they would enable the government to bring about an improvement in the rates of exchange and India's terms of trade by contracting the supply of currency in India, although no formal theoretical explanation was offered of how the reduction in the money supply in India would affect the international demand for rupees. In fact, these measures were initially unsuccessful, and it was not until 1898 that the exchange rate touched the official par. Thereafter, the way was left clear for the gradual and reluctant adoption of the Gold Exchange Standard which ultimately provided India with one of the most perfect mechanisms regulating the supply and demand for foreign exchange. The essence of the system depended on the government's obligation to maintain the fixed rates of exchange in terms of gold to rupees within the gold export and import points, any abnormal fluctuations being smoothed out through official intervention out of the gold reserves in London and silver in India.

On the Indian side, the initial criticisms took three forms: first, that raising the exchange in terms of silver would restrict India's growing textile trade with silver-using countries such as China; secondly, that a possible fall in internal prices would harm the cultivators and make their position as leading debtors in the economy an onerous one, and, finally, an irrational feeling that the Indian finances were being adjusted not in her true interests but in those of her British administrators and foreign investors who had savings and profits to remit home. Time was to show that these fears were unfounded. The prices in China adjusted themselves in terms of gold and India's exports to China continued to grow.[37] Similarly, in India, a sustained rise in internal prices set in during the closing years of the century.[38]

However, the most serious criticism of the Indian currency system was made by a British economist, namely Keynes himself, who pointed out that in the absence of widespread use of bank deposits and cheques, the effect of the closure of the mints was to make the supply of money within the country absolutely inelastic. The only way that an increase could be brought about in the money supply was through the purchase of the Secretary of State's Council Bills in London which were then cashed out of the reserves held by the government in India. The effect of this was to accentuate the existing situation where the seasonal demand for money required for moving crops at harvest time led to a sudden and steep rise in the rates of discount. It also made the Indian money market unduly dependent on the London market and subject to marginal fluctuations in the rates of interest and premium on gold price. The final question then arises whether this inflexibility of the money market with its accompanying high interest rates did not retard India's industrial growth in the early years of the twentieth century. But to answer this would really be an exercise in the application of the theory of capital and is therefore beyond the objective of this chapter.

Notes

1. R. C. Dutt, 1906, *The Economic History of India in the Victorian Age* (London), p. xiv.

2. Ibid., p.535.

3. Cf. K. N. Chaudhuri, 1963, 'The East India Company and the Export of Treasure in the Early Seventeenth Century', *Economic History Review,* 2nd series, vol. 16, p. 27.

4. Cf. K. N. Chaudhuri, 1966, 'India's Foreign Trade and the Cessation of the East India Company's Trading Activities', *Economic History Review,* 2nd series, vol. 19, p. 347.

5. See G. A. Prinsep, 1823, *Remarks on the External Commerce and Exchange of Bengal* (London).

6. On this point, see Morris D. Morris, 1963, 'Towards a Reinterpretation of Nineteenth Century Indian Economic History', *Journal of Economic History,* vol. 23, p. 613.

7. *Select Committee on the East India Company's Relief, Parliamentary Papers,* 1840, vii (353), qq. 1310, 3915–20.

8. John Crawfurd, 1837, *Sketch of the Commercial Resources and Monetary and Mercantile System of British India* (London), p. 26.

9. *Report of the Indian Famine Commission,* 1880, p. i.

10. L. J. Jenks, 1963, *The Migration of British Capital to 1875* (London and New York), reprint, p. 227; D. Thorner, 1955, 'The Pattern of Railway Development in India', *Far Eastern Quarterly,* vol. 14,

p. 214; P. Ray, 1934, *India's Foreign Trade since 1870* (London), p. 37.

11. Charles Kindleberger, 1961, 'Foreign Trade and Economic Growth', *Economic History Review,* vol. 14, p. 289; Charles Kindleberger, 1962, *Foreign Trade and the National Economy* (New Haven and London), p. 104.

12. Cf. Bipan Chandra, 1966, *The Rise and Growth of Economic Nationalism in India* (New Delhi), p. 58.

13. W. F. Stolper and Paul A. Samuelson, 1941, 'Protection and Real Wages', *Review of Economic Studies,* 1941; also printed in *Readings in the Theory of International Trade,* American Economic Association, London, 1961.

14. J. M. Campbell, 1880, *District Gazette: Nasik,* pp. 142–4.

15. Kindleberger, 1961, ' Foreign Trade and Economic Growth'.

16. Charles Kindleberger, 1951, 'Group Behaviour and International Trade', *Journal of Political Economy,* vol. 59. For the tariff question, see S. B. Saul, 1960, *Studies in British Overseas Trade* (Liverpool), p. 198.

17. *The Indian Economist,* 11 October 1869, p. 80.

18. W. F. Marriot, 'Indian Political Economy and Finance', India Office Library, *East India Tracts,* vol. 503.

19. Cf. Chaudhuri, 1966, 'India's Foreign Trade'.

20. *S.C. on the East India Company's Relief, Parliamentary Papers,* 1840, VII, qq. 1441–4; see also the evidence of Charles Trevelyan, ibid., p. v.

21. Ibid.

22. For figures of exports and imports for this period, see T. Took and W. Newmarch, 1857, *A History of Prices* (London), Appendix XXIII, pp. 712–36; F. J. Atkinson, 1897, 'Silver Prices in India', *Journal of the Royal Statistical Society.*

23. For Naoroji's various writings, see *Poverty and Un-British Rule in India* (new edition, Delhi), 1962; for a general discussion of the drain controversy, see J. R. Mclane, 1963, 'The Drain of Wealth and Indian Nationalism at the Turn of the Century', in Tapan Raychaudhuri, *Contributions to Indian Economic History* (Calcutta), vol. II (chapter 3).

24. Bipan Chandra, 1966, *The Rise and Growth of Economic Nationalism in India,* p. 661.

25. Dutt, 1906, *The Economic History of India in the Victorian Age,* p. xiv.

26. Sir Theodore Morison, 1911 *The Economic Transition in India* (London), ch. 8, ix.

27. Kindleberger, op. cit., p. 195.

28. For a discussion of the theoretical problems and the bibliography, see H. G. Johnson, 1958, *International Trade and Economic Growth* (London), Part II; R. C. O. Matthews, 1954, *A Study in Trade Cycle History* (Cambridge), chs 1 and 9.

29. Professor Johnson's discussion of the problem is confined to the correction of a possible deficit since the emergence of a balance of payment surplus does not normally raise pressing problems of policy, Johnson, op. cit.

30. B. N. Ganguli, 1965, *Dadabhai Naoroji and the Drain Theory* (Bombay), p. 16.

31. Kindleberger, op. cit.; H. Myint, 1958, 'The "Classical Theory" of International Trade and the Underdeveloped Countries', *Economic Journal,* pp. 317–37.

32. Sir Thomas Munro, 1881, 'Condition of Salem', in *Selections from his Minutes and other Official Writings,* edited by Alexander J. Arbuthnot (London), vol. I.

33. Saul, 1960, *Studies in British Overseas Trade,* ch. 5.

34. J. M. Keynes, 1913, *Indian Currency and Finance* (London).

35. *S.C. on the East India Company's Relief, Parliamentary Papers,* 1840, VII, p. v.

36. See Saul, 1960, *Studies in British Overseas Trade;* Ray, 1934, *India's Foreign Trade since 1870,* p. 183.

37. *Report of the Indian Tariff Board (Cotton Textile Industry Enquiry, 1927),* Bombay, 1927, vol. I, Report, p. 95.

38. Cf. K. L. Datta, 1914, *Report on Rise of Prices and Wages in India* (Calcutta), vol. I.

3

The Drain of Wealth and Indian Nationalism at the Turn of the Century*

John McLane

Between the passing of the Councils Act of 1892 and the partition of Bengal, the economic aspects of British rule, rather than the political, most occupied the attention of Indian nationalists. The severe famines of 1897 and 1899–1900 gave weight to Indian complaints about the 'drain' of wealth to England and the over-assessment of the land. The 'drain' gained special prominence during the 1890s because of the increasing amount of Indian revenues required to pay the Home Charges. The persistent complaint punctuating many writings and speeches between 1895 and 1910 was that India was being 'drained', 'throttled', 'bled', 'sucked', and 'exploited' of her wealth, and that the British were removing the surplus capital without which no economy could develop.

In the description of the 'drain' which follows, it is important to remember that few officials were impressed by the drain argument. Lord Curzon, for instance, described as 'nonsense' the idea that India 'is bleeding under British rule'.[1] Sir John Strachey thought that 'The payments made by India are the result and the evidence of the benefits which she derives from her

---

* Previously published in *Contributions to Indian Economic History*, vol. 2.

connection with England. In place of constant anarchy, bloodshed, and rapine, we have given her peace, order, and justice; and if our Government were to cease, all the miseries from which she has been saved would inevitably and instantly return. Her payments in England are nothing more than the return for the foreign capital in its broadest sense which is invested in India, including as capital not only money, but all advantages which have to be paid for such as the intelligence, strength, and energy on which good administration and commercial prosperity depend'.[2]

But if officials were not usually sympathetic to the 'drain' argument, the nationalists were not convinced by the Strachey thesis either. In 1904 R. C. Dutt was urging 'Retrenchment and Representation'[3] at the same time that Lord Curzon was increasing government expenditure and saying that political reform had progressed as far was possible.[4] With this wide measure of disagreement between the official and the nationalist outlook, the ultimate solution could only be a political one.

The key to the drain was to be found in the financial arrangements between the United Kingdom and India. These arrangements were submitted to a variety of analyses between 1895 and 1905. In 1895 the Welby Commission was appointed to inquire into the military and civil expenditure in England on behalf of India and 'the apportionment of charge between the governments of the United Kingdom and India for purposes in which both are interested'. The appointment of this Royal Commission followed a demand by the Indian Parliamentary Committee, of which William Wedderburn and Dadabhai Naoroji were members, for an inquiry into the economic condition of India.[5] Wedderburn, Naoroji, and W. S. Caine were members of the Welby Commission, and H. Morgan-Browne (Secretary to the British Committee of the Indian National Congress), G. K. Gokhale, G. Subramania Iyer, D. E. Wacha, Surendranath Banerjea, and Naoroji appeared before it as witnesses. The final Report, which was presented in 1900, was not signed by Wedderburn, Caine, and Naoroji who appended their own Report, declaring their disappointment that the Welby Commission did not consider 'whether the Government of India, with all its machinery as then existing in India, had, or had not, promoted the general prosperity of the people in its charge, and whether India was better or worse off by being a province of the British Crown'.[6]

The drain and its consequences were discussed in numerous speeches and in several books during the period under review. Among the principal books were R. C. Dutt's *England and India: A Record of Progress during a Hundred Years* (1897), *The Economic History of British India* (1902), *and India in the Victorian Age: An Economic History of the People* (1904); William Digby's *'Prosperous' British India* (1901); and Dadabhai Naoroji's *Poverty and Un-British Rule in India* (1901). The drain was also referred to, although in less detail, in Prithwis Chandra Ray's *The Poverty Problem in India* (1895), M. G. Ranade's *Essays in Indian Economics* (1899), and G. Subramania Iyer's *Some Economic Aspects of British Rule in India* (1903).

It is necessary to understand what an Indian nationalist meant when he used the word 'drain'. The most common meaning attached to the word was the wealth which left India for which there was no equivalent return in merchandise or treasure. By this definition, the drain equalled the surplus of exports over imports or the visible balance of trade.[7] In the ten years, 1899–1900 to 1908–09,[8] the value of India's exports annually exceeded its imports by an average of £15,051,000. This should not be regarded as the amount by which India was impoverished each year. In the years 1903 to 1908, the following countries also had large annual export surpluses: Brazil (£14,099,000), Australian Commonwealth (£19,898,340), Russian Empire (£33,175,000), and the United States (£98,698,000).[9] An export surplus is frequently a feature of the trade of a country in the early stages of industrial development.

Sometimes the 'drain' was used to include, besides the visible balance of trade, estimates of the interest paid to England on private capital investment and the remittances of European non-officials. Naoroji apparently was doing this in 1901 when he stated that the annual drain was £30,000,000[10] although the average export surplus in the preceding four years had been only about £13,000,000 per annum.[11]

Naoroji, and the other persons who followed him in estimating the drain at £30,000,000, seem not to have understood the mechanics of private remittances. In the first place, private remittances to Europe were not much in excess of fresh European investment in India so that, in balance, the amount of private money leaving India was not large.[12] Secondly, most of the private remittances were made through Exchange banks. The European in India wishing to make a remittance would pay rupees into the Indian branch of an Exchange bank and receive a bill payable in sterling in London. The London branch would honour the bill from money received from the sale of Indian goods in the United Kingdom or from bullion imported from India.[13] In either case, the actual transfer of capital would be shown in the trade figures. Thus, to count the money remitted privately in this manner as part of the drain would be to count it twice.

Sometimes the word 'drain' was used figuratively and included expenditure in India on such items as the Army or European Agency.[14] But the usual meaning was surplus of exports for which India received no commercial equivalent.

Theodore Morison devoted two chapters of his book, *The Economic Transition in India* (1911), to the drain. He made a distinction between the 'actual' and the 'potential' drain. The actual drain was the excess of export, or £15,051,000 per annum from 1899–1900 to 1908–09. The potential drain which Morison computed consisted of, besides the excess of exports, the increase of the Government of India's capital liabilities in England (£4,193,000 per annum), the 'interest on private capital, earnings of English merchants and professional men, and freights earned by English ships in Indian waters'. The potential drain represented the amount by which India's exports would have had to exceed her imports in order to avoid borrowing capital abroad to meet her foreign obligations. Morison estimated the potential drain to be £21,000,000 per annum for the years 1899–1900 to 1908–09. In arriving at this figure he guessed that the amount of foreign capital invested privately in India was at most £2,000,000 or one-half as large as the amount borrowed by the Indian government in England.[15] Dr Anstey regards Morison's discussion as one of the most intelligent analysis of the drain.

Neither Anstey nor Morison regards the drain as impoverishing. On the contrary, they both believe the money spent on European agency, railway development, and defence, as well spent on the whole.[16]

As already indicated, a surplus of exports was not necessarily incompatible with increasing prosperity. A country with such a surplus would accumulate credit abroad. Actually, it was the Home Charges, on which India's foreign credit was spent, that Indian nationalists objected to. In order to pay the Home Charges, the Government of India, in the years 1899–1900 to 1908–09, not only paid to England £15,051,000 representing the annual balance of trade, but it also had to borrow in England enough to pay the remainder of the £18,598,000 representing the average annual Home Charges.[17] In these years, the Home Charges usually amounted to more than one-fourth of the total expenditure of the Government of India.[18]

The surplus of exports was transformed into credit for India through the sale of what were known as Council Bills. When an importer in Europe wanted rupees to pay for his imports from India, he paid sterling to the Secretary of State in London in return for Council Bills. These bills were then presented at the government treasury in India where the holder received rupees out of the Indian revenues in exchange for the bills. In this way, the Secretary of State obtained most of the money required to pay the Home Charges.[19]

Exchange difficulties between 1873 and 1898 added a considerable burden to the amount paid from the Indian revenues for the Home Charges. Until 1893 India was in a silver standard and England was on a gold standard so that India had to meet her obligations in England in gold. As long as the gold value of silver remained constant, this arrangement was satisfactory to India. But after 1883 the value of silver began to depreciate. The result was that India was forced to remit more silver (that is, spend more rupees) in order to meet the same obligations in England. In 1873–4 the exchange value had been about 2s. By 1892–3 the exchange value had fallen to 1s. 2d.[20] This meant that in 1892–3 the Government of India had to raise Rs 264,780,000 to meet the Home Charges of £16,532,000. Had the exchange rate of 1873–4 still prevailed, the government would have had to spend Rs 177,529,000, or Rs 87,260,000 less for the 1892–3 Home Charges.[21] In 1893 a committee was appointed under the presidency of Lord Herschell to consider the problem, and in accordance with the committee's recommendations the Government of India closed the mints to the free coining of silver in 1893.

As the government ceased to add to the number of rupees in circulation, the demand for rupees began to grow, the price of rupees rose, and by 1899 the exchange value of the rupee had reached the desired 1s. 4d. After 1898 the exchange rate was maintained for fifteen years at 1s. 4d. with only minor fluctuations.[22]

The stabilization of the rupee at 1s. 4d. saved the Indian tax-payer large sums of money on the remittances to England. But the currency legislation affected the cotton goods trade unfavourably and this obscured for some of the Congress supporters the benefit conferred upon balance of payments by the currency reforms. When the gold value of silver had been low, Indian exporters and manufacturers had been at an advantage in selling to gold standard countries. For the same reason, the Government of India and importers had lost through exchange. After the gold value of the rupee increased, the Indian cotton industry no longer possessed its former advantage. It was actually at a disadvantage in its principal market, China, which continued on the silver standard, and sought its cotton goods increasingly from its own mills or from Japan, rather than from gold standard countries like India. The temporary decline of the Chinese demand for Indian yarns and cottons was one of the reasons for the five-year slump after 1900 in the Bombay mills,[23] and the nationalists blamed the government's currency legislation for the difficulties in the one major industry in which Indian investment predominated over foreign.[24]

It would be misleading to suggest that the Home Charges exactly or even approximately represented the amount by which India was impoverished or exploited. An analysis of the components of the Home Charges shows that some of the charges were similar to those paid voluntarily by independent countries.

The Home Charges consisted in 1901–02 of the following items. The year 1901–02 is taken as the year between 1899–1900 and 1908–09 in which the Home Charges most closely approximate to the annual average for that decade.

Railways, interest and annuities	£6,416,373
Interest on debt (excluding that on the railway debt)	3,003,782
Management of debt	48,628
Army services	4,383,059
Stores	1,918,206
Civil charges, furloughs, pensions, allowances, and miscellaneous	1,370,903
Charges on account of Departments in India	227,704
Total	£17,368,655[25]

The Home Charges may be divided between two categories: the 'economic' payments and the 'political' payments.[26] The economic payments consisted of the interest on the railway and the permanent debt, the management of the debt, and the stores, or in other words, foreign expenditure of a type which any independent country might make in the early stages of industrial development and railway building.[27] The political charges would be the military, administrative, and civil charges, pensions, and allowances which India could not presumably have paid as an independent country. If such a hypothetical division is made for the year 1901–02, the economic charge was £10,386,989, and £6,981,666 was the political charge.

The individual items of the Home Charges may be examined. The largest item was the railway charge and it was increasing rapidly in the period under review. In 1899–1900 it was £5,913,780: by 1908–09 railway payments in England amounted to £8,249,846. However, the nature of the payments was changing. In the former year £2,172,336 of the railway expenditure had been interest paid on guaranteed lines, while in the latter year none of the expenditure was on guaranteed lines.[28] The early railway lines had been built by European companies whose profits were guaranteed by the East India Company at the rate of 5 per cent. Private European capital probably could not have been attracted at the mid-century without a guarantee, and 5 per cent was a low rate of interest for railways before 1870.[29] But the arrangement was unsatisfactory from several points of view. The government took the risk without the opportunity of receiving the profits while the companies reaped the profits with little incentive to economy. Daniel Throner has labelled the guarantee system as private enterprise at public risk.[30] During the latter half of the century, the Secretary of State for India found that India could borrow in London at lower rates of interest for state railways and that private companies would enter contracts on terms more advantageous to India. In guaranteeing the early railways, the right had been reserved to purchase the lines after the lapse of certain periods of time, and the Secretary of State exercised this power so that by the end of 1907, the last of the guaranteed railways had been bought up.[31] With the decline of payments on the guaranteed railways and the increase in the volume of traffic, the public works of India began after 1900 to show a profit to the public revenues for the first time. In 1900–1901, there was slight profit; in 1901–02 it was £750,000; and in 1905–06, they earned India £2,000,000.[32]

India borrowed in England at a lower rate of interest than other foreign countries did. In the early years of the twentieth century, Japan, for instance, paid 4.5 to 5 per cent on its foreign loans while India paid about 3.5 per cent.[33] The yield to British investors on Indian railways in 1907 was 3.87 per cent; on colonial railways, 4.0 per cent; on America railways, 4.5 per cent; and on other foreign railways, 4.7 per cent.[34] Thus, at the beginning of the century, Indian nationalists had less reason to complain about the current rate of interest paid to foreign capitalists. Furthermore, they could no longer say that railroads were unprofitable to the State.

Rather, it was the priority given to railway construction and the public debt incurred by the earlier and more extravagant expenditure which was open to criticism. It was complained that the total outlay before 1902 on railways had been £226,000,000 compared to £24,000,000 spent on irrigation works,[35] that some railways were built for military purposes and could not be expected to yield a commercial return,[36] and that other railways were built at the request of English manufacturers who wanted to open Indian markets to cheap, British manufactured goods, thereby hastening the de-industrialization of India and converting her into a producer of raw materials only.[37]

While the railway or 'productive' debt was increasing, the ordinary or 'unproductive' debt was decreasing. The ordinary debt had included the £12,000,000 owed to the stockholders of the old East India Company, the cost of suppressing the mutiny, and expenses arising out of other wars. The ordinary debt stood at £96,000,000 in 1862; by 1897 it had been reduced to £72,721,161, or by more than 24 per cent. In the same period, the rate of interest paid on the debt declined from 4.543 per cent to 3.393 per cent. In consequence, the annual charge of interest declined by 50 per cent not including exchange, or by 16 per cent including exchange.[38] By 1909, the ordinary, or unproductive debt had been reduced still further, to £37,700,000.[39]

Looking now at the total Permanent Debt of India, including the productive and unproductive debt, and the debt held in India as well as in England, it will be seen that it was growing rapidly in the period under review, and that it was increasing more rapidly in England than in India. In 1898–1900 the total Permanent Debt in India was Rs 112,475 million; in 1908–09 it was Rs 134,566 million. In England during the same period, the debt rose from £119.64 million to £160.97 million.[40] Even these figures do not give an adequate idea of the degree to which the Indian government depended on foreign capital. The Welby Commission reported that 'out of Rs 103,000,000 borrowed in India, Rs 25,000,000 was actually held at home [United Kingdom], that Rs 48,000,000 was held by Europeans in India, and that only Rs 30,000,000 was held by Natives of India'.[41] Why was more of the government's capital not borrowed from Indians themselves? The most important reason was that English interest rates were lower than Indian ones. The Government of India could borrow in England at the rate of between 3 and 4 per cent. In Bombay, according to Wacha, capital could be borrowed for as little as

4 to 5 per cent but in most places Indians wanted 6, 7, 8, or 9 per cent.[42] A study is needed of the efforts, or lack of them, made by the government to raise Indian capital. Again, a word of caution is needed about the significance of the Indian debt and the interest paid on it. India's public debt was small compared to that of the United Kingdom, and the interest India paid to the United Kingdom on private and public loans was only a fraction of the £60,000,000 or so which the United States was annually remitting to Europe in about 1910 as interest.[43] It is a truism, but nevertheless worth repeating, that the significance of India's foreign obligations was not be found in their absolute size. The question is whether India should have put surplus capital back into her economy at once, or invested it in railways in the hope of future economic expansion.

M. G. Ranade was among the minority of nationalists who felt that 'far from complaining, we have reason to be thankful that we have a Creditor who supplies our needs at such a low rate of intersest'.[44] A more common view was that foreign investment was more or less the same as foreign exploitation. The *Power and the Guardian* of Calcutta made this point when it said that from the point of view of an Indian, an influx of British capital 'will be one of those irreparable evils which make their sinister influence felt upon distant generations. It is doubtful if the indigenous population will ever have strength enough to shake off the financial bondage which the larger and freer influx of foreign capital will necessarily impose upon the country. What the zealous capitalist calls increased material prosperity is from another point of view nothing but greater exploitation'.[45]

The next item of the Home Charges—the £4,383,059 in 1901–02 for Army services—was the section of the charges open to easy attack. In 1900 India employed about one-third of the whole British Army. The Indian revenues were charged with the cost of training these men in England (16,000 men a year in 1890), with a major share of the pensions, with their transport to and from India, and with all expenses incurred by the troops between the day they left England and the day they returned, or for an average of six years per man. Between 1875–6 and 1896–7, the net Army expenditure in England rose from £3,476,000 to £4,133,000. Because of the fall in the exchange value of the Rupee, this meant that the cost to India increased from Rs38,580,000 to Rs 68,650,000. In the same period, the total Army expenditure in England and India, including exchange increased from Rs 162,590,000 to Rs 259,730,000.[46]

Much of the increase had nothing to do with the direct defence of India, and it was not only the nationalists who complained of this. In one of the numerous formal representations made by the Government of India about military costs,[47] Lord Lansdowne's government expressed its opinion to the Secretary of state that:

> The revenues of India have been charged with the cost of many charges in organization not specially necessary for the efficiency of the army in this country, and with the cost of troops employed in Imperial service beyond the limits of India. Millions of money have been spent on increasing the army in India, or armaments, and on fortifications, to provide for the security of India, not against domestic enemies, or to prevent the incursions of the warlike peoples of adjoining countries, but to maintain the supremacy of British power in the East.[48]

On 18 July 1900, about one-tenth (23,022) of the Indian Army were serving outside of India, including 9186 men in South Africa and 10,616 in China, although in these particular instances the Home Government paid the costs.[49] The manner in which expenses for military expeditions beyond India's borders were divided before 1895 may be seen in Table 3.1.

In 1900, upon the recommendation of the Welby Commission, India was relieved of a total of £257,000 on account of the Home Charges. This sum included one-half the cost of transporting troops to and from India (£130,000) and one-half the military charge for Aden (£72,000). The Congress and the Government of India were disappointed with the relief granted. The Government of India protested to the Secretary of State that the £257,000 'falls far short of according to India the just and liberal treatment which was claimed for her'.[50]

Table 3.1 Expenditures on overseas military expeditions, 1838–6

Expedition	Date	Ordinary charges		Extraordinary charges	
		Paid by India	Paid by England	Paid by India	Paid by England
1st Afghanistan	1838–42	All	None	All	None
1st China	1839–40	All	None	None	All
2nd China	1856–7	None	All	None	All
Persia	1856	All	None	Half	Half
3rd China	1859	None except expenses of Indian Navy vessels	All	None	All
Abyssinia	1867–8	All	None	None	All
Perak	1875	All	None	None	All (by Colonial government)
Malta	1878	None	All	None	All
2nd Afghanistan	1878–80	All	None	All but £5,000,000	£5,000,000
Egypt	1882	All	None	All but £5000	£5000
Soudan	1885–6	All	None	None	All

Source: Indian Expenditure Commission, Vol.II, First Report, Appendix 45, No. 13, Sub-Appendix, para. 123, Governor General in Council to Secretary of State, 20 August 1895.

The slight relief given on account of the Home Charges was more than offset by the decision to increase the pay of the British Army. The increase, which ultimately meant an additional charge of £786,000 per annum on the Indian revenues, was unsuccessfully resisted by Lord Curzon's government.[51] A still further, although temporary, increase in the military expenditure occurred in 1904–05 and 1905–06 with the reorganization of the Indian Army. The reorganization involved an additional expenditure for India of £869,932 in India, and £1,401,933 in England. Altogether the net Indian military expenditure in England and India grew from £15,376,473 in 1899–1900 to £19,602,988 in 1908–09.[52]

The history of India's economic relation with Great Britain generated at least as much nationalist indignation as the contemporary financial arrangements between the two countries. R. C. Dutt gave organized expression to the prevailing belief about the early period in *The Economic History of British India*. He rejected the notion that India's 'intense poverty' and 'repeated famines' could be explained by factors such as increasing population, drought, peasant improvidence, and alienation of land to the moneylender. The narrowing of India's sources of wealth was due to other reasons.

India in the eighteenth century was a great manufacturing as well as a great agricultural country, and the products of the Indian loom supplied the market of Asia and of Europe. It is unfortunately true that the East Indian Company and the British Parliament, following the selfish commercial policy of a hundred years ago, discouraged Indian manufacturers in the early years of British rule in order to encourage the rising manufacturers of England. Their fixed policy, pursued down the last decade of the eighteenth century and the first decades of the nineteenth, was to make India subservient to the industries of Great Britain, and to make the Indian people grow raw produce only, in order to supply material for the looms and manufactories of Great Britain. This policy was pursued with unwavering resolution and with fatal success: orders were sent out, to force Indian artisans to work in the Company's factories; commercial residents were legally vested with extensive powers over villagers and communities of Indian weavers; prohibitive tariffs excluded Indian silk and cotton goods from England; English goods were admitted into India free of duty or on payment of a nominal duty.[53]

Four Western writers were often invoked in support of nationalist views. H. H. Wilson's continuation of Mill's *History of British India* was used to prove that Indian textiles were kept out of British markets by prohibitive duties while India was prevented from protecting her own industry.

> The foreign manufacturer employed the arm of political injustice to keep down and ultimately strangle a competitor with whom he could not have competed on equal terms. Had Indian goods not been kept out of England, the mills of Paisley and Manchester would have been stopped in their outset, and could scarcely have been again set in motion, even by the power of steam.[54]

Robert Montgomery Martin[55] and Sir George Wingate[56] were quoted about the exaction of tribute from India. Finally, Brooks Adams' view that plunder from India was instrumental in financing Europe's industrial revolution was accepted.[57]

The 'Moral Drain'

The portion of the Home Charges expended on pensions, furlough allowances, exchange compensation allowances, and on the employment of foreign agency in general was objected to because it represented to nationalists both a denial of the promises of equality contained in the Queen's Proclamation of 1858 and an extravagant means of running the government. The cost of foreign agency was higher than is sometimes realized. Probably in no other country in the world were civil servants paid so liberally. In Algeria, for instance, the highest judicial officer, the First President of the Court of Appeal, received £720 and a furnished house each year while the Chief Justice of Bengal earned £4911, including exchange compensation allowance.[58] Other comparisons between French salaries in Algeria and British salaries in India reinforce this point.[59] In 1892 a Parliamentary Return was prepared showing the amount of money received from the revenues of India in 1889–90 by persons earning Rs 1000 or more. In the total in Table 3.2, sums paid in England have been converted from sterling into rupees at the rate of 1s. 4d.[60]

Table 3.2   *European salaries in India (in Rs)*

Paid by the Government, 1889–90	
Annual salaries paid to Europeans in India	87,714,431
Absentee allowances paid to Europeans in India	4,636,314
Pensions paid to Europeans in India	2,328,882*
Amount paid to Europeans in England	55,660,170
	150,339,797
Paid by the Railway Companies, 1889–90	
Amount paid to Europeans in India	11,606,891
Amount paid to Europeans in England	817,830
	12,424,721
Total paid to Europeans from the Revenues of India, 1889–90	162,764,518**
Total government expenditure in England and India, 1889–90	824,731,700

* Eurasian pensions are included in this figure.

** East India (Salaries) Return of the number of all persons who received from the Revenues of India, during the year 1889–90, annual allowances . . . of which the amount was not less than 1000 rupees for each person.

Source: British Parliamentary Papers, House of Commons 192 of 1892.

Dadabhai Naoroji called the exclusion of Indians from position of responsibility India's 'moral drain'. By employing Europeans where Indians could perform the job, he said, the British government was stunting the capabilities and intelligence of the Indians.[61] In 1900 Naoroji wrote to Lord Hamilton, the Secretary of State, hinting that if the pledges of equality were not honoured, India might 'under the persistence of the present evil bleeding fall from the British frying pan into the Russian fire or free itself from a destructive rule'.[62]

In the Indian Legislative Council in 1904, Lord Curzon vehemently denied that Indians had received an inadequate share of the civil employment. He stated that in 1867 there had been 13,431 government posts in India with a salary above Rs 75, and of these, Europeans and Eurasians held 55 per cent. In 1903 the total number of posts was 28,278, of which only 42 per cent were held by Europeans and Eurasians. Curzon demonstrated the improvement of the Indian position in another way. He said that the aggregate pay of the European government servants had increased by 6 per cent since 1867 while the pay of the 'Natives' had grown by 191 per cent. Curzon thought that these and other figures he produced proved

> how honestly and faithfully the British government had fulfilled its pledges, and how hollow is the charge which we so often hear of a ban of exclusion against the children of the soil .... Will anyone tell me in the face of these figures that our administration is unduly favourable to the European or grudging to the native element? I hold, on the contrary, that it is characterised by a liberality unexampled in the world.

Curzon rested his case largely on the unquestioned increase in the proportion of Indians in subordinate positions, which Indians coveted, and Lord Curzon had definite views on the racial superiority of Europeans which disqualified all but a few Indians from holding these positions. Those few Indians who could proceed to England and pass the civil service examinations might be employed.

> The highest ranks of civil employment in India ... must nevertheless, as a rule be held by Englishmen, for the reason that they possess, partly by heredity, partly by upbringing, and partly by education, the knowledge of the principles of Government, the habits of mind and the vigour of character, which are essential for the task, and that, the rule of India being a British rule, and any other rule being in the circumstances of the case impossible, the tone and standard should be set by those who have created and are responsible for it.

Curzon believed that 'the greatest peril with which our administration is confronted' was 'the system under which every year an increasing number of the 900 and odd higher posts that were meant and ought to have been exclusively and specifically reserved for Europeans, are being filched away by the superior wits of the Native in the English examinations'.[63] Curzon realized regretfully that the time had passed when a racial qualification could be placed on the entrances to the civil services. But the Government of India found a number of reasons for keeping

Indians out of the higher posts in the Forest, Customs, Salt, Opium, Postal, Telegraph, Survey, Jail and Police Departments.[64] Apart from the necessity of sitting for the ICS examination in the United Kingdom, there were other barriers to Indians. For instance, the Post Office Department preferred to send Europeans to arrange postal services during military operations in China, Africa, and the North-west Frontier. Again, in some areas of Assam and Bihar, travel could be done only with the assistance of the planters, and this ruled out Indians for assignments in these areas.[65] In the Preventive Branch of the Customs Department, Europeans were preferred because of their ability to withstand 'great exposure in all weather' and the need to enforce customs and port rules on European officers and sailors. Indians were not permitted to sit for Police Department examinations in London. Most central and district jails were run by medical officers,[66] and the Indian Medical Service was open only to those persons 'registered in the United Kingdom under the Medical Acts'.[67] Other departments needed Europeans because Indian performances had not 'been found to be altogether satisfactory' because of 'the high standard of scientific accuracy' required, 'the rough and solitary life', the poor quality of Indian applicants, and the need for 'energy and physical capacity'.[68]

G. Subramania Iyer contributed an article to the *Hindustan Review and Kayastha Samachar* in which he contradicted Lord Curzon's statement that Europeans were not unduly favoured in the Civil Service.[69] Using the same figures as Curzon had, Iyer proved that the number of posts carrying salaries of Rs 1000 or above which were held by Europeans and Eurasians had increased more between 1867 and 1903 than the number held by Indians. The increase in the Public Works Department for Europeans and Eurasians had been 133, for Indians 11; the increase in the Land Revenues Department for Europeans and Eurasians had been 95, for Indians 19; in the Medical Department (Civil) the increase had been 95 and 6, respectively; in the State Railways, 95 and 0, respectively. In only one department—the Judicial—had the number of Indians holding positions with salaries over Rs 1000 gained more than the number of Europeans and Eurasians. Taking the total net increases of all such positions between 1867 and 1903, the Europeans and Eurasians increased their share by 591, Indians by 84.[70]

In conclusion, it may be said that an important part of the background to the disorders beginning in 1905 was the firm rejection of two of the major demands of the Indian National Congress. The Congress had asked for a vast reduction of the Home Charges; instead India was relieved of only £257,000. The Congress had demanded the Indianization of the civil services; Lord Curzon, in reply, gave an unqualified, and perhaps unparalleled, public assertion of the racial basis of employment in the higher positions of the Civil Service.

Notes

1. Curzon's speech to the Anjuman-i-Islamia, Lahore, Enclosure to Curzon to Hamilton, 5 April 1899, MSS.Eur. 510/1.
2. John Strachey, 1903, *India: Its Administration and Progress,* p. 195.
3. Romesh Dutt, 1904, *India in the Victorian Age: An Economic History of the People,* p. 612.
4. Curzon's speech on the 1904–05 Budget Statement, 30 March 1904, *Progs. of the Legislative Council of the Governor-General,* 1904, p. 560.
5. *India,* vol. VII, no. 12 (Dec. 1896).
6. Report by Sir W. Wedderburn, W. S. Caine, and D. Naoroji, Para. 3. *Indian Expenditure Commission,* vol. IV, *Final Report of the Royal Commission on the Administration of the Expenditure of India* (d. 131 of 1900).
7. The drain was defined as the surplus of exports by R. C. Dutt, 1904, *India in the Victorian Age,* p. 528; Dadabhai Naoroji, 1901, *Poverty and un-British Rule in India,* p. 34; and William Digby, 1901, *'Prosperous' British India,* p. 16. This is also the definition accepted by C. J. Hamilton, 1919, *The Trade Relations between England and India (1600–1896),* p. 136, and by Holden Furber, 1951, *John Company at Work,* p. 304.
8. This period is used rather than a period covering the 1890s because the 1890s are unrepresentative and would be less illuminating due to the exchange crisis and the fall in exports during the famine years.

9. Quoted from the Financial and Commercial Supplement of the *London Times*, 30 September 1910, by Theodore Morison, 1911, *The Economic Transition in India*, p. 206.

10. Naoroji 1901, *Poverty and un-British Rule*, p. viii.

11. Dutt, 1904, *India in the Victorian Age*, p. 528.

12. Sir George Cambell estimated in 1887 (*The British Empire*, p. 70) that the private remittances were about balanced by the flow of fresh capital into India from Europe. Quoted by Digby, 1901, *Prosperous British India*, p. 231.

13. Vera Anstey, 1952, *The Economic Development of India*, 4th ed., pp. 116–17.

14. A. J. Wilson seemed to be doing this when he set the drain at £35,000,000 annually, *An Empire in Pawn*, p. 64.

15. Morison, 1911, *The Economic Transition*, pp. 197–203.

16. Anstey, 1952, *The Economic Development of India*, Appendix G, pp. 599–600. Morison, 1911, *The Economic Transition*, pp. 240–1.

17. Morison, 1911, *The Economic Transition*, pp. 196–8.

18. General Statement of the Gross Expenditure charged against Revenue in India and England, *Statistical Abstract relating to British India from 1899–1900 to 1908–09*, (d. 5345 of 1910), pp. 50–1.

19. The Secretary of State sold Council Bills to be drawn on the Indian Treasury at the annual rate of £17,500,000 from 1899–1900 to 1909–10. Sir John Strachey, 1911, *India: Its Administration and Progress*, pp. 210–11.

20. H. H. Dodwell, ed., *The Cambridge History of India*, vol. vi. The Indian Empire, 1858–1918, with chapters on the development of administration, 1818–58, Cambridge, 1932, p. 321.

21. Strachey, 1911, *India: Its Administration and Progress*, p. 197.

22. Final Report of the Royal Commission on Indian Finance and Currency, 1914 (Chamberlain Commission), d. 7236 to 1914, paras 15–20.

23. D. H. Buchanan, 1934, *The Development of Capitalist Enterprise in India*, pp. 155, 200.

24. See speech by Vithaldas Damodardas Thakarsey, *Report of the 19th Indian National Congress*, p. 99.

25. India Office, *Statement Exhibiting the Moral and Material Progress and Condition in British India*, 1901–02, HMSO, London, 1902.

26. Theodore Morison, 1911, *The Economic Transition*, pp. 236–7, suggested these categories.

27. It is not intended to suggest that an independent India would have spent as much as British India did on these items.

28. India Office, *Statistical Abstracts Relating to British India, 1908–09*, HMSO, London, 1909.

29. W. J. MacPherson, 1935, 'Investment in Indian Railways, 1845–1875', *Economic History Review*, 2nd Ser., vol. VIII, no. 2, p. 181.

30. Daniel Thorner, 1950, *Investment in Empire: British Railway and Steam Shipping Enterprise in India: 1825–1849*, p. 168.

31. *Statistical Abstract . . . 1899–1900 to 1908–09*, note, p. 49. The practice of guaranteeing railway profits was abandoned in 1869.

32. *Cambridge History of India*, vol. VI, pp. 325–6.

33. Morison, 1911, *The Economic Transition*, p. 239.

34. Albert H. Imlah, 1952, 'British Balance of Payments and Export of Capital, 1816–1913', *Economic History Review*, 2nd Ser., vol. 5, no. 2.

35. Dutt, 1904, *India in the Victorian Age*, p. 550.

36. Speech of D. E. Wacha, *Report of the 17th Indian National Congress*, p. 46. The North-Western Railway, a large part of which was classified as military, accounted for a net charge to the government of Rs 25.33 crore up to the end of 1900. The net charge of all other State Railways to the end of 1900 was Rs 6.08 crore. Statement of Financial Statistical of State Railways . . . for and to the end of the year 1900, *Supplement to Gazette of India*, 6 July 1901.

37. For a fuller nationalist view, see D. E. Wacha, 1912, *Indian Railway Finance*. W. J. MacPherson gives instances in which British commercial groups influenced railway policy in directions not necessarily beneficial to India. 'Investment in Indian Railways, 1845–1875', *Economic History Review*, 2nd Ser., vol. III, no. 2, p. 185.

38. *Indian Expenditure Commission*, vol. IV, *Final Report*, paras 121–9.

39. Strachey, 1911, *India: Its Administration and Progress*, p. 251.

40. *Statistical Abstract . . . 1899–1900 to 1908–09*, p. 267.

41. *Indian Expenditure Commission*, vol. IV, *Final Report*, para. 350.

42. *Indian Expenditure Commission*, vol. III, *Minutes of Evidence*, Q. 17566.

43. Morison, 1911, *The Economic Transition,* p. 215.
44. Inaugural Address to the 1st Industrial Conference, Poona, 1890. M. G. Ranade, 1899, *Essays on Indian Economics: A Collection of Essays and Speeches,* p. 186. Ranade also said that although there was 'good cause for complaint' about the Home Charges for pensions, administration, and defence, 'we should not forget the fact that we are enabled by reason of this British connection to levy an equivalent tribute from China by our Opium Monopoly'.
45. *Power and the Guardian,* 15 July 1899, Thagi and Dakaiti Department Selections from the Native Newspapers, 24 July 1899, Political and Secret Letters from India, vol. 115.
46. *Indian Expenditure Commission,* vol. IV, *Final Report,* paras 218–27.
47. See Suakin Expedition: Correspondence between the Government of India and the Secretary of State in Council regarding the incidence of the cost of Indian troops when employed out of India, H. of C. 8131 of 1896.
48. *Indian Expenditure Commission,* vol. II, *First Report,* C. 8259 of 1896, Appendix 45, no. 1, Government of India to Secretary of State, no. 70, 25 March 1890, para. 21. Government protests against the financial arrangements with the United Kingdom were a favourite source of ammunition for nationalist-speakers. This particular despatch of Lansdowne's was quoted by Srinivas Rao at the 1902 Congress. *Report of 18th I.N.C.,* p. 103.
49. Curzon to Hamilton, 15 July and 15 August 1900, MSS, Eur. D. 510/5.
50. *Indian Expenditure Commission, Copy of Further Correspondence . . . H. of C.* 169 of 1902, no. 3, Government of India to Secretary of State, 6 July 1901.
51. East India (Liability for Increase in British Soldiers' Pay), *Return of the Correspondence . . . H. of C.* 237 of 1903.
52. *Statistical Abstract . . . 1988–1900 to 1908–09,* pp. 68–9. In 1904, in the Governor-General's Legislative Council, the Military Member, Sir Edmond Elles, made a rather feeble attempt to prove the military expenditure was decreasing in proportion to revenue receipts, and not as Gokhale had alleged, increasing. To support this tendentious point, Elles selected as the starting point for his comparison the years 1896–7 to 1899–1900 when revenue was low due to famine and plague, and when military spending

was high as a result of the Frontier Wars. Abstract of the Governor-General's Legislative Council Progs., vol. LXIII, 30 March 1904, p. 625.

53. R. C. Dutt, 1908, *The Economic History of British India,* pp. vii–viii.
54. James S. Mill, 1848, *The History of British India . . . with notes and continuation by Horace Hayman Wilson,* quoted in R. C. Dutt, 1908, *Economic History of India under Early British Rule,* pp. 362–3, and by P. M. Mehta, Industrial Exhibition of 1902, *Report of the 18th I.N.C.,* p. 160.
55. *The Political, Commercial and Financial Condition of the Anglo-Eastern Empire,* in 1832 (1832) and *The Indian Empire: History, Topography, Geology . . .,* 3 vols. (1858–61), cited by Naoroji, 1901, *Poverty and Un-British Rule in India,* p. viii; Digby, 1901, *'Prosperous' British India,* pp. xxi, 81; and Dutt, 1908, *The Economic History of British India,* pp. 289–90, 409–10.
56. Goerge Wingate, 1859, *A Few Words on our Financial Relations with India,* p. 8. Cited by Naoroji, 1901, *Poverty and Un-British Rule in India,* pp. viii–ix; Dutt, 1901, *'Prosperous' British India,* pp. 419–20; and Dutt, 1904, *India in the Victorian Age,* pp. xvi, 214, 219.
57. Brooks Adams, 1896, *Law of Civilisation and Decay: An Essay on History,* chap. x, cited by Digby, 1901, *'Prosperous' British India,* pp. 31–3; also in Surendranath Banerjee's Presidential Address, *Report on the 18th I. N. C.,* p. 43. The view of Brooks Adams is controverted by C. J. Hamilton, 1919, *The Trade Relations between England and India,* pp. 167–71.
58. *India List and India Office List for 1902,* p. 174.
59. Strachey, 1903, *India: Its Administration and Progress,* p. 84, Note 1.
60. The actual rate of exchange for 1889–90 was $1s. 4\frac{5}{66}d$. R. C. Dutt (*Economic History of India under Early British Rule,* p. 444) converted the figures from the Parliamentary Return into sterling at the rate of 2s., thus exaggerating the amount received by the Europeans.
61. Naoroji, 1901, *Poverty and Un-British Rule in India,* pp. 56–8.
62. Naoroji to Hamilton, 12 Oct. 1900. *Bengalee,* 4 June 1901.
63. Curzon to Hamilton, 23 April 1900, MSS. Eur. D. 51015.
64. See Honorary Secretary, Indian Association, to Secretary, Govt. of India, Home Dept., 18 Dec. 1899. Enclosure to C. W. Bolton, Secretary, Govt. of Bengal, to Govt. of India, Home Dept., 9 March

1899, Dec. Prog. no. 236. Also, J. P. Hewett, Secretary, Govt. of India, to Secretary, Govt. of Bengal, 20 Dec. 1900. Dec. Prog. no. 237, India Home Prog., Public, vol. 5874.

65. A. U. Fanshawe, Director General of Post Office of India, to Secretary, Govt. of India, Finance and Commerce Dept., 25 April 1898, Oct., Prog. no. 290, India Home Prog., Public, vol. 5640.

66. J. P. Hewett to Secretary, Govt. of Bengal, 20 Dec. 1900, op. cit.

67. Governor General in Council of Secretary of State, 13 Oct. 1898, Oct. Prog. no. 168, India Home Prog., Public, vol. 5414.

68. J. P. Hewett to Secretary, Govt. of Bengal, 20 Dec. 1900, op. cit.

69. G. Subramania Iyer, 1904, 'Employment of Indians in the Public Service—Fiction and Fact', *Hindustan Review and Kayastha Samachar,* vol. x, no. 4 (Oct.), p. 327.

70. These figures are compiled from the tables appended to Subramania Iyer, 1904, 'Employment of Indians in the Public Service, pp. 330–44.

For India, the beginning of the 1890s marked a period when British rule appeared to be fairly well-entrenched in terms of mechanisms to extract resources from the domestic economy. This was reflected in the growing volume of Home Charges (or contractual overseas expenses) of the Indian government, the actual value of which was around £18 million by the turn of the century. This sum was substantial relative to the level of national income of India which was estimated at £120 million in 1900.[1]

Institutional support for transferring financial resources was provided by the exchange banks, operating in the City of London and in the financial centres of India (mainly Calcutta or Bombay). These banks financed the growing financial transactions—both public and private—between the two countries. In London, all the sterling funds due for remittance to India (mainly on account of export surpluses) were mopped up through the intermediation of the exchange banks and the India Office, under the direct surveillance of the British government. No less significant, however, was the influence of the financial centre, the City of London, which circumscribed the sphere of operation of the India Office. The Home Charges of the Indian government were disbursed in London in sterling procured from the exchange earnings, while the unspent part was maintained as a steady and growing sterling balance with the Bank of England. Funds deployed by the India Office, especially as cash reserves and other sterling assets in the City, had a significant role in easing the liquidity situation in London City. (The Indian government's involvement in the London money market was considered crucial for maintaining, in accord with imperial interests, the market trends in silver. The Indian government was actually forbidden, even during situations of silver shortages at home, to procure silver from the market which would have produced sharp increases in silver prices.)

In section 4.1 we provide an account of the model of effecting the transfers, through specially instituted devices—Council Bills (henceforth CB) which settled the remittances. Attention is drawn to the legal–contractual aspects supporting the network of financial settlements across the two nations, especially in the

4

Tributes and Transfers from Colonial India*

Sunanda Sen

This chapter makes an attempt to identify and measure the tributes which flowed from colonial India. Evidence of transfer of the tributes will be offered in this chapter, reinforcing our central thesis that expropriation and transfer of surplus in an Empire–colony set-up was an ongoing process.

We have chosen 1890–1914—years of high finance in the world economy—as the period of our analysis. During this period, banks and industries in the advanced countries were geared, for the first time in history, to maximize the rates of return on investment which was also invested overseas. This period marked the heyday of finance capital in Europe and witnessed the coming of age of the financial institutions, especially in the City of London, which provided for a multilateral clearing of trade and capital flows across the Empire and other overseas nations.

Our method of analyzing the process of expropriation of surplus and its transfer overseas is relevant in understanding both the Empire–colony configurations and the neo-colonial relationships. Parallels drawn between the colonial mode of surplus extraction and neo-colonialism in the periphery lends topicality to our research on late nineteenth- and early twentieth-century experiences.

* Previously published in Sunanda Sen, *Colonies and the Empire: India 1890–1914*, Orient Longman, Hyderabad, 1992, pp. 15–70.

context of the colonial regime in India. The crucial role of the exchange banks and trading houses is unveiled in the process, all of which were significantly controlled by Europeans. Financial transfers to England, legalized under the pretext of the manifold claims on the Indian government, were entirely met through export earnings in London. A closer analysis reveals the underlying process of political domination in which the government as well as private individuals in Britain wielded the power to set the norms for transactions with the colonies. As will be indicated in this chapter, it is possible to identify an element of unilateral transfer in what can otherwise be viewed as a regular flow of remittances between the two countries. The official and private agencies in both countries took active interest in ensuring, through the CB network, a channel for the steady flow of financial transfers between India and Britain. Additional support was lent through private financial institutions (like exchange banks) which were mostly controlled by Anglo-Indian or European commercial and financial interests in India. It is thus convincing to take, at its face value, the generalization arrived at at the end of Section 4.1 that the major instruments of financial transfers between the two governments were, by and large, initiated at the behest of the British government or the European commercial agencies (which included the banks). Attempts to lay bare the specific political context of the various financial transactions bring to focus the subservient colonial status of the country in relation to Britain, in terms of both administrative and commercial arrangements. Our approach towards understanding external economic transactions rejects mechanistic interpretations of these arrangements which are often evident in other similar studies.[2] The specific slant in our emphasis on political factors behind the international economic transactions in colonial India, while germane to the nationalist writings on Indian economic history, was hardly spelt out in these studies. Section 4.2 draws attention to the implications of silver currency in India, especially during the period of depreciating silver.

Section 4.3 identifies and measures the flow of financial transfers between the two countries. For the sake of convenience it has been subdivided into two subheads, addressing two specific questions. In Section 4.3.1 we look into the details of the 'Expenditure Abroad', the compelling factor behind financial transfers. While a major part of these transfers consisted of interest payments on productive loans, incurred to meet productive expenditure (railways and irrigation) in the past, closer analysis reveals that even such interest payments could be classified as unproductive expenditure. Unearthing some accounting devices, which were used in the official budget, we find it possible to conclude that almost the entire amount of the Home Charges could be regarded as unilateral transfers from India. Section 4.3.2 addresses the question posed by Indian nationalists around the turn of last century concerning the so-called drain of wealth from India. We have sought to bring out the basic strength as well as weaknesses of the nationalist position on this question. We have contested the claim of the nationalists that: (a) the whole of India's export surplus remained unpaid, and (b) the entire amount of Home Charges, including servicing of irrigation and railway loans, was part of a political tribute. Both issues can be examined by looking into budgetary transfers. The first claim is found to be formally invalid since exporters were, in fact, duly paid through the mediation of exchange banks. But the practice of using local tax revenue to settle net export earnings within the country imparted a deflationary bias in terms of aggregate demand in the economy. In fact, the unilateral transfer of the tribute (comprising Home Charges) created, in addition to an equivalent transfer or drain of wealth, a potential for income contraction. The second claim is examined as we look into the details of the controversy on the drain. Attention, in particular, is paid to the sharp attacks on the nationalist arguments by both Alfred Marshall and John Maynard Keynes in their official papers and other writings (which include private correspondence). That Keynes was an official at the India Office did not detract from the analytical rigour of his writings and correspondence on Indian currency. Incidentally, both Keynes and Marshall lent full support to the prevailing monetary arrangements in British India. A general ethos thus prevailed amongst officials and intellectuals in England which provided uncritical support to the British Empire. The view clearly dismissed the ongoing questioning of British rule in India. For Keynes, inflow of long-term capital into India was solid evidence of what could be characterized as a 'reverse' drain of wealth from England.[3] We have contrasted this view with that held by the nationalists[4] in their theory relating to the drain.

Section 4.4 dwells on quantification of resource transfers from India. We have tried to arrive at an indirect measure by relying on the estimates that are available for external trade and other economic transactions over the period 1899–1900 to 1908–09. Data compiled by Theodore Morison, and revised later by Keynes, on a 'Conjectural Balance Sheet for India'[5] have been used to test out our arguments on external transfers. Statistics on current account transactions in the above estimates do not, somehow, tally with the figures available from India Office sources on remittances. This has led us to cross-check and reconstruct the official series on India's trade data. Our doubts on the issue seem to have a point as Keynes himself appears to have been baffled over the same issue. In his private correspondence with an India Office official, he pointed out an inconsistency between India's official trade returns and the India Office's records on Council Bill remittances—a controversy of which we became aware at a late stage of our research.[6] It was indeed reassuring to discover that Keynes pointed to the same type of limitations in India's official trade data as have been identified by us in our attempt at constructing a new series of such data. Problems in reconciling the CB series and the trade data even after possible corrections to the latter led us to treat the remittance figures at the India Office[7] as a better approximation of net transfers from India. (Our practice of treating the data on remittances as a surrogate for data on trade balance between the two countries can be justified by the prevailing legal–institutional system in colonial India which entailed the use of her entire trade surplus to meet the Home Charges in England.) Our analysis in the rest of this chapter confirms the hypothesis that there is evidence of a continuing flow of transfers from colonial India.

4.1   Formal Control over Remittances: The Council Bill Device

India's trade and exchange links with the rest of the world appear to have achieved a fair degree of sophistication by the 1890s. The decade witnessed the emergence of a whole network of banks and business houses in India, largely controlled by Europeans, which supported official attempts to achieve a smooth flow of remittances between the two countries. By the turn of the century, official remittances to England on account of the overseas liabilities were nearly as large as the sum spent to meet official liabilities in India. Increases in contractual overseas payments—the typical pattern of which around 1900 can be judged from data given in Table 4.1—indicate that regularity in overseas remittances was essential for managing the external relations of the government. Payments abroad covered administrative charges at the India Office and other external liabilities, some of which were contractual in nature. Administrative arrangements to ensure a steady homeward flow of the earnings of the commercial community and other European residents in India were highly convenient. A brief account of the changing arrangements for remittances is given below.

A formal device was employed by the British rulers to siphon off the sterling proceeds of India's export surpluses to England. This marked the beginning of the CBs drawn on the Treasury in India and sold by the India Office in London to exchange banks desirous of remitting (on behalf of their agents) the proceeds of India's net export earnings. In India the bills were honoured by the Treasury where the exchange banks were reimbursed in Indian rupees out of the fiscal revenue earmarked in the domestic budget. The new system of remittance reduced the significance of flows of treasure which, along with the trade bills, were ordinarily the means of settling the balance of payment. The CBs were sold in London every Wednesday by the Secretary of State (SOS) at the India Office against offers in sterling from exchange banks. The prevailing exchange rate and currency system in India permitted, until the mints were closed to unlimited coinage of rupees by an official decree of June 1893, a parallel flow of remittances via flow of treasure (which included both gold and silver). Thus, till June 1893, silver rupees were available on demand from the mint against bullion offered by the remitting public. The exchange value of the rupee fluctuated in sterling according to the movements in the relative prices of the two metals in the world market. The price of the CBs in rupees were closely monitored by the India Office, in order that the network of remittances under CBs was never unprofitable as compared to direct remittances through flow of treasure (gold and silver bullions as well as gold coins).

Problems encountered by the ruling government and European residents in India in the face of sharp declines in the rupee rate (which drifted downwards with the drop in the gold price and in the price of silver since the 1870s) led to the appointment of a Royal Committee on Indian Currency in 1893. This committee, known as the Herschell Committee, recommended closure of the Indian mint to the public so that no coins could be minted on public demand. While the exchange value of the rupee was officially announced at 1s. 4d., minting of coins was left entirely to official discretion after 1893. As mints were closed in 1893, the unit price of the CBs sold was appropriately adjusted, allowing for the costs of remittance. (Rates fixed for the alternate route of remittance, i.e., telegraphic transfers, were similarly adjusted.) The volume of CBs sold by the SOS went up over the years, providing the India Office direct access to the sterling proceeds of India's net export earnings. (The earlier practice—during East India Company rule—of selling bills of exchange on India effectively achieved for the Company a similar goal of collecting the sterling proceeds of India's net exports in London.) During the earlier years, the maximum value of CBs sold during a year was limited to the annual Home Charges. The CBs were later allowed by the Act of 1905 to exceed the Home Charges and thus CBs sold were up to a value which was acceptable in the market (see Table 4.1 for CBs sold during 1861-1914). The CBs, therefore, provided a route for retaining in England the entire amount of India's export surplus which now could even build up externally held assets for the India Office. Actual use of these assets, however, was severely constrained by the directives of the Bank of England, which soon gained an authority over the financial policies of the Indian government. Purchase of sterling securities by the India Office improved, in general, the investment climate in the City. We will return to these aspects of India's financial links with Britain during the period of 'mature colonialism'[8] in the late nineteenth century after we have discussed the essence of the mechanism and the magnitude of the financial transfers.

Remittances through Council Bills were based on an undertaking by the Indian treasury that all bills drawn on it were to be reimbursed by it in Indian rupees. Funds earmarked in the annual budget as 'Expenditure Abroad' were used to honour the CBs in India, thus releasing the sterling proceeds (of the sales of CBs) for disbursement in England. Fiscal problems of providing for the Home Charges in rupees were sorted out in 1893 when uncertainties regarding the rupee rate were removed. Home Charges, however, continued to grow in absolute terms in sterling resulting in proportionate increases in the domestic expenditure earmarked for overseas disbursements. The process, in terms of a simple Keynesian framework, implied a leakage in the income stream, as could be caused by an equivalent surplus budget. Compounded by the monetary squeeze and credit stringencies which resulted from the policies followed by the ruling government, the colonial economy had reasons to experience a sluggishness in demand and a related depression in output growth.

The intricacies of the remittance scheme under the Council Bills or of their counterparts, the Reverse Councils (which were sold in years of adverse trade), persuade us to pay a little more attention to the mechanism. Figure 4.1 shows the network of payments and compensations which can be described in the following seven steps:

(a) CBs sold by the India Office to exchange banks served as a device to retain in London India's sterling revenue from net export earnings abroad.

(b) In India, the Treasury paid to the exchange banks an equivalent sum in rupees as the CBs were produced for encashment. Implicit in the device was a transfer or compensation; while the budgetary sources of revenue in India provided for the entire payments to exporters on account of their net export earnings abroad, equivalent revenue was kept back in sterling at the India Office in England. The rupee payments were the counterpart funds to sterling disbursed (in England) under the budgetary head of Expenditure Abroad (or Home Charges).

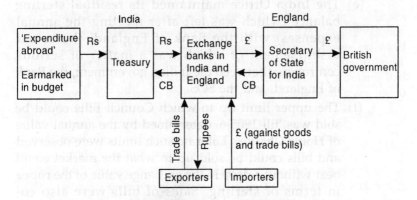

Fig. 4.1 *Mode of remittance between England and India during British rule*

(c) Bills sold by the SOS were denominated in sterling, the rupee value of which was consistent with the exchange value of the currency. Before 1893, when mints in India were open to unlimited coinage of silver currency, CBs provided an alternate channel of remittance, supplementing the other option of a direct settlement by shipments of gold and silver bullion or gold coins. It had thus always been customary as well as compulsory on the part of the SOS to maintain the price of the CBs at a level which was consistent with the prevailing rupee–sterling rate.

(d) In England, the India Office's annual expenditure abroad, known as Home Charges, included the Indian government's official liabilities to Britain. The more important heads of such expenditure (given in Table 4.1) included interest payments and debt management on past loans. In addition, Home Charges included payment of salaries and pensions to British officials employed with the (Indian) government, the India Office's administrative expenses, and finally, the charges on account of Britain's defence activities in India and abroad.

(e) The India Office maintained its residual sterling balance (which was left after meeting the annual expenses) with the Bank of England, the actual disbursement of which was a matter of serious controversy between the Indian government, the Bank of England, and the SOS.

(f) The upper limit up to which Council Bills could be sold was, till 1905-6, determined by the annual value of Home Charges. Later no such limits were observed and bills could be sold up to what the market could bear without a drop in the exchange value of the rupee in terms of sterling. Sales of bills were also co-ordinated to transfer gold from the Treasury and from the two official currency reserves in India to their counterparts in London where gold could be put to use for purchase of sterling securities, providing additional sources of liquidity to the financial system in the London City.

(g) Sales of CBs on India gave way to Reverse Council Bills (RCBs) on England during 1907–08. The period was an unusual one with trade deficits for India, largely as a result of extensive droughts and crop shortfalls in the country. The practice was one of stopping the sale of CBs in London and their substitution by RCBs. These bills could be encashed in sterling at the India Office. The unusual step was taken to meet the country's trade deficit and also to maintain the rupee rate at its official peg. In the absence of RCBs, the trade deficits would have put pressure on the rupee rate.

The singularities of this remittance scheme and the Indian currency system were commented upon by Keynes who, among other contemporaries, was also highly appreciative of the device: '. . . remittances by means of Council Bills is a feature peculiar to the Indian system [arising] partly from the historical circumstances that the Government of India is the successor of a trading company, partly from the necessity . . . of making very large remittances to England.' Furthermore, '. . . rupees to this amount, being part of the revenue from taxation, etc. accumulate in the Indian treasuries. This value is remitted to England by selling for sterling in London bills which can be cashed in Calcutta. Thus the Government of India pays out rupees in Calcutta where the bills are presented, and the Secretary of State's balances in the Bank of England are swelled by a corresponding amount.'[9]

It is reasonable at this stage to distinguish between two possible approaches to the mode of external settlements by Council Bills. In terms of the first approach, the CBs, in combination with ordinary trade bills (also known as bills of exchange), can be viewed as ordinary means of settling India's external trade and payments. Council Bills and trade bills, along with the domestic budget, were the three chief instruments available to finance the country's external economic transactions, and were used by a set of three official agents which included the India Office (or the SOS) in London, the exchange banks and trading houses operating between the two countries, and finally, the Treasury in India.

We have offered, above, an alternative view on Council Bills, based on considerations which completely change the interpretation of the CB network as a mode of remittance. This former view reflects an awareness that, implicit in the CBs— apparently settled on a simple basis of reciprocity—was an imperial design to plough back the entire proceeds of India's export surplus and to retain it in England. In Section 4.3.1 we pose the question of whether the process was at all legitimate, an answer to which helps us to identify the element of unilateral transfer in the flow of remittances between the two countries. The issue, as pointed out earlier in this chapter, can only be sorted out by recognizing the political realities of the Empire–colony relationship between India and Britain.

4.2 Depreciating Silver and the Fiscal Burden on the Indian Government: 1870–92

The CB network provided a handy tool to the finance department of the Indian government as it closed the mints to free coinage in 1893 on the recommendations of the Royal Committee on Indian Currency. The committee, under the chairmanship of Lord Herschell, wanted to delink the rupee rate from world silver prices that fell in world markets with the steady displacement of silver by gold and the breakdown of bimetallism in the major industrialized nations of the West during the 1870s. As already hinted, maintaining silver currency in India implied a considerable strain on the country's fiscal resources, with almost half (or more) of official expenditure determined by contractual liabilities in sterling. It was, therefore, necessary to raise additional revenue which could meet the escalation in the rupee cost of sterling caused by the depreciating rupee. Moreover, the European community in India was concerned at the depreciated sterling value of their rupee remittances, and this provided additional grounds for a change in the official currency policy. Implementing the recommendations of the Herschell Committee in 1893 by delinking the rupee rate from market fluctuations in silver prices thus proved to be a mutually convenient solution to the government as well as European residents in India. The continued use of silver as the metallic base for coins in India (and in China) suited the interests of silver producing countries in the West which, according to one study, constituted an integral part of imperial designs in the East.[10]

Measures implemented during 1893–8 to stabilize the rupee at 1s. 4d. included the following:

(a) A willingness on the part of the Indian Treasury to convert all incoming CBs at the official exchange rate. It is worth pointing out the implicit anomaly in the functioning of the gold exchange standard in India as conversion of rupees into sterling was ruled out by the government, presumably on grounds of the poor rating of the rupee in the world currency market. The official attitude indicated the prevailing state of colonial economic policies in India which ruled out all connections between export surpluses and the market strength or weakness of the rupee.

(b) Measures were taken to demonetize the rupee, as was recommended by the Herschell Committee, in order to stabilize the rupee rate at the officially announced peg of 1s. 4d. Rupee coins worth Rs 10 million were melted while fresh coinage of the rupee was altogether stopped—the second measure amounting, according to a private estimate, to a net withdrawal of Rs 525 million from circulation during 1893–8. The package of measures, however, did not succeed in stabilizing the rupee before the reversal in world gold prices which started during 1898.

The closure of the mints in 1893 to coinage on public demand strengthened the demand for CBs in England as a form of remittance. The other route via treasure flows, however, continued, as can be verified from Table 4.1. While treasure inflows helped sustain hoarding (or other industrial uses) of the metals, coinage was resumed in 1898 and sustained the regular source of demand for imports of silver in India. Gold sovereigns, however, were accepted by the Treasury as revenue—a policy which channelized most of the gold sovereign imports into official reserves. The changing composition of reserves which resulted from disproportionate increases in the share of gold sovereigns called for further changes in the official currency policy in India which now aimed at transferring them to England by using the Council Bills remittance network.

4.3 The Pattern of Financial Settlements between India and England around 1900: Direction, Sources, and Magnitude of Net Flows

In this section we draw attention to the pattern and magnitude of what we have identified as the flow of unilateral transfers from colonial India around 1900. It clearly requires more than a conventional textbook approach to look for an element of transfer in what were apparently legitimate contractual payments to the British government and its officials for 'services' provided and paid for under Home Charges. An analysis of the specific political context of the so-called 'services' reveals an element of expropriation legitimized under colonial rule. Interestingly, the relatively non-controversial component of the Home Charges, viz. that on servicing official loans contracted in the past for productive purposes seems, on a closer analysis, to have been a result of accounting transfers. Such transfers were deliberately used to hide the extent of borrowing to meet the unproductive expenditure of the Indian government. Use of the net export earnings to meet unproductive expenditure amounts to an act of unrequited exports or unilateral transfers—one without any quid pro quo (as indicated in Section 4.3.1). Understandably, it is relatively difficult to arrive at a measure of unilateral transfers. The difficulties are compounded by the limitations of trade data and the consequent problems of compiling India's balance of payments by a 'residual approach'.[11] Problems of using the official trade statistics of colonial India led us to base our measure of the transfer on estimates of remittance flows through sales of Council Bills at the India Office—records that were obviously more accurate compared to trade data. We will return to this theme in Section 4.4 which deals with the magnitude of transfers.

Table 4.1 *Pattern of overseas expenditure under Home Charges: 1861–2 to 1913–14 (£ million)*

Items	Annual averages			
	1861–2 to 1874–5	1875–6 to 1897–8	1898–9 to 1913–14	1910–11
(1)	*(2)*	*(3)*	*(4)*	*(5)*
1. Interest charges and debt management: chargeable under head of	5.7	7.9	9.4	11.1
(a) railways and irrigation	3.5	5.3	6.9	8.8 (0.1)
(b) other interest	2.2	2.6	2.5	2.3
2. Stores purchased in England against revenue and for railways	1.1	1.2	1.6	1.0
3. Civil administration in India Office (excluding pensions)	0.2	0.6	0.2	0.1
4. Army and marine charges:	2.6	3.5	4.2	4.1
(a) effective charges including Home Charges for British officials in India				1.1
(b) Non-effective charges				3.0
5. Pensions and furlough	0.9	1.7	2.3	2.3
6. Total expenditure under Home Charges (items 1 to 5)	10.5	14.9	17.7	18.6

Note: Figure in brackets in col. 5 refers to irrigation.

Sources: Cols. 2 to 4, Dharma Kumar, 'The Fiscal System', in Dharma Kumar, ed., 1983, *Cambridge Economic History of India (1757–1920)*, vol. II, p. 938. Col. 5 is taken from the Explanatory Memorandum, annually submitted by the Under-Secretary of State for India, cited in Theodore Morison, 1911, *Economic Transition in India*, London, p. 234.

4.3.1 *Transfers from India and 'Expenditure Abroad'*

The flow of finance between India and England was to a large extent determined by the sum annually remitted abroad to meet the government's Home Charges in England. Since the latter absorbed nearly the entire amount of India's overseas trade surplus, it is worth enquiring into its political legitimacy by scrutinizing the individual heads of expenses under the Home Charges. The criterion of political legitimacy is given by the justifiability of such expenses in terms of the separate identity of India as a self-governing territory, as was often claimed by the British. Payments made out to procure goods or services which were absorbed by the national economy (in its separate identity shorn of colonial rule) were all warranted in terms of this criterion. Logically, the remaining charges which were directly related to the maintenance and promotion of the commercial and political interests of the British Empire could be identified as unilateral transfers from the national economy since these were never reimbursed or repaid in any form.

Let us dwell a little on the actual pattern of financial flows between England and colonial India during the half century preceding the First World War. As already explained, all official expenses of the Indian government in England were earmarked, in the India budget, as 'Expenditure Abroad' by the India Office, which procured the sterling equivalents through sales of Council Bills in London. In Table 4.1 we have provided the details of overseas expenses during 1861–2 to 1913-14. The items listed under the different subheads can be divided into the following three major categories: (a) civil administration (items 3 and 5); (b) defence (item 4); and (c) productive expenditure and/or management of debt chargeable under productive heads (item 1 excluding [b] plus item 2).

Quantitatively, the weight of debt service charges in respect of railway and irrigation loans appears to be predominant in the aggregate overseas expenditure during the period. These loans were chargeable under productive heads. The relative significance of the three categories (a) to (c) can be assessed from their respective weights which stood at 1:1:3 during 1910–11, indicating the very crucial importance of the expenditure designated as 'productive' in determining the magnitude of Home Charges, most of which was thus incurred on servicing irrigation and railway loans. In the year 1910-11, out of a total expenditure of £18.6 million on Home Charges, more than 60 per cent was spent in servicing past loans. At £8.7 million, railways alone accounted for around 47 per cent of the total expenditure. Interest payments and debt management in respect of other types of loans accounted for another £2.3 million, thus bringing expenditure under this head to £11.1 million, a sum which was substantial compared to other current productive expenditure earmarked for purchase of stores for railways, which at £1.0 million, was only 5.6 per cent of the total. Expenditure on defence, designated as 'Army and Marine Charges', comprised the second major component, which, at £4.1 million, constituted about 21 per cent while the third important component, viz. pensions and furlough, along with current civil expenditure stood at £2.4 million or 12 per cent of total overseas expenditure for 1910–11. The distribution of the expenses reflects the overall pattern of Home Charges during the pre-World War period.

One can argue, presumably without being accused of a nationalist bias, that most of the civil and military expenditures of the Indian government in England (items 3, 4, and 5 in Table 4.1) listed as (a) and (b) above, which accounted for one-third of overseas expenditure, were in the interest of the British.[12] The argument excludes the local expenses in rupees connected with the maintenance of the civilian government in India, which would clearly have been warranted even under a national government. Later in this section, we survey some of the current controversies on the expediency and justifiability of the enormous share of British military expenses which had to be borne by India.

Looking at the table one can identify about one-third of over-seas expenses (which included defence and civil administration) as directly caused by British rule in India. This certainly does not warrant condemning the entire amount of Home Charges as a 'drain of wealth' from India as the nationalists had argued.[13] It has to be remembered that nearly three-fifths of the overseas expenditure was accounted for by 'interest charges and debt management' against productive loans for investment in railways and irrigation. Unless these payments can also be attributed to the machinations of the ruling imperial power in India, it would not be logical to attribute the entire amount (or even the major part) of the Home Charges as expropriations due to foreign rule. It is interesting to note that a distinction was maintained in contemporary official reports between productive and unproductive categories[14] of official loans in India. When the money borrowed was spent on public works like railways and irrigation, loans were treated as productive. Borrowing for all other purposes including administration, was categorized as unproductive. We do not, at this point, want to enter into a debate as to whether in India, expenditure in railways was oriented to serve national interests. Rather, we prefer to reserve our judgement on the extreme position taken by the nationalists that the entire amount of Home Charges, including the substantial sum incurred to service productive loans, were all a drain of wealth from the national economy.

It is worth mentioning, at this point, a rather curious device of accounting transfers which was hidden in the budgetary practices of the Indian government during the period. The practice, initially recommended by a select committee of the British Parliament in 1867, amounted, for practical purposes, to a camouflaging—one where borrowings under productive heads were used, in effect, to cancel old unproductive debt while public works expenditure was in reality financed by a revenue surplus. In terms of the recommendation of the 1867 select committee, '. . . all capital expenditure on productive works supplied from revenue should be treated in the accounts *as if it had been borrowed*, that a sum equal to that which was thus supplied should be *transferred* from the ordinary debt to the productive public works debt, and that interest on that sum be charged on the works' (italics added).[15] In the year 1880–1 the Government of India added Rs 5.4 million as outstanding productive loans—a sum which was simultaneously recovered from current revenue and utilized to cancel unproductive loans, the proceeds of which were spent on unproductive heads before 1867.[16] Since then new loans shown against productive heads of expenditure were floated in the market, and the proceeds made available to finance capital projects (despite the availability of revenue surplus for the purpose). The notional (or accounting) transfers implicit in the scheme included the following stages:

Stage 1: A hypothetical sum, say Rs 100, is transferred from the revenue account to finance an equivalent expenditure on public works in the capital account of the domestic budget.

Stage 2: An expenditure of Rs 100 on public works in India and England is shown in the capital account.

Stage 3: Additional borrowings, under productive heads, worth Rs 100 cover the capital expenditure.

Stage 4: Revenue from the above borrowings is used to repay and cancel old unproductive loans which now goes down, as a consequence, by Rs 100.

The adaption of the procedure described above in managing the government's finances led, as could be expected, to a relative increase in the size of productive debt which was held as a proportion of the aggregate debt in rupees and sterling. The absolute figures for productive debt went up from £5.4 million to £159.3 million over 1867–97, and its share in total debt went up from 6.4 per cent to 63.3 per cent over the same period (see Table 4.2).[17] *The underlying process was the outcome of a policy contrived by the colonial rulers to camouflage the extent of public borrowings to finance politically sensitive and commercially unviable expenditures of the government.* Most of these expenditures, connected with the subservient political status of India in relation to Britain, were but overtly political in origin. It is pertinent to argue, by the same logic, that the servicing of productive debt, which accounted for almost two-thirds of the aggregate Home Charges by 1913, was in effect financing unproductive expenditure. Thus the interest paid and the debt managed were, truly speaking, not in respect of productive debt, since the latter was a surrogate for the amount spent and borrowed in the past for unproductive purposes. This fact, we think, can be used as a very important step in constructing an argument on the justifiability or otherwise of the Home Charges from a national angle.

Table 4.2 *Changes in the composition of public debt in India: 1867–97*

(£ million)

	1867	1897
Ordinary or unproductive	90.6(93.3)	72.7 (31.4)
Productive (public works)	5.4 (6.7)	159.3 (63.6)
Total	96.0	232.0

(Figures in brackets are in percentages)

Note: 1. According to Balfour returns, unproductive debts held in March 1867 and 1897 were £92.5 million and £63.7 million respectively. The divergent movements in the shares under the two heads over the period were thus sharper under the Balfour returns.

2. Rupee figures converted into sterling at Rs 10:£1 and Rs 15:£1 for 1867 and 1897 respectively.

Source: Welby Commission, pp. 44, 47–8.

With notional transfers incorporated in the budget, revenue earmarked to finance public works was, in effect, used to subsidize unproductive expenditure by cancelling old and unproductive debt. Hence, a natural tendency on the part of the government was to feel encouraged in continuing with its growing level of unproductive expenses in the two countries and covering them by taxes or loans (in rupee or sterling) raised from the market. (All productive expenses, it might be recalled, were statutorily covered by fresh loans raised in the market.) Moreover, raising of sterling loans to cover capital expenditure and the subsequent transfers under service heads led to the possibility of sterling borrowed in excess being retained by the SOS in London. Sterling loans contracted against public works expenditures in India, which was statutory under the select committee's recommendations, increased the India Office's liquidity in England because a part of the public works expenses was met in rupees.

Outstanding loans of the Indian government held in sterling rose sharply relative to rupee loans during 1890–1913.[18] This was evident in the meagre 10 per cent increase in rupee loans over the period, which contrasted with the 32 per cent increase in sterling loans. Table 4.2 reveals the marked increases in outstanding loans under productive heads, matched by a simultaneous decline in unproductive loans. It was thus natural that interest charges and management of productive debt comprised nearly 60 per cent of the Home Charges around 1910–11 (see Table 4.1).

Current expenditure, classified as unproductive in the government budget, was spread under three heads. These included famine relief, military operations, and civil administration. Interestingly enough, while the outstanding debt shown under unproductive heads went down over 1867–97, the scale of unproductive expenses, especially on overseas military operations, went up over the period 1861–2 to 1913–14. Contrasted with the annual average expenditure of £2.6 million spent on 'Army and Marine' over 1861–2 to 1874–5, the expenditure under the same head was substantially higher later, with annual averages of £3.5 million and £4.2 million respectively between 1875–6 to 1897–8 and 1898–9 to 1913–14 (Table 4.1). The increased expenditure on Army and Marine was clearly encouraged by the provision for notional transfers incorporated in the budget. As pointed out above, the practice amounted to 'subsidizing' unproductive heads of expenditure because of the facility to fund the latter through new debt under productive heads. This created a tendency on the part of the government to continue with its growing level of unproductive expenditure in India and England. Thus sterling loans, contracted against public works expenditure in India (which was only statutory), increased liquidity at the India Office in England.

The Welby Commission's analysis of the implications of fiscal transfers between productive and unproductive heads of expenditure (as well as of borrowing) puts to test the basis of the rather politically charged thesis advanced by John Strachey—a contemporary British official. According to him, most of the increases in India's public debt between 1862 and 1909 were related to public works expenditure. Basing his argument on a rather simplistic use of official data on India's outstanding public debt and its distribution under productive and unproductive heads, Strachey drew attention to the fact that all increases in aggregate public debt occurring over the period 1862–1909 were matched by a fall in the unproductive category by £60 million (see also Table 4.2). Clearly, the argument is disproved if attention is paid to the accounting transfers mentioned above. The rate of return on irrigation projects, calculated by what came to be known as the Strachey method, was put at 0.2 per cent for 1885–6, and was thus considered rather low, especially when compared to the opportunity cost of capital employed elsewhere during the period. Calculation of returns under the Strachey method, according to the Welby Commission, entailed an underestimation and could be revised upwards to 2.2 per cent per annum by redefining the surplus on public works (given the fact that money spent on public works was actually not borrowed and was chargeable under revenue). Thus interest charges on borrowed capital, ordinarily treated as an item of cost, were no longer relevant in determining the rate of return on public works. The rate of return calculated by the Welby Commission on irrigation was, therefore, at a higher level—at 2.2 per cent over the same period. The calculation removed, to a large extent, the impression created under the Strachey thesis that much of the public works expenditure in India was non-remunerative.[19]

The select committee's recommendation of showing all capital expenditure on public works as new loans also encouraged a different kind of financial transfer within the official budget. Funds initially allocated to the Famine Relief Fund—initiated in 1874 at the suggestion of Lord Northbrook—were often set aside for expenditure on irrigation and railways.[20] Thus, out of the Rs 500 million allocated to the Famine Relief Fund between 1881–2 and 1923–4, the amount spent on direct relief was as little as 47 per cent while 21 per cent and 4 per cent respectively were spent on irrigation and protective railways.[21] For John and Richard Strachey, both ardent advocates of the Empire, such expenses could be justified as being incurred for '. . . the construction of canals and railways required for the protection of districts, especially liable to drought and consequent scarcity'.[22]

Of the total outstanding public debt held by the Government of India, the proportion held as sterling loans rose from 27 per cent (1860) to 47 per cent (1890), and to 59 per cent (1913).[23] This implied a fall in rupee loans as a part of total outstanding public debt held. It was thus only natural to find a rising trend in the debt charges on sterling loans over the period. Incidentally, it is worth mentioning here that the records available on rupee loans subscribed by the European community indicate that around 1899, resident Europeans had subscribed to Rs 480 million of such loans (which was 46.6 per cent of the total rupee loans floated by the Indian government). Their overseas counterparts managed to pool another Rs 270 million (26.2 per cent) of the total rupee loans.[24] The predominance of Europeans was but natural in the other category of public loans, viz. those which were denominated in sterling and sold in London. The national bourgeoisie thus posed no effective threat to the European rentier class or to the commercial public who enjoyed a clear superiority in the Indian subcontinent.

The above discussion on interest charges and debt management—the major component of Home Charges—brings us logically to the second most important component of Home Charges, viz. overseas expenditure on military operations. This alone accounted for more than a quarter of aggregate Home Charges over 1898–9 to 1913–14, as we can see from row 4 of Table 4.1. An interesting debate was going on during the period amongst the different departments of the British government regarding the justifiability of levying the costs of the military operations of the Empire on the Indian government. It brings to mind a parallel debate amongst nationalists and contemporary British officials on the justifiability of Home Charges as a whole. Interestingly enough, the Welby Commission's views on the more general issue of apportioning Home Charges was very different from the official stand of the British rulers. The Commission drew attention to several anomalies in the prevailing pattern of military expenses, and especially to the share borne by India.[25] Following are some of the observations which, on a closer look, touch upon some critical points relating to apportioning of official military expenses:

(a) Aggregate official overseas expenditure on 'Defence and Foreign Affairs' exceeded the official expenditure on civil charges, administration, pensions, and public works chargeable to revenue (compare sum of rows 2, 3, and 5 with row 4 in Table 4.1).

(b) During the period under consideration, the Indian government was increasingly involved in British defence and foreign affairs. This implied a proportionate and absolute rise in expenditure on related items (row 4 in Table 4.1).[26]

(c) The Welby Commission was openly critical of the fact that most of the expenses of administration in overseas British territories (like Aden and in China, and Persia) were borne by India, and pointed out that 'the practice had no parallel in our relations with other colonies or dependencies'. Often the share borne by India was much larger than that borne by Britain—a fact pointed out by the commission.[27]

Senior officials of the Indian government were quite aware, by the turn of the century, of the financial responsibilities of the Indian government in the military and foreign administration of the Empire. Differences were thus only inevitable, even between the Indian government and an British government officials, on the political justice in the 'apportioning' of expenses. The debate provided interesting revelations of the actual pattern of expenditure:

(a) Payments for Indian troops stationed outside the country were questioned by the Secretary of State. Despatches to the Indian government from Lord Hamilton (30 June 1896) and Lord Cross (3 February 1887), and the speech delivered by Henry Fowler at the British parliament on 6 July 1896 all expressed a similar attitude.[28]

(b) 'Effective charges', consisting of the capitation cost to repay to the British exchequer the actual cost incurred by the War Office at home in raising and maintaining the British forces in India, were a matter of dispute, and the original rate, fixed at 10s per person, was revised at the end of a series of Indian government despatches over 1870–90 and the deliberations of a committee set up under Lord Northbrook. The new rate was fixed at 7s. 4d in 1890–1.[29]

(c) 'Non-effective charges', on which payments had to be made by the Indian government to the War Office in London to meet 'pensions of officers and soldiers of British forces in respect to their service to India', was another source of discord on financial matters between the India Office and the British government.[30]

(d) Disagreements relating to the apportioning of 'Naval Charges' led Lord Salisbury, the prime minister of England, to arrange a conference in 1891 of officials from the India Office, the British Foreign Office, the Treasury, and the British Admiralty. (Incidentally, a mutiny broke out in the Indian Navy in 1862, at the end of which naval defence was handed over to the Admiralty in Britain.) The meeting was, however, inconclusive and in 1894 the India Office had to accept, unconditionally, the views expressed by Lord Rosebury, the new prime minister of Britain.[31]

We have so far focused our attention on two major heads of expenditure under the Home Charges—the costs of interest payment and debt management, as well as those of defence and foreign administration. It is only logical at this point to discuss the remaining heads of expenses relating to the management of civil administration in England and incurred mostly to meet the costs of the India Office. The amount spent annually on civil administration (excluding pensions paid out) averaged around £200,000 over 1898–9 to 1913–14. This sum was a little more than 1 per cent of the average annual Home Charges £17.7 million over the same period. Despite being a relatively small part of the Home Charges, India Office expenses drew disproportionate attention and turned out to be a politically sensitive issue. A rather progressive view was taken by the Welby Commission on the matter, which represented a radical departure from the contemporary British view. This position is evident in the following extract from the report: '. . . in order that there may be no ground for allegation that India is treated less favourably than other parts of Her Majesty's Empire, we recommend that Parliament should be asked to make a contribution towards the charge of the India Office'.[32] Interestingly enough, the Welby Commission chose to remain silent on matters relating to direct expenditures on defence (which contrasted with its critical look at the costs of foreign missions and those on managing the India Office), probably in deference to the view dominant in England. The Commission could thus avoid the dilemma experienced by the Indian government in its attempts to denounce, because of financial hardship, the various liabilities emerging out of India's 'association' with the 'British Crown'. A minority in the Commission submitted a note of dissent to the main report, the foremost among whom was Dadabhai Naoroji, the nationalist spokesman, who successfully persuaded Sir Wedderburn and Mr Caine, two British members of the Commission, to sign the note of dissent.[33]

Our discussion so far on the nature of the Home Charges, the resistance on the part of Indian government officials to the financial commitments arising therefrom, the difficulties experienced by them in view of the official British position supporting such expenses, and finally, deviations from the official line of thinking on the part of the Royal Commission (Welby Commission) as expressed in their *Report on Indian Expenditure* make it evident that the authority and justifiability of imposing these charges on India were questioned even by the British.

Economic historians, writing in the imperialist tradition, were naturally on the defensive on this count and about financial arrangements during the period. We may mention in this connection the work of Theodore Morison, who was a contemporary, and of Vera Anstey, who wrote in the 1940s. Both authors identified a 'political' content in the expenditure and borrowing patterns of the government. A distinction was drawn by Morison between debts under 'economic' and under 'political' heads. Of a total debt of £17.2 million outstanding in 1910–11, £10.3 million comprised 'economic debt', the proceeds of which were used to meet expenditures in the past such as '. . . an independent country might make in the early stages of industrial

development and railway building'. The remaining £6.9 million
was deemed to have been spent on 'political heads . . . related to
the lack of independent status for the nation'.[34] Attention was
drawn in Vera Anstey's work to such official expenses as were
incurred on 'particular civil and military items . . . on account of
the military expenses of conquering India and interest payments
on the debentures of the East India Company, taken out by the
Crown after the Mutiny and *unjustly* debited from India' (italics
added). Again, '. . . it is reasonable to argue that payments on
account of the military expenses of conquering India and interest
payments on the debentures of the East India Company, taken
out by the Crown after the Mutiny ought never to have been
charged to the Indian revenues'.[35] Questions raised by Vera
Anstey on the justifiability of certain expenses of the Indian
government abroad stand in sharp contrast to the analysis of
Theodore Morison whose distinctions between 'economic' and
'political' debts were never extended to a questioning of the
latter. Thus, in Morison's view, the £7 million which India paid
because of her 'political connections with England', was in the
nature of a 'political drain' and in return for the 'freedom from
external aggression, and peace and order within the borders'.
On the 'economic debt' Morison pointed out that 'such [economic]
borrowing was probably justifiable by the same logic as with
the political heads under Home Charges'.[36]

Morison's approach was consistent with the general view
prevailing amongst the British on the rather sensitive issue of
the period, viz. that of the justifiability of overseas expenditure
related to the British Empire and its apportioning between India
and England. However, the functional distinction between
'economic' and 'political' debts was widely in use in the debate
current amongst the nationalists and official spokesmen of the
period. The shift from an unquestioned approval in Morison
(1911) to a moderately critical look at the 'political' debt (and
overseas expenses) in Vera Anstey (1942) can be traced to the
controversies current during the interim period. Even Vera Anstey
had to concede that 'political, administrative and commercial
connections with England . . . far outweighed the corresponding
payments',[37] presumably the Home Charges. The cautious and

conservative stance of Anstey continues the condescending note of the Welby Commission on the huge military involvement of the Indian government in the upkeep of the British Empire. (Incidentally, the Commission also maintained a distance from sensitive issues like the 'drain' of wealth.) Most contemporaries, British and Indians alike, writing outside the nationalist tradition apparently seem to have shared the conviction that the Home Charges were mostly payments for invisibles purchased by India. Morison was no exception and his writings reflected a total rejection of any plea whatsoever that could question the responsibilities laid on the Indian government to finance the Home Charges. Incidentally, this attitude was shared by his contemporary John Maynard Keynes, who, as mentioned earlier, commented extensively on Morison's work in the *Economic Journal* of 1909.[38]

The British official position on the legitimacy of the Empire and the Home Charges on colonies was, in principle, never in doubt in the mainstream literature of the period. It, however, underplayed the discontent and contradictions, even at the level of intra-governmental despatches between the Indian government and the SOS in London which often openly expressed displeasure over the military expenses. A picture of apparently harmonious relations also leaves out the critical analysis of the Welby Commission. A survey of the official reports or correspondences relating to the period reflect the undercurrents of tension in administering the financial arrangements, which became a more sensitive issue because of growing nationalist sentiments against these arrangements.

We conclude the present section with a summary of our impressions on the issues pertaining to 'overseas expenditure' by India. These concern (a) the dilemma of the Indian government in conceding to and abiding by the demands of the imperial authorities; (b) the revelations by the Welby Commission of the various accounting transfers practised by the Indian government; and (c) the characterization by imperialist historians of the financial administration in British India. Our observations strengthen the thesis that most of India's 'Expenditure Abroad' during the period was political in origin and was avoidable in the absence of colonial rule. The above lends support to the proposition advanced earlier in this section that such expenditure constituted an element of unilateral transfer from the point of view of the national economy.

4.3.2 The Nationalist Argument on 'Drain of Wealth' Revisited

Nationalist perceptions on what they had chosen to describe as a 'drain of wealth' from India can now be reassessed. We propose to reopen the arguments put forward[39] on the issue and relate them to our position on 'transfer of resources' from colonial India.

Attention was drawn in the seventeenth century and earlier by mercantilist writers on the possibilities of acquiring 'Treasure by Foreign Trade'.[40] Writings defending the East India Company's practices were all centred around the mercantilist notion of drain as a net outflow of precious metals. Thus the early writings on the subject by Thomas Mun and Josiah Child in England emphasized that Britain's exports of specie to India fetched, in effect, a net inflow of the same to the country—earned through re-exports of Indian wares to European markets. Notions of drain in terms of an outflow of precious metals were often considered as too narrow, even in eighteenth- and nineteenth-century writings on Indo-British economic relations. Thus, despite net inflows of silver as well as gold to India, external payments were considered responsible for a conceivable drain of wealth from the national economy and were attacked by various writers. Indian government expenditure abroad and other private remittances by Europeans were quantitatively not significant before the Indian mutiny and the takeover of the East India Company by the Crown during 1857–8. However, East India Company administration was evidently exploitative. This was indicated by the sharp public criticism from British officials like George Wingate who pointed to the '. . . *tribute* paid to Great Britain . . . (as) . . . the most objectionable feature in our existing policy' (italics added). Thus the '. . . cruel, crushing effects of the tribute upon India' entailed a policy with 'taxes raised in one country and spent in another' which implied 'an absolute loss and extinction of the whole amount withdrawn from the taxed country'.[41] Tribute from India increased to significant proportions by the early nineteenth century and a large number of British civilian officers were concerned about the large outflow of funds from India. We may recall, in this connection, the writings and representations of Lord Cornwallis (the governor-general of India in 1790), Frederick John Shore (a Bengal civilian, writing in 1837), Saville Marriot (a revenue commissioner of the Deccan), and C. J. Hamilton (a British economist writing in 1919).[42] Thus tribute paid out by India was often recognized in the commentary offered by some Englishmen. For understandable reasons, writings by the British stopped short of questioning the tribute—an attitude which was in line with the prevailing ethos of British rule in India. Questions raised in the late nineteenth century by Indian nationalists regarding the propriety of British claims were based on a conceptualization of drain which was very different from the specie form prevalent in the writings of mercantilists. The awareness shown by British administrators of the tribute paid by British India helped the nationalists to articulate their challenge, which questioned the very basis of the British Empire in India. In Europe the pace of the Industrial Revolution and the consolidation of industrial capitalism led to the rise of free trade doctrines which advanced the role of comparative advantage in transmitting growth. The nationalists used these paradigms to highlight the experience of India under colonialism. In the West, similar dissents were articulated in the context of the Irish economy of the eighteenth and nineteenth centuries.[43] Thus mercantilist preoccupations of the earlier centuries with the drain of specie gave way, in later writings, to a theoretical perception in which the drain was identified as unilateral transfers effected through commodity trade. This shift in position was evident in the writings on Irish colonies during the nineteenth century. A similar recognition of the drain ran parallel in the Indian context as the nationalists started writing, during the second half of the nineteenth century, about the intensity of famines in India and their incidence on poverty, and about the lack of fairness in the steady flow of remittances from India, a large part of which was connected with the upkeep of the British Empire. Incidentally, the complacency and self-righteousness of British officials who relied on the Strachey thesis about the benevolence of the British administration of public works programmes (despite their low rates of return) suffered a jolt with India experiencing some of the severest famines of the century over the same period.[44]

Writings by the nationalist writers in India, as could be expected, were at various levels of sophistication and political expediency. From an analytical angle, Dadabhai Naoroji's writings provided one of the earliest but relatively complete versions of the nationalist argument.[45] Emphasizing the drain of wealth from India through its export surplus which he believed remained unpaid or unrequited from the angle of the domestic economy, Naoroji also drew attention to the profits on the export trade. These profits, mostly enjoyed by Europeans, were also viewed as a part of the drain. According to Dadabhai Naoroji, 'Profits on India's export trade' (which ranged between 15 and 20 per cent of export earnings during 1883–92) were entirely appropriated by the Europeans. Imports were also overpriced during these years by at least 10 per cent. The two components, along with the unpaid (unrequited) margin of export earnings (which was another 30 per cent of the latter) comprised, according to Naoroji, the drain from India. It ranged, according to him, between £20 million and £30 million. The estimate was clearly larger than the annual averages of export surpluses which stood, according to official statistics, at £17 million in the 1870s. We are tempted, probably at the risk of reproducing what might be considered as a piece of rhetoric, to quote the following passage from Naoroji's work: 'This, then, is the way the treasure goes, and poor British India gets all the abuse—insult added to injury. The candle burns not only at both ends but at all parts.'[46]

Naoroji's notion of drain, which had a wider coverage than those of other nationalists, was relatively difficult to quantify. Since profits in export trade and the overcharging of imports were both subject to the varying degrees of monopoly enjoyed by the respective traders, these were difficult to estimate. In a recent work on India's economic relations over the second half of the nineteenth century, Banerji has stressed the need to look at the drain of wealth from India from an 'alternative' angle in order that the researcher could examine the 'entire spectrum of payments abroad' and identify varying elements of drain in them.[47]

The political leverage they enjoyed in colonial India was clearly an important factor behind the ability of the British to extract monopoly profits (in both internal and external trade) and to earn high salaries. Thus the Indian government was committed, despite financial stresses in the domestic economy, to meet a myriad of overseas liabilities, most of which, as noted earlier, had their origin in the political subordination of India. This alternative notion of drain, according to Banerji, was potentially capable of capturing the element of compulsion in the colonial economy to procure net export earnings in order to make them available for settling overseas liabilities.

That export surpluses did not have a positive impact on the national economy—since net earnings from exports were all retained abroad (to meet the Home Charges and other expenses of the India Office)—provided the core of the argument for nationalists ranging from Naoroji to Dutt. All of them were critical of the prevailing procedure which, for practical purposes, amounted to remitting India's tax revenue abroad (see Fig. 4.1 and the related arguments). The above may, in fact, be interpreted as an anticipation of a Keynesian effective demand argument which was voiced in nationalist protests against prevailing financial practices.[48] The argument also contests the very basis of the notion of gains from free trade—one which was evidently denied to India under colonial rule. The nationalists, however, did not spell out their critique of free trade doctrines. Nor did they visualize the parallel surplus expropriation process within the economy—one which left very little potential for domestic investment. The issue gains a special perspective in some recent writings where these nationalist views are identified with an anti-imperialist position.[49]

While the drain of wealth from colonial India had far-reaching consequences for the domestic economy, it is nonetheless important to arrive at a measure of the flow of drain-related remittances. The flow, in our judgement, provides a good indicator of the possible extent of expropriation and spoliation of the colonized economy.[50]

The prevailing financial arrangements in British India were questioned by nationalist writers on three major grounds. First, in British India most of the significant positions in civil administration, in defence services, and in commercially profitable ventures were controlled by Europeans. The related income enjoyed by the latter, which was considered as a 'moral drain' by Naoroji, was seen by nationalists as a cost to British India. In terms of Naoroji's estimates, the sum comprised about one-sixth of total expenses of the Indian government disbursed between England and India.[51]

Second, the Indian government was forced, under British rule, to meet a long list of official overseas expenses, described as Home Charges.

Third, India's net export earnings in sterling were never brought back to the country. This aspect confirmed the existence of unrequited (unpaid) exports from India, the proceeds of which, according to the nationalists, financed the flow of unilateral transfers from the country. The magnitude of the drain of wealth from India was thus approximated by the annual value of its export surpluses.

The nationalist arguments were articulated in the charter of demands put forward by the Indian National Congress around the turn of the century. The demands included (a) a reduction of Home Charges (which were considered excessive), and (b) the Indianization of civil services.[52] Lord Curzon, the then governor-general of India, however, asserted that of the salaried sections receiving Rs 75 and above per annum in 1867, about 55 per cent were either Europeans or Eurasians. The proportion fell, according to Curzon, to 43 per cent in 1903. G. Subramania Iyer, the Indian nationalist, was quick to point out that the real picture was exactly the opposite—with the share of Europeans rising over 1867–1903, provided one only considered the jobs fetching Rs 1000 and above. The Indian National Congress's demands were wholly rejected by the ruling government.[53]

Notwithstanding the stand taken by the nationalists in their challenges to the old imperialist order and colonial rule in India, the drain theory, which identified India's export surpluses as unilateral transfers (or unrequited exports) from the country can, in our view, be faulted on the following two grounds. First, it is not logical to argue that India's export surplus remained unpaid. Revenues against such surpluses were duly remitted under the Council Bill schema (see Fig. 4.1 and Section 4.1) and actually paid out via the intermediation of exchange banks to exporters in India. Revenue earmarked in the domestic budget as 'Expenditure Abroad' was, however, effectively transferred abroad with Home Charges met in sterling without the necessity of an actual sterling remittance to England. Hence India's export surpluses, which roughly indicated the magnitude and direction of financial transfer from the country, should by no means be deemed to constitute the transfer itself.

Second, it is difficult to accept, at its face value, the nationalist contention that the entire amount of Home Charges (including the sum spent in the servicing of productive loans) represented a drain of wealth to the national economy. Indeed, the absolutist position of the nationalists and their outright condemnation of public works programmes in India appears untenable, especially when one considers the material implications of public works programmes for the domestic economy. One can here address the broader question as to whether public works expenditure programmes on railways and irrigation brought any net benefits to India. The available analysis of railroad investment in India fails to provide a conclusive thesis on the matter. The Indian government's purchases of erstwhile guaranteed railway companies in 1907 has often been cited as an indirect example of profitability. Profits, however, fructified only after the step was taken. It has also been pointed out that during this period concessional finance was often provided by Britain to meet the cost of railroad construction in India.[54] Railways have, in general, been viewed as 'profitable' ventures, capable of reducing discrepancies between social and private returns. To Vera Anstey, interest paid on productive loans (which covered expenditure on railways) 'brought in more revenue than suffices to cover the interest charges . . . (it) does not contain any net drain from India. In addition railways and irrigation works have been of immense benefit to the country . . . the money could not have been raised as cheaply anywhere else as in London.'[55] The above view contrasts with the position held by nationalists on Indian railways who point at the fact that the network of railway tracks laid in India more often served British commercial interests and not the national interest.[56] It was often a common official practice to buy the entire amount of railway stores (raw materials, machinery, etc.) in England—a device which entailed an equivalent expenditure abroad to procure imports. The above considerably minimized the possible expansionary (multiplier) effects of initial railway investment in the national economy.[57] The arguments are by no means unfounded and one comes across, even in a more balanced study on Indian railways, comments such as '. . . railroad building in India did not give rise to a flood of satellite innovations and it destroyed more occupational opportunities than it opened up'.[58] The developments probably led a British contemporary to admit that 'next to Australia, India is the largest consumer of Britain for locomotives . . . . We have supplied all the material and all the equipments and we reaped the profits very largely.'[59] The earlier years of railway construction in India were often geared to the strategic or political exigencies of British rulers in India, some evidence of which comes out clearly in the following statement from Lord Hardinge, the governor-general, in 1846: 'In this country . . . the facility of rapid concentration of infantry and artillery and stores may be [treated as] the cheap prevention of insurrection, the speedy termination of war, or the safety of the Empire.'[60] Similarly, the strategic value of railways led Lord Dalhousie, the governor-general of India, to state in 1853 that railroads would provide 'full intelligence of any event to be transmitted to government at five times the speed now possible; as well as the concentration of its military strength on every given point, in as many days as it would now require months to effect'.[61] Interestingly enough, despite expansions which covered ventures along non-rewarding tracks, the railways turned out to be a financially profitable proposition as was evident from the literature.

The diametrically opposite views on the implications of railroad investment in India have been mentioned above to serve an illustrative purpose. We certainly did not want to provide the whole debate on railway investment in India. Our purpose was to highlight the difficulty, even from a nationalist angle, of ignoring the material indicators of changes in the Indian economy which were introduced by the railways (say, in terms of the increased traffic provided by growing transportation facilities connecting the hinterland and the port, in the movement of goods in internal trade within the economy, and finally, with the relative standardization of prices, often at higher levels, for commodities grown in the interior areas). Some of these aspects were stressed by Marx as indicative of progress (actual or potential) in his attempt to identify the 'regenerative' role of railroad construction in Asian colonies. (Incidentally, Marx's comments on Indian railways have been viewed with scepticism in the controversy over Marx's position on Asian colonialism.)[62] Our discussion shows the logical difficulty in accepting what we view as the rather absolutist position of the nationalists that the entire sum of Home Charges (including the servicing of the loans needed to finance public works including railways[63] or irrigation) could be reckoned as a drain of wealth from India.

A possible way of avoiding the impasse faced by the nationalists in their attempts to identify the drain can be found if we refer to the accounting transfers which were practised by the Indian government in the context of the domestic budget. As mentioned above, in British India accumulation of 'productive' debt had been achieved with equivalent cancellation of unproductive debt. Evidence of the above was provided by the Welby Commission. Thus interest and debt management charges on loans which in the past were contracted to meet railway and irrigation works (none of which could, by any fervour of nationalism, be branded as wholly related to British interests) were, in fact, services on unproductive or 'ordinary' debt. The surreptitious underplaying of the compounding or the servicing of unproductive loans lends credence to the argument that the entire amount of Home Charges covering both productive and unproductive heads of expenditure was attributable to colonial expropriation. The position, interestingly, removes the major fallacy or dilemma of the nationalists in their outright condemnation of public works expenditure and the servicing of related loans in India.

Before concluding our analysis of the nationalist position relating to the drain, we feel tempted to draw attention to the question of what has been described as a 'moral drain'. The dominance of Europeans in most of the remunerative occupations in British India[64] implied a regular expropriation as well as remittance of the privately appropriated surplus. This led to outflows of funds on private account, the overall magnitude of which was large enough to balance (according to unofficial estimates) the private inflows of capital over the decade preceding 1908-9.[65] This aspect of the drain of wealth received relatively less attention from nationalists who, for political reasons, were more concerned with official remittances. A related flow concerns the surplus appropriated by British residents in India, and especially those who opted to spend their earnings within the country. To the extent the above are overlooked, the nationalist approach to the drain leaves out, in our judgement, an important aspect of the imperial impact on the Indian economy, with European residents controlling a sizeable part of the surplus. Colonial policies in India also generated a layer of surplus which was enjoyed by Indians in various capacities— through their land rights or through the relatively superior positions they enjoyed in government or business. As the demands of the Indian National Congress made it evident, nationalists wanted to curtail the extent of European domination in government and business. It was, however, less important to them as to whether such domination also provided a source of private remittance. Similarly, they were concerned even less with how imperial connections transplanted to Indian soil, the machinations of an exploitative system where the loot was appropriated by Indians as well.

4.4 On Quantifying Resource Transfers from India

In this section we will make an attempt to assess the quantitative magnitudes of resource transfers from India. A rough measure of the transfers will be approximated from the available series on external trade, capital flows, and remittances from the country.

A parallel process in Britain—the recipient country—might be worth considering at this point. We have offered below a brief digression on the 'reverse flow of capital', experienced by Britain—the lender nation—which started receiving net inflows of funds from abroad since the mid-nineteenth century. Incidentally, our findings relating to the Indian experience refute the position that during the period under consideration, India was receiving, on a net basis, foreign investment from abroad. We will later counter the extreme position held by Keynes that India's borrowings implied an equivalent 'drain from England'.[66]

It may not be out of place to digress, at this stage, on two specific dimensions which are important for the resource transfer issue. The first concerns the perceptions relating to the external economic transactions of Britain over the period. The second relates to a broader context and points at the need to avoid possible ambiguities in interpreting the international accounts of individual nations. The two aspects would help in our understanding of resource transfers between colonial India and Britain.

In the literature on theories of imperialism, there is mention of a 'reverse flow'[67] of capital, experienced by mature capitalist economies like Britain. Britain's early start as a capital-exporting nation initiated steady inflows of income to the country, the magnitude of which outstripped the flow of her overseas investment by the middle of the nineteenth century. Looking at British national accounts statistics for 1870, the country's overseas investment (I_f) was less than her investment income from abroad (i). (Thus I_f at £55 million was clearly much larger than i at £35 million during the year.)[68] The picture conforms to its mirror-image, the pattern relating to net financial (and real) outflows from colonies like India.

It is interesting to relate the above thesis on reverse flow to the argument that investment income flows from abroad were supporting British domestic investment or consumption. Thus, during 1870, the sum of British overseas and domestic investment was actually smaller than the sum of savings of domestic origin and investment income from abroad. In symbols, $(I_d + I_f) <$ $(S_d + i)$ where I_d and S_d respectively indicate gross domestic fixed capital formation and savings of domestic origin. Looking at the data for 1870,[69] we get the following:

I_d : £64 million

I_f : £55 million

S_d : £111 million

i : £35 million

The excess of $(S_d + i)$ at £146 million over aggregate investment $(I_d + I_f)$ at £119 million indicates the possibility that overseas investment income was used to supplement domestic consumption during the year in Britain. It is not difficult, in this context, to find indirect evidence of distinct improvements which were taking place, by the late nineteenth century, in consumption standards of the British working class. Aggregate consumption of items like tea, which had a low income elasticity of demand, went up—a fact which indicates that tea entered the consumption basket of a wider section of British people, a large section of whom were presumably from the upcoming working classes.[70]

We now refer to the second theme relating to basic principles governing the external accounts of nations including double-entry bookkeeping devices. Credits (claims) arising from an outflow of real resources (exports) from a nation ordinarily gives rise to a claim over an inflow of financial resources. These inflows could lead to the following possibilities: (a) imports of goods and service; (b) purchase of foreign assets (for example, securities, gold or foreign currencies) deposited with the domestic/foreign monetary system; and (c) unilateral transfers abroad. Of the three, only the first contributes to the current flow of consumption or investment in the domestic economy while the second and third options release resources to the rest of the world. In fact, a use of export proceeds for (b) amounts to lending on a short-term basis by the domestic economy over the period during which the foreign assets are held. Option (c) transfers abroad, on a permanent basis, the country's claims over the corresponding export earnings. Exports which finance this category of transactions are thus without a quid pro quo. In other words, real transfers (via exports) make possible unilateral transfers in financial terms.

We now get back to our task of quantitative identification of such transfers, if any, from British India. As revealed earlier in this chapter, most of the expenses of the India Office (that is, the Home Charges) can be attributed to imperial interests. We have already analysed the details of India's expenditure abroad. As has been argued earlier, even the servicing of productive loans were, in reality, geared towards the upkeep of the Empire. The interpretation follows as we keep in mind the expenditure under different heads.

Flows of remittances between India and England were regularly recorded in the value of Council Bills sold in England. Since the sterling proceeds of CB sales remained in England with the India Office, the above effected a flow from India to England, with bills being reimbursed in rupees at the Indian Treasury. In addition, sterling could also be procured by the India Office through its borrowings in the London capital market. Remittances largely channelized through the sale of CBs (and trade bills) could in principle be supplemented by net flows of gold and silver. The overall picture relating to the flow of remittances and their components for India can be stylized in terms of the following equation:

$$B_T + K_f = CB, \tag{4.1}$$

where B_T and K_f respectively indicate the balance of India's trade in commodity plus treasure, and the flow of net capital imports during each period. The left hand side of the equation records the demand for the flow of remittances during each period. Sale of CBs by the SOS, recorded on the right hand side, measures the actual flow of remittances between the two countries which settled the balance of trade and other payments. Since K_f

provided a part of import finance over the same period, the flow of K_f released the same value of export earnings which could be remitted to India. Thus the sum $(B_T + K_f)$ measures the net remittances sent through CBs sold in England. However, in terms of institutional arrangements, CB sales in England were not followed by actual remittances of sterling to India. Instead, India's claim was settled within the country by drawing on budgetary resources, earmarked as expenditure abroad. Clearly, the availability of foreign finance in the form of external borrowings (K_f) effectively increased the stock of sterling with the SOS. To provide an example, a hypothetical merchandise surplus at an annual value of £100 could be partly financed or settled by net imports of treasure worth £25 over the same period, thus leaving a balance of £75. Again, direct borrowing of sterling by the SOS might amount to £25 which could settle an equal value of imports. The final settling of remittances then would amount to £100 (derived as the sum of trade and treasure balance plus foreign borrowings) which had to be transacted by CBs. Since the whole of the sterling proceeds of CB sales were maintained in England, if spending by the SOS fell short of the value of those sterling proceeds (from sale of CBs and official borrowings) the SOS's reserves were likely to go up in London.

We can put back, in equation (4.1), figures which relate to the annual averages for the respective flows of B_t, K_f and CB during 1898–1908. Alternatively, we can compare the time series relating to CB and B_T over a longer period and find out the discrepancy (which, in principle, should reflect the net flows of foreign capital). The latter method provides a basis for cross-checking the margin of accuracy in the statistics by looking into their internal consistency. Incidentally, among the sources of statistics, data provided on the CB series by the SOS's office, or even the data on K_f collected by private researchers from the London stock market (and other sources), are usually more dependable than official trade statistics originally collected from customs returns.

Data on India's capital flows (K_f) during the period, as are available from different sources, do not seem to tally (see Table 4.4). Using the available estimates of gross and net capital flows, Theodore Morison constructed, for the first time, international accounts for India. This was described by him as a 'Conjectural Balance Sheet of India 1898–1908'. The data were cross-checked and corrected by Keynes in the *Economic Journal* (1909).[71] We have rearranged them, in the following pages, in order to assess the magnitudes of financial flows from India during the above period. Later, we have used the same data source to test the validity of equation 4.1, which also cross-checks the internal consistency of the statistics.

Separate estimates of capital flows, done by Paish (for 1908–09) and by Pandit (for 1905–06), are provided in Table 4.4. Discrepancies in data, especially relating to the capital accounts, led Pandit to construct, in 1937, an indirect estimate of India's 'balance of indebtedness'.[72] Thus data on the current account for 1905–06 were utilized to construct, on a residual basis, the size of official and private capital inflows (or, the 'balance of indebtedness') which financed, ex post, the remaining items in the country's balance of payments. Comparing the data sources relating to the available estimates on different components of India's external payments in Table 4.4, we get the impression that the annual averages relating to capital inflows during 1899–1900 to 1908–09 were much lower in the Keynes–Morison estimate than those provided by Paish (for 1908–09) and by Pandit (for 1905–06).

For both Keynes and Morison, the inflow of foreign capital curtailed the size of 'potential' drain to the level of the 'actual'. The authors defined the actual drain as external liabilities which remained to be met after using capital flows for the purpose of settling the potential drain which measured the annual liabilities against Home Charges and other private liabilities. Incidentally, the notion of drain in Keynes or Morison had none of the political or moral overtones present in the nationalist literature. As calculated by Keynes (or Morison), the size of potential drain for the decade ending in 1908–09 was £213.4 million. This came down to an actual drain of £150.5 million with sums of £41.9 million (official) and £21.0 million (private) borrowed abroad. The distinction drawn between actual and potential drain was probably to stress the crucial role of foreign capital inflows in financing a part of India's liabilities abroad. This position is in conflict with our observation that India was transferring, on a net basis, a substantial inflow of resources to the rest of the world over the same period.

Keynes and Morison's point regarding the prevailing net inflow of capital to India was very much an accepted thesis. Pandit[73] has estimated the outstanding 'balance of indebtedness' for India, which at £16.6 million recorded the inflow of capital to the country over 1905–06. The indirect method used earlier by Viner was used by Pandit for arriving at this estimate. Pandit's calculations, however, seem to be subject to double counting.[74] Our corrections bring the figure down to £6.1 million (a figure which was comparable to the respective sums of £8.6 million and £6.2 million obtained by Keynes and Morison as annual averages for net capital inflows for the decade ending 1908–09).[75] As a point of contrast, Paish's figure of capital flows stood at £14.3 million for 1908–09, which appears as a gross overestimate (for details, see Table 4.4).

The preceding account of the data relating to capital inflows for India is based on the presumption that the country was receiving, on a net basis, capital from overseas. We have deliberately highlighted such positions in order to contrast them with the arguments advanced earlier in this chapter that the colonial economy was ordained, over the period, to part with resources through (unilateral) transfers abroad. Obviously, the differences between the two approaches lie in the respective characterization of the nature of claims on colonial India.

Data provided by Keynes (and Morison) for the 'Conjectural Balance of Payments of India' over 1898–1908 can be arranged in terms of the following format:

$$LTC_m^o = H + M + \Delta R - B_T - \left(LTC_m^v - i \right), \tag{4.2}$$

where the right hand side sums up the figures on Home Charges (H), miscellaneous payments abroad (M), accumulations of reserves in London (ΔR), and subtracts from the sum arrived at, the net balance on commodity trade plus treasure (B_T) and the gross inflows of capital on private account (LTC_m^p) less interest payments (i) on private loans. The balance is financed by gross imports of capital under official heads (LTC_m^o) as given by the left hand side of the equation. Interest charges on LTC_m^o are included in the Home Charges and hence listed on the other side.

Before putting, in equation 4.2 above, the respective figures provided by Keynes and Morison for 1898–1908, we once again focus attention on the general impression created by pro-British and other writings on India that the country in general was receiving net inflows of capital from abroad. Scholars including Paish (who estimated the country-wise flow of British overseas investment at the end of the first decade of the twentieth century) and Y. S. Pandit, among others, subscribed to this view. The position on net inflows of overseas capital fits in with the slant in the Keynes–Morison data on India's international accounts which also matches equation 4.2. Net inflow of official capital (LTC_m^o) on the left hand side of equation 4.3 thus provides the net finance for the rest of the items in India's 'conjectural balance sheet'. Keynes's data, put against the respective symbols in equation 4.2, appear as follows:

$$4.1 = 15.7 + 1.4 + 1.6 - 14.6 - (4.5 - 4.5) \tag{4.3}$$

Each entry in equation (4.3) relates to the respective annual averages during 1898–1908 and is given in units of millions of pound sterling.

What impression do we have from equations 4.2 and 4.3 for India's international accounts over the decade 1898 to 1908–09? While gross inflows of capital on the private account (LTC_m^p) at £4.1 million (annual average) were netted out by the annual average for interest payments (i)—which was exactly of the same value—the merchandise and treasure balance (B_T) calculated at £14.6 million was inadequate to meet the liabilities on account of Home Charges (H), miscellaneous payments (M), and reserve accretions (ΔR). The net sum due was thus financed by inflows of long-term official capital (LTC_m^o) of £4.1 million.

Table 4.3   *Balance of trade (merchandise and treasure) and Council Bills sold*

(million £)

	Council Bills sold	Official series on balance of trade	Adjusted series on balance of trade
	1	*2*	*3*
1894–5	16.9	20.3	20.5
1895–6	17.6	20.3	20.2
1896–7	15.5	14.3	14.3
1897–8	9.5	9.5	9.5
1898–9	18.6	23.5	20.3
1899–1900	19.0	16.8	17.5
1900–01	13.3	14.7	11.6
1901–02	18.5	21.1	20.3
1902–03	18.4	22.3	20.9
1903–04	23.8	29.5	26.5
1904–05	24.4	23.9	23.0
1905–06	32.1	29.4	25.9
1906–07	33.1	31.1	17.2
1907–08	16.2	13.3	4.5
1908–09	13.9	10.0	6.0
1909–10	27.0	26.4	24.2
1910–11	26.7	31.9	29.9
1911–12	27.0	30.8	24.7
1912–13	25.7	27.5	19.9

Sources: Col. 1: Royal Commission on Indian Finance and Currency, London, 1914, *Evidence and appendices*, vol. 3, p. 232; col. 3: *Statistical Abstracts of British India*, adjusted as explained in note (e) of Table 4.4.

In the approach to India's international accounts outlined above, all international payments are treated at par. Thus Home Charges, miscellaneous payments, and payments towards reserve accumulations are all recognized as debt entries. Expressed in present-day language, Home Charges are viewed as payments for ordinary (contractual) services—a perspective which was common in the imperialist historiography on India. The position, viewed from our frame of analysis, neglects the political overtone of the specific transactions in the external accounts of a country. The resulting trite and mechanistic description of a nation's international accounts does not, however, necessarily dispel the value-loaded premises. By treating Home Charges as ordinary invisibles, the above analysis of India's international payments did indirectly subscribe to the political context which was dominant in the imperialist perception of British India. It was thus not accidental that imports of long-term official capital were viewed by Keynes and others as net inflows of external finance in India's international accounts.

Conclusions arrived at earlier (in Section 4.3) on the identifiability of Home Charges as tributes from colonial India allow us to substitute the symbol for Home Charges (H), by that for tributes (T) in equation 4.2. Rearranging, we get

$$B_T = T + M + \Delta R - B_L \qquad (4.4)$$

where the net lending balance in the capital account (B_L) is defined as the sum $(LTC_m^o + LTC_m^p - i)$ in equation 4.2, while H has been substituted by T. The remaining symbols read the same as in equation 4.2.

In terms of the rearranged payments balance in equation 4.4, the trade surplus (B_T) provides the source of net finance which meets unilateral transfers or the tribute (T), the reserve accumulations (ΔR), and payments under miscellaneous heads (M), after using, for the same purpose, the lending balance from abroad (B_L). The corresponding estimate, in units of pound millions, is:

$$14.6 = 15.7 + 1.4 + 1.6 - 4.1 \qquad (4.5)$$

where the figures are the annual averages, based on Keynes's statistics mentioned above.

Equations 4.4 and 4.5 shed new light on the pattern of utilization of India's export surpluses during the period 1898–9 to 1908–9. The surplus in commodity trade which remained after paying for the net imports of treasure seems to have been spent on settling the tribute and the acquisition of financial assets in sterling (apart from meeting miscellaneous payments, the magnitude of which was smaller). None of the major expenses (including those on reserve accumulations) had much relevance in terms of material well-being in the national economy, as we have discussed in Section 4.3. The country's exchange receipt, from $(B_T + B_L)$ in the above equations, was thus financing the sum of $(T + \Delta R)$ and M, largely reflecting its obligations to the Empire.

We can now cross-check the data and try to assess the magnitude of the tribute from India. In terms of the rearranged balance of payments in equations 4.4 and 4.5, the tribute seems to be roughly of the same value as that of the trade surplus on trade and treasure. Incidentally, B_T at £14.6 million was derived by Keynes after revising official trade statistics (which, according to Keynes, was an overestimate since it left out the import surpluses in India's land-borne trade).[76] We return to the point later in this section.

Let us look again at equation 4.1 where CB sales are equated to the sum of B_T and K_f. The value of CBs sold annually, as pointed out, was supposed to yield this sum. Relating the arrangement to the political processes in colonial India, the flows of remittances (in the CBs) thus seem to have sustained the flow of the imperial loot from British India, divested in forms which had very little significance from a national angle.

We now make use of equation 4.1 as a device to cross-check data. Let us put back the values of CB, B_T, and K_f from Keynes's estimates. Now the annual average relating to CB during 1898–1908 was £23.2 million—a figure much larger than the sum $(B_T + K_f)$ at £18.2 million. How does one explain this rather serious anomaly between the two sources of statistics on remittances? Observing that the discrepancies between the CB and the official B_T series seem to exceed the capital inflows (K_f), we have tried to construct a new series for India's trade data. Our calculations yield a new average for B_T in equation 4.5 at £17.3 million. The gap between the two sides of equation 4.4, however, still persists, reflecting the excess of CB sales, at £23.2 million, over remittances solicited against $(B_T + K_f)$, the revised sum of which now stands at £21.4 million.

A digression can be provided here as a plea for further research on the quality of India's trade statistics available for the colonial period. In our view the official statistics are faulty on four grounds: (a) They exclude statistics on land-borne trade which, in contrast to seaborne trade, consistently showed a deficit balance for India; (b) They exclude purchases (imports) of official stores by the SOS in London; (c) They exclude re-exports; and finally, (d) the fixed rate of exchange at £1 = Rs 15, which in official statistics converts the sterling values of India's trade, did not actually prevail till 1898 when the declining rupee rate in sterling finally stabilized to 1s. 4d. (which was equivalent to £1 = Rs 15). Keynes, incidentally, had been aware of the omission of re-exports and made a reference to the gap in the memorandum he submitted to the India Office in 1913, regarding 'inaccuracies of seaborne trade by India'.[77] He also mentioned the 'serious discrepancies' in the declared (c.i.f.) values for imports probably due to an under-reporting of the profit margin enjoyed by foreign suppliers at the stage of entry of imports. The points raised by Keynes were, however, not all incorporated in the new series he worked out for the period 1898–1908, since the latter was adjusted for the omission of land-borne trade only.

Discrepancies in India's trade data and their inconsistency with figures for remittances (CBs) available from the India Office (which represented a more reliable source) prepare the ground for rejecting estimates of tributes on the basis of trade data (as suggested in equation 4.4). Incidentally, our pointer to the unexplained gaps between the CB and the B_T series, plus the capital inflows (K_f) in equation 4.1 sounds rather convincing as we draw attention to the controversy between Keynes and his colleagues at the India Office—Lionel Abrahams and James Mackay—on the same question. The observed gap between CB sales and the official series for B_T could, according to Keynes, reflect inflows of foreign capital—a route which, incidentally, we have also taken in equation 4.1 to indicate the links between CB and other transactions. Officials at the SOS's office, however, maintained a different position and they pointed out, in reply to Keynes's letters, the following: (a) export values recorded by the customs department in India, which provided trade data, had a tendency 'to lie' since the prices reported in the value columns relating to exports tended to lag behind the actual export prices which were consistently rising during the period; and (b) imports were, in part, paid for directly through proceeds of sterling loans raised in London. This could have exaggerated the value of imports in the official series which ignored such practices. A newspaper clipping on parliamentary questions for 1910, which was maintained by Keynes in his private papers, mentions a certain unease, prevailing at the India Office circles, on the question of CB sales in excess of Home Charges. (The Under-secretary of State at the India Office was asked a question in Parliament by Rupert Gwynne, on the use of CB proceeds beyond the financing of Home Charges. Surprisingly enough, Keynes ignored all such issues including the limitations of trade data in his own work on Indian currency and finance completed in 1913.)[78]

Considering the reliability of the alternative sources of statistics, it would be appropriate to use the annual values of CB sales (net of capital imports) as a tentative measure of the annual flows of financial transfers or tributes from colonial India. In terms of equation 4.1, the flow is indicated by $(CB - K_f)$. Data limitations compel us to confine our attention to 1898–1908. During this period, an annual average of £19.8 million (representing about 2.3 per cent of India's national income) had been the value of CB sales net of capital imports—a sum which was remitted abroad as unilateral transfer. The sum exceeded the annual averages for India's net export earnings from trade and treasure, estimated by us at £17.3 million over the same period. The transfers, however, had a wider range of implications on the domestic economy than are captured by the quantitative magnitudes. Thus we should consider the transformations in the colonial economy which came about with rising exports and the newly opened up opportunities for expropriation of surpluses in the agrarian economy. In the present chapter we have confined our analysis to the financial aspects of export expansion. Our conclusions support the thesis on the use of colonies as sources of surplus which were appropriated by the metropolitan economy in the age of finance capital.

In terms of the prevailing financial arrangements in British India, unspent sterling reserves (R) of the SOS were regularly deposited at the Bank of England. By the policy adopted in 1905, CB sales were no longer restricted to the size of annual Home Charges. Thus the sale of CBs, which served as the vehicle for the transfer of financial resources between India and England, could, after 1905, be utilized to finance flows of expenditure of the India Office as well as accumulations in the India Office's reserves in London. Both proved convenient to the City of London. Interestingly enough, official reserves maintained in London had very little effect on expansion of currency. In fact, between 1893 and 1898, minting of new coins was virtually suspended in India for reasons connected with the prevailing exchange policy of the government. Location of gold reserves in England was sought to be justified, in official circles, by its ready availability for silver purchases needed for India. In reality, the Bank of England was reluctant to let the SOS take out its own deposits for purchase of silver. The rather limited options open to the India Office to use its growing reserves at the Bank of England, especially for purchase of silver in the London market, soon became a sensitive as well as a highly confidential issue around 1912–13. Difficulties of procuring silver from the London market even constrained the capacity of the Indian Treasury to honour (redeem) the Council Bills presented to it. The Bank of England on its part was interested in the overall liquidity situation of the City of London which was dependent on regular injections of India Office deposits. The SOS even demonstrated a conscious attempt to keep out Indian silver merchants from the London market by denying them silver purchase contracts. Instead, the banks worked out an arrangement which favoured some London-based European merchants having closer contact with the SOS. On the whole, accumulation of reserves by the SOS had very little, if any, impact on money supply in India. The link between official gold reserves in the London branch of the Paper Currency Reserve (PCR) and issue of paper money in India, though legalized in terms of the official legislation in 1905, made almost no dent on money supply because of the limited circulation of paper currency in India. While about one-third of the value of India's imports in each year comprised precious metals or gold coins, a large proportion of the treasure found its way to the unusually large hoards maintained by private individuals in India. The residual was used for new coinage at the mints. However, such imports did not contribute to the nation's capacity for current consumption or investment—a fact which also applied to India's official reserves maintained in London.

Table 4.4   Comparative estimates of selected items in India's balance of payments: 1899–1900 to 1908–09

(million £)

S.no.	Items	Keynes (annual average 1899–1900 to 1908–09)	Morison (annual average 1899–1900 to 1908–09)	Pandit (1905–06)	Paish (1908–09)	Official and CB trade series (1899–1900 to 1908–09)	Official series re-estimated by author
(1)	(2)	(3)	(4)	(5)	(6)	(7)	(8)
1.	Home Charges less purchase of stores in England	15.7	15.7	15.5			
2.	Private capital inflows	4.5	2.1				
3.	Private capital outflows [including miscellaneous payments for services (f)]	5.5	5.6 (net)	1.3 (16.9) $^g/_b$	9.7 (4.7) $^h/_c$		
4.	Official capital inflow	4.1	4.1		4.3 (5.3)		
5.	Change in official reserves held in London	1.6		1.0			
6.	Rupee debt repatriated by India (i)	0.4	0.4 $^i/_e$				

Contd.

Table 4.4 contd.

S.no.	Items	Keynes (annual average 1899–1900 to 1908–09)	Morison (annual average 1899–1900 to 1908–09)	Pandit (1905–06)	Paish (1908–09)	Official and CB trade series (1899–1900 to 1908–09)	Official series re-estimated by author
(1)	(2)	(3)	(4)	(5)	(6)	(7)	(8)
7.	Export surplus including treasure and official transaction (k)	15.0	15.0	21.8	21.2		17.3 ^{e}/g
8.	Land-borne trade (excess of imports over exports)	0.4	0.8				(m)/(h)
9.	Council Bills sold in London					23.9	23.9
10.	Railway annuities			5.6			
11.	Balance of non-commercial transactions			5.7 (0.8) ^{n}/i			
12.	Balance of indebtedness (comparable private and official capital imports)			16.6 (6.1)			

Contd.

Table 4.4 contd.

Notes and Sources: (a) Keynes (1911); (b) Morison (1911); (c) Pandit (1937); (d) Paish (1909); (e) The adjusted series on trade data corrects the official series for exchange rate fluctuations till 1898. Omissions in the latter for data on land-borne trade, re-exports, and government purchases (stores) are corrected in the adjusted series. See Table 4.3 for the discrepancy between the official and the adjusted series on trade data; (f) Private remittances of interest and of miscellaneous payments are recorded in Keynes's data as £4.5 million and £1.0 million respectively; (g) Figures in brackets refer to Pandit's estimates for Home Charges and freights; (h) Paish (1909) did not provide the details of private or official flows. His estimates for official flows, consistently larger than comparable estimates from other sources, relate to transactions for investment in railways and other types of borrowing by government and the municipalities (interest payments are recorded in brackets); (i) Represents additional payments by way of repatriation; (j) Estimates by Morison, though mentioned in text, are not used in his conjectural estimates, as pointed out by Keynes; (k) Official transactions include expenditure in England on stores. Imports, as ordinarily recorded, are on a c.i.f. basis. This introduces an element of double counting in Morison's estimate, since he considers the freight separately under invisibles as well (item 3). See Keynes (1911) for a mention of the above point. Figures for export surplus (row 7) reported under Keynes and Morison are exclusive of land-borne trade. Hence Keynes's figures for balance of trade for sea- and land-borne trade (inclusive of treasure and stores) amount to £14.6 million, as pointed out in the text above; (l) Exclusive of freight; (m) Our estimates on land-borne trade are already covered by data reported under (7) which is the adjusted series. This, however, is not true of the official series which excludes, among others, data on land-borne trade which had a negative balance. Data reported in Table 4.4 may not exactly match because of rounding off; (n) Reported separately as net non-commercial remittances through exchange banks at £0.8 million. On a clear analysis Pandit's data include railway annuities separately (at £5.6 million), since they are already included under Home Charges at £16.9 million under row (3) above. Second, they count under the head of balance of non-commercial transaction payments through exchange banks at £0.8 million which in reality were already covered by Home Charges, ordinarily transacted by exchange banks. The corrected figure relating to Pandit's balance of indebtedness is reported as £6.1 million in row (12).

Notes

1. Raymond W. Goldsmith, 1983, *The Financial Development of India 1860–1977,* (Delhi), 1983, p. 6. The original figure was Rs 18.13 billion for 1900 and we have converted it into sterling at an exchange rate of Rs 15 to the pound sterling.

2. See K. N. Chaudhuri, 1968, 'India's International Economy in the Nineteenth Century: A Historical Survey', *Modern Asian Studies,* vol. 2, no. 1, pp. 31–50 (Chapter 2 in this volume).

3. 'As a matter of fact . . . it is the inflow of capital, the "drain" from England into India which drives them (prices) up'. J. M. Keynes, 1909, 'Rise in Prices 1907–09', *Economic Journal,* quoted in the *Madras Mail,* 10 April 1909.

4. Amongst the more significant writings that present nationalist arguments, we include: R. C. Dutt, 1960, *The Economic History of India,* vol. II (Delhi); C. L. Parekh, ed., 1887, D. Naoroji, *Essays, Speeches and Writings* (Bombay); D. Naoroji, 1901, *Poverty and Un-British Rule in India* (London); M. G. Ranade, 1898, *Essays on Indian Economics* (Bombay).

5. Theodore Morison, 1911, *Economic Transition in India* (London), pp. 186, 197, 202; J. M. Keynes, 1911, 'Review of Theodore Morison: Economic Transition in India', *Economic Journal.*

6. See Keynes Papers at the Marshall Library, Cambridge files IB/2 and IB/3. In a memorandum to the India Office, dated 20 May, 1913, inaccuracies of seaborne trade data were noticed by Keynes. Also see J. M. Keynes, 1910, 'Notes on Seaborne Trade of India', in supplement to *Indian Trade Journal,* 22 September.

7. This includes statistics for Council Bills (or Reverse Council Bills) sold (or bought) by the India Office, the value of which measured the India Office's records on remittances between India and England.

8. Burton Stein and David Washbrook, 1987, 'Eighteenth Century India: Historiography, Perspectives, and Propositions', mimeo (London).

9. J. M. Keynes, 1913, *Collected Writings of John Maynard Keynes,* vol. I; *Indian Currency and Finance* (London), p. 72.

10. Marcello de Cecco, 1974, *Money and Empire: The International Gold Standard, 1890–1914* (Oxford).

11. See amongst other works on the residual approach to construct capital accounts transactions, Jacob Viner, 1924, *Canada's*

Balance of International Indebtedness, 1900–1913 (Cambridge, Mass.), ch. v; Y. S. Pandit, 1937, *India's Balance of Indebtedness 1898–1913* (London).

12. Even Vera Anstey, who subscribed very little to nationalist claims regarding a drain of wealth from British India, spoke of an 'unjust' debiting from India on political grounds which was related to military and other similar spending. Vera Anstey, 1921, *Economic Development of India* (London), Appendix G, pp. 109–11.

13. In addition to those cited in note 4, see the following for more recent work on the subject: B. N. Ganguli, 1965, *Dadabhai Naoroji and the Drain Theory* (Bombay); Bipan Chandra, 1966, *Rise and Growth of Economic Nationalism* (New Delhi); A. K. Banerji, 1982, *Aspects of Indo-British Economic Relations* (Bombay), pp. 176–206.

14. See for an officially accepted distinction between productive and unproductive loans, *Final Report of Royal Commission on Expenditure of India* (under the chairmanship of Lord Welby), London, 1900, pp. 44–5.

15. Select Committee Report to Parliament. Cited in Welby Commission, ibid., pp. 44, 45, 71.

16. Ibid.

17. Additional transfer towards debt retirement included, in 1874, cancellation of a £12 million East India Company debt, presumably through funds drawn from the revenue account of the budget. See also Welby Commission, pp. 44–8, 71 for statistics cited in this paragraph.

18. Goldsmith, 1983, *Financial Development*, p. 40.

   In 1857 there was the first world stock market crisis. It originated in a boom in USA . . . caused by a rapid increase in gold production and an enormous railway construction (21,000 miles were built in eight years). A large number of banks, many of them unsold, had been opened. The failure of many of these American banks and the fall in the value of railway securities (many of them held by British investors) brought the crisis to England and gave rise to heavy demands on the Bank's reserves. It was necessary to suspend the Act of 1844 and issue notes beyond the amount which could be backed by gold.

   J. L. Gayler, Irene Richards, and J. A. Morris, 1975, *A Sketch-Map Economic History of Britain* (London), p. 175. See also, for a succinct account of the Great Depression of 1873–95, Michel

Beaud, 1984, *A History of Capitalism 1500–1980* (London), pp. 117–22.

It is not difficult to see an element of causality as well as 'financial prudence' in the Select Committee's recommendation to the British Parliament in 1874 for conversion of the Indian government's unproductive loans to productive ones.

19. Welby Commission, *Final Report*, p. 71. See also, John and Richard Strachey, 1822, *The Finances and Public Works of India* (London).
20. Ibid., p. 259.
21. Dharma Kumar, 1982, 'The Fiscal system', in *Cambridge Economic History of India*, Dharma Kumar and Meghnad Desai, eds, vol. II, 1757–1970 (Delhi), pp. 934–5.
22. John and Richard Strachey, 1822, *Financial and Public Works*, p. 259.
23. Goldsmith, 1983, *Financial Development*, p. 40.
24. Welby Commission, *Final Report*, pp. 40–5, 47, 48.
25. Ibid., pp.90–128.
26.

	1862-3	*Annual average 1883-5*
Expenditure on defence and foreign affairs	16.5	19.1
Expenditure on civil charges including public works expenditure chargeable to revenue	13.0	18.8

(in Rs million)

27. India bore the entire amount of charges, both civil and military, for British administration in Aden during the period. India's share of expenses in British missions in Persia during 1891 and 1893–4 to 1895–6 was one-and-a-half times the amount contributed by the British. Similarly, a large part of expenditure on the British consular establishments in China was borne by India. Also, India met a substantial part of charges on 'postal and telegraphic services' in Zanzibar, Mauritius, the Red Sea, the Euphrates, Tigris, and Karuph area, and consular expenses in Jeddah, Chiengmai, and Surinam. Welby Commission, *Final Report*, p. 91.
28. Ibid., pp. 90–128, 151.

29. Ibid., p. 95.

30. Ibid., pp. 90–128.

31. Ibid., pp. 116–17.

32. Ibid., p. 81. In its memorandum to the Welby Commission, the select committee on Indian finance argued that '. . . there is no true partnership, at any rate, no freedom of contract between England and India, that the Indian authorities have scarcely any voice at all in the adoption of military reforms; and that there is not that identity of interest in measures . . . which is essential for partnership'. The point was cited from an earlier despatch of the Indian government, dated 10 August 1883 and 25 March 1890, to the British government. Ibid., pp. 90–128.

33. Ibid., p. 151.

34. Theodore Morison, 1911, *Economic Transition*, pp. 237–41.

35. Anstey, 1942, *Economic Development of India*, pp. 509–10.

36. Morison, 1911, *Economic Transition*, pp. 237–41.

37. Anstey, *Economic Development*.

38. See note 5.

39. Mention may be made here of a few Western writers of the nineteenth century whose arguments support the nationalist contention: H. H. Wilson, 'On Tariff-free Entry of Textiles', cited in J. S. Mill, *History of British India*, vol. III; Montgomery Martin, *The Political, Commercial and Financial Aspects of the Anglo-East Empire in 1832*; George Wingate, 1859, *A Few Words about the Financial Relations with India* (London); Brooks Adams, 1896, *Law of Civilisation and Decay: An Essay in History* (New York). Sources relating to nationalist literature are provided in notes (4) and (13).

40. Thomas Mun, 1664, *England's Treasure by Forraign Trade*. See also, amongst other mercantilist authors, Josiah Child, 1775, *Discourse of Trade*.

41. Memorandum submitted by W. Martin (App. II) to the Indian Currency Commission, 1889, *Minutes of Evidence*, Pt. III.

42. See also for details, B. N. Ganguli, *Naoroji and Drain Theory*, and Banerji, 1982, *Indo-British Economic Relations*, pp. 97–8.

43. See, for an interesting parallel drawn between 'drain of wealth' in Ireland and India and the literature thereon, B. N. Ganguli, 1965, *Naoroji and Drain Theory*, pp. 51–9.

44. In the first half of nineteenth century, there were seven famines, with an estimated total of one and a half million deaths from famine. In the second half of nineteenth century, there were twenty-four famines (six between 1851 and 1876, and eighteen between 1876 and 1900), with an estimated total, according to official records, of over 20 million deaths.

R. P. Dutt, 1970, *India Today* (Calcutta), p. 125. See also William Digby, 1901, *Prosperous British India*. Interestingly enough, a British viceroy in India, Lord Northbrook was remarkably complacent on the question of Indian famines by 1874: '. . . whatever means we may take to obviate or mitigate them, it must, under present circumstance, be looked upon as inevitable that famines will from time to time occur.' John and Richard Strachey, 1822, *Finances and Public Works*, p. 259.

45. Naoroji, 1901, *Un-British Rule*.

46. Ibid., pp. 177, 233.

47. Banerji, 1982, *Indo-British Economic Relations*, pp. 185–91.

48. See for example, Dutt, *Economic History*, p. xiv.

When taxes are raised and spent in a country the money circulates among the people, fructifies trades, industries, and agriculture, and in one shape or another reaches the mass of the people. But when taxes raised in a country are remitted out of it, the money is lost to the country for ever, it does not stimulate her trade or industries, or reach the people in any form.

Also R. C. Dutt, 1885, 'A plea for the spoliation of India', *JPSS*, vol. VIII, no. 3, p. 17. The arguments of the nationalists echoed the following views expressed by George Wingate in his minute of evidence to the Fowler Committee on Indian currency, '. . . taxes raised in a country and spent in another . . . constitute . . . an absolute loss and extinction of the whole amount withdrawn from the taxed country . . . the cruel, crushing effect of the tribute upon India.' Memorandum submitted to the Indian Currency Committee, 1898 (App. II) by W. Martin as *Minutes of Evidence*, Part III.

49. Bipan Chandra, 1979, 'Reinterpretations of Indian Economic History', in Bipan Chandra, ed., *Nationalism and Colonialism in Modern India* (Delhi), pp. 28–73.

50. See, for a preview of the present work, Sunanda Sen, 1982, 'Trade as a Handmaiden of Colonialism: India during Late Nineteenth

Century to First World War', *Studies in History*, vol. IV, no. 1, January–June.

51. Letter from Dadabhai Naoroji to Lord Hamilton dated 12 October 1900 cited by John McLane, 1963, 'The Drain of Wealth and Indian Nationalism at the Turn of the Century', in T. Roychaudhury, ed., *Contributions to Indian Economic History*, vol. II (Calcutta) (chapter 3 in this volume).

52. McLane, 1963, *Drain of Wealth*, p. 40 (pp. 109–10 in this volume).

53. *Bengalee*, 4 June 1903 cited in McAlpin, *Price Movements*, pp. 39–40, in Dharma Kumar, ed., *Cambridge Economic History of India*.

54. McLane, 1963, *Drain of Wealth*, pp. 28–9 (pp. 99–100 in this volume).

55. Anstey, 1942, *Economic Development*, pp. 509–10.

56. W. J. MacPherson, 1955, 'Investment in Indian Railways: 1845–75', *Economic History Review*, pp. 181, 185.

57. Arun Bose, 1975, 'Foreign Capital', in V. B. Singh, ed., *Economic History of India 1857–1956* (Delhi), p. 504.

58. L. H. Jenks, 1944, 'British Experience with Foreign Investment', *Journal of Economic History*, December.

59. Henry Bearmont cited in Bose, 1975, 'Foreign Capital', p. 511.

60. Cited in Vinod Dubey, 1975, 'Railways', in V. B. Singh, *Economic History*, p. 328.

61. Daniel R. Headrick, 1983, *The Tools of Empire: Technology and European Empire in the Nineteenth Century* (New York), p. 182.

62. According to a recent interpretation, later-day Marxists ignored the dialectical method of Marx, as was evident in his attempt to incorporate both the regenerative as well as the destructive role of capitalism in the colonies. Thus the charge of 'blinkered ethnocentricity' against Marx can be dispelled by recognizing the fact that '. . . the idea of the "cunning reason" (List der Vernunft) duly set "right way up", enabled him (Marx) to condemn capitalism and colonialism from the point of view of those who suffer them, and at the same time to consider them as important progressive forces from the point of view of objective historical movements'. See Umbretto Melotti, 1977, *Marx and the Third World* (London), p. 118. Also see Karl Marx, 'The Future Results of the British Rule in India', in *Marx-Engels Reader*, pp. 583–4 (cited in Melotti, 1972, *Marx*, p. 193). Thus Marx goes to the extent of making the following statement, 'England has to fulfil a double mission in India: *one destructive, the other*

regenerating—the annihilation of old Asiatic society, and the laying of the foundations of Western society in Asia . . . . Steam has brought India into regular and rapid communication with Europe, has connected its chief ports with those of the whole south-eastern ocean, and has revindicated it from the isolated position which was the prime cause of its stagnation,' cited in Melotti, 1977, *Marx,* p. 115 (italics added).

63. See for different positions on the economic implication of railways in British India, L. H. Jenks, 1927, *The Migration of British Capital* (New York); Daniel Thorner, 1950, *Investment in Empire* (Philadelphia); MacPherson, 1955, 'Investment in Indian Railways'; John Hurd II, 'Railways and the Expansion of Markets in India 1861–1921', *Explorations in Economic History,* July. See also Headrick, 1983, *Tools of Empire.*

64. On the salary structure for Europeans and others during 1887–1913, see A. K. Bagchi, 1985, *Private Investment in India,* p. 168.

65. See Keynes, 1911, 'Review of Morison' and Morison, 1911, *Economic Transition.*

66. Keynes, 1909, 'Rise in Prices'. See also *Madras Mail,* 10 April 1909 in Keynes Papers, files IB/2 and IB/3 at the Marshall Library, Cambridge.

67. Michael Barrat-Brown, 1974, *Economics of Imperialism* (Harmondsworth), pp. 170–93, and Michael Barrat-Brown, 1972, *Essays on Imperialism* (Nottingham), p. 68. Also see Michael Barratt-Brown, 1984, *Models in Political Economy* (Harmondsworth), p. 88.

68. See for data on S_d, I_d, and I_f, H. Feinstein, 1972, *National Income, Output and Employment in the UK* (Cambridge), p. 85. For data on i, see B. R. Mitchell, 1962, *Abstract of British Historical Statistics* (Cambridge), p. 333.

69. See note 68.

70. See for statistics on tea consumption, Mitchell, 1962, *British Historical Statistics.* For the general argument on a possible rise in the standard of living of the working classes in the late nineteenth century, see E. J. Hobsbawm, 1964, *Labouring Men: Studies in the History of Labour* (London), pp. 120–5, 272–303; E. P. Thompson, 1963, *The Making of the English Working Class* (London), part II.

71. Morison, 1911, *Economic Transition;* Keynes, 1911, 'Review of Morison'.

72. Pandit, 1937, *Balance of Indebtedness.*

73. Ibid.

74. In Pandit's calculations, railway annuities are separately calculated as outstanding payments at £5.6 million. The sum, however, is already subsumed under Home Charges and estimated at £15.5 million, a fact which is ignored by Pandit as he adds the two. Second, payments under 'non-commercial transactions' included, in Pandit's estimates, the entire flow of payments through exchange banks—an enumeration which ignores the fact that the exchange banks were instrumental, under the CB scheme, for remittances under commercial transactions (merchandise trade) as well. The above introduced an element of double counting in the figure Pandit arrived at as 'balance of indebtedness' (defined as total credits less total debits). See Pandit, 1937, *Balance of Indebtedness.* See also for other criticisms of Pandit's calculations, Banerji, 1982, *Indo-British Economic Relations*, pp. 190–4.

75. Morison, 1911, *Economic Transition*; Keynes, 1911, 'Review of Morison'.

76. Keynes Papers, files IB/2 and IB/3 at Marshall Library, Cambridge, See also Keynes, 'Note on Seaborne Trade by India', supplement to *Indian Trade Journal*, 22 September 1910, and *Times*, 9 November 1914.

77. Ibid.

78. J. M. Keynes, 1913, *Indian Currency and Finance.*

5

The Great Depression (1873–96) and the Third World: with Special Reference to India[*]

Amiya K. Bagchi

Introduction

The expression 'Great Depression', used to characterize the period 1873–96, was coined primarily with reference to the state of Great Britain, the leading imperial country of the nineteenth century. Whether a similar characterization of other capitalist countries of the world can be made for the same period is doubtful. Even for Great Britain, the applicability of the term for the 1873–96 period has been questioned (Saul, 1969). It has been pointed out that while prices fell in that country, the fall was not uniform. The index number of prices constructed by P. Rousseaux fell from 128 in 1872 to 81 in 1887; but it rose again up to 1891 when it reached a figure of 86, and then fell up to 1895, when it reached a low of 72 (Mitchell and Deane, 1976, pp. 471–3). The fall in prices in the period 1872–95 in any case

* Previously published in *Social Science Information*, 18, 2 (1979), pp. 197–218.

I am indebted to Sri Ashok Chakrabarty and to other members of the Historical Research Cell, State Bank of India, Calcutta for help in preparing this chapter, and to Drs Saugata Mukherjee and Sunanda Sen for comments on an earlier draft. None of them are responsible for any remaining errors.

came in the wake of a period of rising prices since 1850. Furthermore, the fall in prices helped raise the standard of living of British wage-earners, who by now formed the major part of the population. However, the percentage of persistent unemployment to total working force was higher during the period of the Great Depression than it was at any time between, say, 1830 and 1920. It is also known that the growth of industrial production decelerated in Britain during the period under review, but then it had shown a decelerating tendency in all the years since the 1830s (Saul, 1969, p. 36).

Even if the Great Depression can be accepted as an expression roughly characterizing economic change in Britain during 1873–96, it is misleading as a characterization of economic growth in the other advanced capitalist countries. In this chapter I shall try to draw attention to some of the relatively neglected interrelations of international capitalism during the period, and certain neglected processes of adjustment in which the third world played a very important part. We begin by briefly recounting some important developments in the structure and processes of international capitalism.

First, this period witnessed the consolidation of the centre of industrial capitalism. This capitalist centre consists roughly of Britain, France, Germany, the Netherlands, Belgium and the Scandinavian countries, the USA, Canada, and Australia. Even in 1851, no other country except Britain and Belgium could be properly called industrialized, since in only perhaps these two countries did the non-agricultural population exceed the agricultural. By 1900, many other countries had attained the status of industrialized nations. It was in the last quarter of the nineteenth century that the USA and Germany forged ahead and overtook Britain in many branches of industrial production. Within this centre, the position of Britain weakened relatively, but British capital played a large part in financing the industrialization of the USA, Canada, Australia, and South Africa.

As is well known, generating an export surplus with colonial dependencies through tribute and trade was a very important means of effecting the transfer of capital from Britain to the colonies of European settlement (Bagchi, 1972). A. W. Flux was one of the first commentators to notice an important change in the structure of trade of imperial countries with their colonies during the period under discussion. In the case of Britain, for example, while imports from Britain constituted 57.5 per cent of total colonial imports over the period 1867–71, the corresponding percentage over the period 1892–6 had declined to 55.3; on the other side, exports to Britain declined from 52.4 per cent over the period 1867–71 to 49.0 per cent over the period 1892–6 (Flux, 1899, pp. 495–7). While this suggests an absolute, though small, decline in Britain's position in the trade of her colonies, the comparison is incomplete because it leaves out of account Britain's earnings from invisible services, connected with trade, such as shipping, insurance, exchange, banking and so on. Moreover, in order to get at the true character of the change, we have to distinguish between Britain's trade with the self-governing dominions such as Canada or Australia, and her trade with the colonies proper. For instance, while the share of Britain in the imports of Canada declined from 49.9 per cent to 33 per cent between 1867–71 and 1892–6, the share of Britain in the imports of India increased between the two dates from 69.2 per cent to 71.9 per cent. A more drastic change is observed in Britain's share in the exports of the two countries. Whereas Britain's share in Canadian exports increased from 31.4 per cent to 54.9 per cent, her share in Indian exports declined from 52.6 per cent to 33.2 per cent between 1867–71 and 1892–6. These changes can be interpreted to mean that Britain's position worsened in the relatively affluent white colonies but improved in the poorer non-white colonies. Since we know that Britain was investing capital in the white colonies and extracting a surplus out of the non-white colonies, it is reasonable to conclude that an export surplus was being engineered by British capital with the non-white colonies so that it could fructify into capital formation in the white colonies. While industrial capitalism was being diffused into new lands, a process of polarization was going on between the emerging advanced capitalist centre and the third world.[1]

Thus the period under consideration displays the contradictory developments of diffusion of industrial capitalism to practically all countries populated by western European migrants (the period 1880–1913 was the peak period of migration from Europe) and the open manifestation of rivalry among the advanced capitalist nations for acquiring colonies. While the scramble for Africa going on in this period has been analysed in some detail, the processes of exploitation in the already conquered lands have not received an equal degree of attention. In this chapter, I shall contend, among other things, that the method of free trade was supplemented by a tributary fiscal apparatus in order to extract an enormous surplus out of India. The long-drawn-out process of demonetization of silver also played a role in extracting a surplus out of India and China. However, none of these exploitative processes were orderly ones; and the human misery caused during this period must be seen as directly resulting from the way in which the metropolitan centre was consolidating itself and differentiating itself from the surrounding world whose progress was decisively retarded for the sake of such consolidation and differentiation.

We shall study the impact of the associated policies on India, with side glances at China. Since India played a pivotal role in the British Empire and hence in the whole capitalist imperialist system, this will, I hope, also illuminate certain areas of policy-making and economic change in other colonies. I shall concentrate on three aspects, the policies regarding trade, those regarding monetary arrangements, and those regarding fiscal systems. It could be said that the sheet-anchor of British policy in India was a tributary fiscal system combined with free trade for India (though not for the self-governing dominions). But complete free trade could not become a reality for India until the British government had overcome the necessity of imposing import duties in order to balance the budget even approximately; the saddling of the Indian finances with an additional debt burden of about £50 million (Dutt, 1963, pp. 157, 272) completely upset Indian budgetary balances in the 1860s. In the 1870s, partly in order to appease Lancashire manufacturers who regarded the rising cotton mills of India with a jaundiced eye, most of the import duties were abolished, even at the cost of embracing a deficit in the current account of the government. The 1860s and 1870s also saw a large extension of the Indian railway system. These measures together allowed British capitalists to penetrate even deeper into India, and both annihilate artisanal manufactures in wide territories and tap the foodgrains and raw materials of interior tracts for the benefit of the metropolitan centre. The demonetization of silver and the acceptance of a gold standard for purposes of international settlement were necessary adjuncts of the consolidation of metropolitan capitalism. But they aggravated the problems of adjustment of third world countries to the new stage of evolution of world capitalism. In effect, the global costs of adjustment to the new monetary order were thrown on to the colonies which were already paying in the form of commercial and fiscal exploitation by the imperialist powers (Triffin, 1969). It is by severely destabilizing the economics of the already conquered colonies as well as by subjugating territories in Africa or Southeast Asia still remaining outside the formal control of European powers that the international capitalist centre sought to overcome contradictions among its own members—old and new. The increasing frequency of famines in India (and partly also in China) should be seen as part of the cost exacted by the metropolitan centre for achieving its own equilibrium, however transitory that equilibrium might turn out to be.

'Silver is for the East, Gold is for the West'

Before industrial capitalism spread to the whole of western Europe and west European settlements overseas, the structures of the non-European and European economies were not radically different. Agriculture was the mainstay of the major part of the population, most people lived in rural areas, and where materials were worked up into artefacts for the use of man, it was done by manual or handicraft methods with the minimal use of machines and without the assistance of non-animal power. After the 1780s Britain began to differ from all other countries in these respects, and after 1850, many other western European countries also increasingly differentiated themselves. The share of agriculture in the national income had probably already declined to less than 50 per cent for Britain, Germany, the Netherlands, and Norway by 1850 or 1860. But in none of the western European countries, except Britain and Belgium, had agriculture ceased to keep less than 50 per cent of the working population occupied (Kuznets, 1971, Tables 21 and 38). In 1860, Australia already had a low share of agriculture in national produce or employment, but it had a very small population at the time. So the diffusion of industrial capitalism from Britain to other parts of western Europe and to overseas European settlements including the USA can be considered to be largely a phenomenon of the second half of the nineteenth century. In this diffusion, the migration of capital supporting the migration of European workers played a very important role. And barring the years 1896–1913, most of this inter-related migration occurred precisely during the period of the so-called Great Depression. By 1900 western Europe, the USA and even Canada and Australia had become very different in their economic and social structures from most of the third world countries of today. In some ways, the most obvious symbol of the consolidation of the capitalist centre and its separation from the colonial periphery was the distinction between the main media of circulation and international payments in the two groups. In particular, while gold came to be adopted as the standard of currency in all western European countries, the USA and Japan, silver remained the standard in the two largest colonial and semi-colonial countries, viz. India and China. This dichotomy in standards and its significance were plainly perceived by many contemporary observers. An anonymous 'Indian Official' (1878) had a full chapter in his book, entitled 'Silver is for the East, gold is for the West'.

The difference between the two monetary standards was highly significant. It revealed itself in at least three ways and further differentiated the two sets of countries: (a) the silver-using countries experienced a mild inflation of internal prices, whereas prices in the gold-using countries generally fell; (b) the rates of exchange of the currencies of the silver-using countries with those using gold generally slid down drastically; and (c) as a consequence of (b), the silver-using countries, which were normally net transferrers of capital to the gold-using ones, had to shoulder an increasing burden in terms of foreign exchange and exports required to finance the transfer.

On the basis of a naive application of neo-classical theory (as developed, for example, by Samuelson, 1952, 1954), the expectation might be formed that the terms of trade of the capital-transferring, silver-using countries should decline. A preliminary calculation made in this respect belied any such expectation (Sen, 1976). There may be some doubts regarding the reliability of the export and import values given by customs authorities since they were notional and had no necessary relation to the actual prices. Assuming that the export and import values are correct, the relative stability of the terms of trade can be explained in terms of the drastic fall in freight rates over this period. To the extent that India and other colonial countries exported low-value raw materials and food and imported in turn high-value manufactured goods, their export values may have benefited more from the decline in freight rates than their imports, assuming that freight rates had a closer relation to bulk than to value.

However, one contention of this chapter is that the terms of trade as they are usually calculated throw little light on the gains made or losses suffered by the people in the colonies; another major contention is that short-term fluctuations in prices and exchange rates are as important in revealing the process of adjustment imposed by the metropolitan centre on the colonial countries as long-term trends. Finally, along with prices and exchange rates, the real direction of flow of resources will have to be determined in order to get at the mechanism of consolidation of industrial capitalism in the metropolitan centre and its retrogression in the rest of the world—particularly the colonial and semi-colonial countries of Asia, Africa, and the Caribbean.

We shall take up the first and third propositions a little later. For the moment, let me describe the difference in the degrees of fluctuation of some very important indices as between the colonial and metropolitan countries and as between magnitudes directly affected by flows of international trade and those not so affected in the colonial countries. I surmised that if in the metropolitan centre, commercial banks and the Bank of England were operating with balances garnered from all over the globe, whereas colonial banks were simply reacting to the shocks imposed on the system by movements of international trade, colonial wars, and uncontrolled nature, then this would be reflected in the relative stability of the bank rate charged by the Bank of England and that charged by the Bank of Bengal (the latter was the most important commercial bank in British India, with important links with the government). This surmise turned out to be correct. An analysis of bank rate changes between 1874 and 1896 is given in Table 5.1.

Table 5.1   *Bank rates, 1874–96*

	Average bank rate (in per cent)	*Standard deviation of bank rates*	*Coefficient of variation of bank rates*	*Number of times the bank rate was changed*
Bank of England[a]	3.50	0.95	0.27	160
Bank of Bengal[b]	6.52	2.13	0.33	270

Sources: a. Mitchell and Deane, 1976, p. 457.
         b. RBI, 1954, p. 691.

It is clear from Table 5.1 that the average bank rate of the Bank of Bengal (which was the bank rate for all of India for all practical purposes) was nearly double that of the bank rate in England; it also fluctuated much more than the bank rate in England. It was higher and more fluctuating in reality than is shown by the figures, for the bank rate on several occasions reached the legal maximum of 12 per cent, and if the legal ceiling were not there, the rate might have gone beyond 12 per cent on a few occasions.

The behaviour of prices in India was influenced by the factors mentioned earlier. Most prices rose internally in terms of silver.

Among them, there were distinctions between products and locations affected directly by international trade factors, and products not so affected. On the whole, prices of export crops at the ports were fairly stable. These included wheat, rice (exported mainly from Burma), cotton, jute, indigo, and opium. Among these crops again, indigo and opium declined in price between 1871 and 1892, and the prices of jute and cotton fluctuated very near those obtained in 1871 (Atkinson, 1897, Appendix C).

An important change took place in the commodity composition and destinations of India's exports. India's exports became far more diversified in respect of countries; it was this diversification that made India's external balance so important for the stability of Britain's imperial balance and of the gold standard mechanism (Saul, 1960). Along with diversification of destinations, there also occurred a change in the composition of commodities, particularly to Great Britain. Food grains became an important part of India's exports from the 1870s onwards. Most of the rice exported was produced in Burma, but some came also from other provinces, particularly Bengal and Madras. Wheat was exported predominantly from the North-Western Provinces (United Provinces) and the Punjab.

The prices of food grains in the period concerned present a complex picture. First, there were the prices at the ports of the superior cereals, particularly wheat and rice. India became a substantial seller of wheat in the international market, but international prices were determined only partly by the state of her supplies. On the whole, it would be right to regard port prices as mainly determined by international factors. In the case of Burma rice also, a similar statement can be made, although in the beginning Burma dominated the international rice market to a large extent. In the case of wheat, increasing supplies from the overseas settlements of Europe, and in the case of rice, increasing supplies from other colonies and semi-colonies of South-east Asia helped keep international prices down.

Even in the case of exportable food crops, internal prices could move very differently from international prices. A famine in a particular area could send prices up to great heights without necessarily affecting export sales to any great extent. In fact, India exported large amounts of food grains even in years when famine depopulated large areas of the country. Part of the explanation lies in that not only the transport network but also the major trade channels were already geared to the export market, and the linkages of trade, transport, and finance between interior areas were as such much weaker than between the hinterland and the ports. The other part of the explanation is that most of the people affected by famine had, of course, no purchasing power with which to make their demand effective, and the state normally saw to it that starving people were deprived of everything they had rather than be allowed to withhold their dues in respect of land revenue.

Among the crops which did not enter into the network of international trade, such as millets and pulses, it is possible to differentiate between those which were major food grains in particular areas and those which acted as supplements rather than as major sources of calories. The former consisted generally of millets, particularly *jowar* and *bajra*, and the latter mainly of pulses. The latter were generally stable in value, except for one or two famine years with a rising trend in the case of *masur* (lentils) and gram. Even in their case, prices could be very variable. For example, the price index of *arhar* at Allahabad (with base: 1871 = 100) changed from 94 in 1877 to 211 in 1878, 181 in 1879 and back to 103 in 1880. Or, in the case of *masur* at Lucknow, the price index could change from 106 in 1876 to 218 in 1878 and move back to 125 in 1880. However, the greatest variations were observed in the case of millets in areas where they formed the staple food of the ordinary people. Thus, the price index of *jowar* at Salem in Madras moved up from 142 in 1876 to 534 in 1877 and fell back to 213 in 1880 and 141 in 1883. Similarly, the price index of *ragi* at Mysore rose from 210 in 1875 to 735 in 1877 and fell back to 187 in 1880. The interspatial variations also seemed to be the greatest in the case of millets; while the 1876-7 famine in Madras was sending all millet prices skyrocketing, in neighbouring Hyderabad apparently the prices of millets and rice continued to be practically on the same level as in 1871, and in fact fell below the 1871 level in the 1880s. (All the index numbers are taken from Atkinson, 1897, Appendix C.)

I have not tried to compare the degree of instability of internal prices in India and in Britain or other advanced capitalist countries. This is partly because the exact measure of instability of prices in India will depend on the regions and baskets of commodities included. Even without such computation, however, it is obvious that internal prices were far more unstable within India than in Britain or other advanced capitalist countries.

While prices of food grains rose in most parts of India, wages of workers did not rise proportionately. This comes out clearly from the indexes of wages published in different issues of the *Prices and Wages in India*, and from the more detailed accounts given in settlement reports and district gazetteers spanning the period (see for example, Nevill, 1921, pp. 45–8; Nevill, 1923, pp. 44–6). Although detailed data on wages of factory or plantation labour have not been processed yet, whatever information we have indicates that such labour also suffered a decline in living standards. For example, the money wages of unskilled labourers in Murree brewery actually fell between 1871 and 1895, while prices rose by a substantial percentage (Atkinson, 1897, p. 118). Thus the wage-earning classes suffered a large decline in earnings over this same period. Their total incomes declined further because of the unemployment let loose by the process of de-industrialization of the economy (Bagchi, 1976).

In this respect also there is a major contrast between India and the advanced capitalist countries. In Britain and in Germany, partly because of a decline in food prices during the period of the Great Depression, real wages of workers rose substantially (for Britain, see Mitchell and Deane, 1976, pp. 343–5; for Germany, Desai, 1968, chapter 4 and Table A.13). While the rise in real wages of employed workers in England was accompanied by some rise in unemployment, this was not severe enough to cancel the gains for workers as a class. Furthermore, taking the Atlantic community as a whole, the situation in respect of unemployment almost certainly improved over the period, although this was often masked by the conversion of underemployment in agriculture into open unemployment.

One of the features of price fluctuations in India that puzzled some contemporary observers was that they persisted in spite of the spread of railways and other types of communication. It has been confirmed by later analysts (for example, Ghosh, 1949) that neither seasonal nor inter-regional variations in prices were greatly moderated by the spread of railroads, although for the important cash crops naturally price movements in major trade centres became more synchronous. British officials often saw a connection between the local monopsony power exercised by traders and the persistence of price fluctuations (see for example, Robertson, 1908, p. 456). But they could not see the pervasiveness of the influence of traders and moneylenders, nor could they see that the whole network of capitalist colonialism introduced and assiduously promoted by the British increased the power of traders, moneylenders, and landlords.[2] Nor have most modern economic historians (for example, Morris, 1974, p. 552n) perceived that the supposed disjunction between the organized and unorganized money markets in British India was largely a myth. The Presidency Banks, other joint-stock banks and the exchange banks needed the native moneylenders and financiers in order to provide them with custom. In times of scarcity, they also profited from the misery of the people, and many bankers recognized this connection. Thus, for example, we read in the annual report of the Agra Bank Limited for the year 1874: 'The first part of the year, owing to the high value of money in India, consequent upon the famine which then prevailed in that country, was favourable to profitable working; but the same cannot be said of the latter half, when, from the reaction which generally follows upon extreme prices, money was comparatively abundant, and more difficulty was experienced in employing it to advantage.' (Agra Bank, 1875).

Transfer of Resources from India to Britain and the Import of Silver

So far we have dealt with instability in India caused by the fact that she (along with other colonies and semi-colonies) had to bear the brunt of residual adjustments when industrial capitalism was being consolidated at the centre.[3] However, the burden of adjustment did not consist simply in having to take care of the peaks and the troughs. It also comprised a large-scale transfer of resources from India and other third world countries to metropolitan countries and thence to the overseas colonies of European settlement. What distinguished India, Indonesia, and other colonies from such countries as Argentina and Brazil, is that much of the transfer took the explicit form of a tribute. Table 5.2 gives figures of the export surplus of India (including Burma) from 1870–1 to 1892–3. I have argued elsewhere that for colonial countries in which the control of foreign trade and of all transactions connected with it was vested with foreign businessmen and in which most of the remittances of profit were outward, that is, from foreigners to their home countries or third countries rather than from indigenous businessmen to the particular countries—the export surplus provides an approximate measure of the drain of incomes abroad (Bagchi, 1977). The essence of this argument was presented by British officials, editors, and Indian nationalists in the nineteenth century (see, for instance, the evidence of Dadabhai Naoroji to the Gold and Silver Commission, 1888). In the Indian case, something like a half of this export surplus was transferred straightaway by Council Bills sold in London by the Secretary of State for India to merchants wanting to make payments in India. The Secretary of State for India used the proceeds to defray the Home Charges, consisting largely of expenses of administering and coercing India. Part of the export surplus was used up in importing silver into India. Contrary to much popular belief, most of the silver imports went into the coining of rupees and thus supporting the expanding colonial payments mechanism (see Table 5.3).

Table 5.2 India's export surplus, Council Bill sales, and silver imports, 1870–1 to 1892–3

	Surplus exports of India		Value obtained from the sale of bills and telegraphic transfers on India		Net imports of silver into India (Rupee values converted at average rate of exchange for Council Bills)
	Rx	£	Rx	£	Rx
	(in tens of rupees)				
1870–1	21,985,579	20,605,026	9,008,500	8,443,509	882,557
1871–2	32,375,072	31,196,080	10,700,000	10,310,339	6,282,868
1872–3	24,763,226	23,477,602	14,702,500	13,939,095	678,016
1873–4	23,332,289	21,729,166	14,265,700	13,285,678	2,324,340
1874–5	21,666,999	20,002,251	11,743,700	10,841,614	4,285,526
1875–6	20,932,737	18,861,268	13,750,000	12,389,613	1,401,440
1876–7	25,594,455	21,870,462	14,890,000	12,695,799	6,151,436
1877–8	25,859,710	22,402,051	11,698,500	10,134,455	12,713,985
1878–9	24,327,417	20,064,037	16,912,361	13,948,565	3,274,830
1879–80	27,430,992	22,814,584	18,350,000	15,261,810	6,545,330
1880–1	24,222,448	20,140,965	18,327,700	15,239,677	6,236,675
1881–2	34,909,876	28,938,832	22,210,935	18,412,429	4,459,008
1882–3	33,397,824	27,170,521	18,585,659	15,120,521	6,085,476

Contd.

Table 5.2 contd.

	Surplus exports of India (in tens of rupees)		Value obtained from the sale of bills and telegraphic transfers on India		Net imports of silver into India (Rupee values converted at average rate of exchange for Council Bills)
	Rx	£	Rx	£	Rx
1883–4	35,417,405	28,829,768	21,621,546	17,599,805	5,213,793
1884–5	30,051,217	24,176,204	17,102,212	13,758,909	5,829,110
1885–6	32,016,304	24,351,067	13,532,537	10,292,692	8,827,808
1886–7	29,767,198	21,632,071	16,700,315	12,136,279	5,200,134
1887–8	28,086,649	19,775,342	21,812,399	15,358,577	6,497,809
1888–9	30,407,853	20,752,093	20,899,122	14,262,859	6,310,773
1889–90	36,836,741	25,426,560	22,418,664	15,474,496	7,549,869
1890–1	31,100,822	23,440,949	21,186,930	15,969,034	10,683,917
1891–2	41,448,553	28,898,276	23,571,437	16,401,538	6,290,342
1892–3	43,896,810	30,605,222	25,989,790	16,224,531	8,031,691

Source: Herschell Committee, 1893, pp. 237–8, 261.

Table 5.3   *Net imports of silver into India and new coinage of rupees, 1870–1 to 1892–3*

Year	Net imports (in tens of rupees)	New coinage (in tens of rupees)
1870–1	941,924	1,718,197
1871–2	6,520,316	1,690,394
1872–3	715,144	3,980,927
1873–4	2,495,824	2,370,007
1874–5	4,642,202	4,896,884
1875–6	1,555,355	2,550,218
1876–7	7,198,872	6,271,122
1877–8	14,676,335	16,180,326
1878–9	3,970,694	7,210,770
1879–80	7,869,742	10,256,968
1880–1	3,892,574	4,249,675
1881–2	5,379,050	2,186,274
1882–3	7,480,227	6,508,457
1883–4	6,405,151	3,663,400
1884–5	7,245,631	5,794,232
1885–6	11,606,629	10,285,566
1886–7	7,155,738	4,616,537
1887–8	9,228,750	10,788,425
1888–9	9,246,679	7,312,255
1889–90	10,937,876	8,551,158
1890–1	14,175,136	13,163,474
1891–2	9,022,184	5,553,970
1892–3	12,863,569	12,705,210
Total	165,225,602	152,504,446

Source: As in Table 5.2.

During the period from 1872 to 1892, the exchange rate for the rupee as measured by the rate on Council Bills slid down from 22.754*d.* to 14.985*d.* The reasons for such a decline lie in: (a) the fall in the price of silver, (b) the free coinage of silver in British Indian mints when more and more countries were either adopting gold coinage for both external and internal purposes or were using gold for external payments and token money (including silver money) for internal payments, and (c) the necessity of transferring larger and larger surpluses from India in the teeth of a falling exchange rate. However, there is more than mere suspicion that the Secretary of State's Council Bills were issued at an exchange rate which was too low, and which acted as a depressive factor on the effective exchange rate (Sen, 1976).

The continued fall in the exchange rate threatened to cause a fiscal crisis in the colonial state apparatus, and this is what ultimately induced the British Indian government to close Indian mints to the free coinage of silver, and gradually move on to the gold exchange or rather, the sterling exchange standard (for an analysis of the process of evolution of the sterling exchange standard, see de Cecco, 1974, chapter 4, reprinted as Chapter 7 in this volume). The balances kept by the Indian government in London then came to play a critical role both in stabilizing London's operations as an international financial centre and in providing a strategic reserve of liquidity for the monetary authorities to work on. However, such stabilization was again achieved by exposing India to the vicissitudes of her own degraded ecology and to the buffeting of international cyclical movements.[4]

In a situation in which the export and import trade and all other operations connected with them were controlled by foreigners, the usual terms of trade calculations on the basis of border prices reveal little about the condition of the ultimate producers. This is why any calculations showing that terms of trade for a particular colonial country were declining, stagnating, or improving will not acquire any meaning until we know how the respective shares of the producers, the consumers, and the traders were changing over time.[5] Such information is difficult to come by, and little work has been done in this direction. What our rather preliminary analysis has indicated is that there is a good ground for believing that many countries of the third world acted as an absorber of shocks that were generated by the consolidation of industrial capitalism in the centre countries, and that the third world transferred a large surplus to the centre countries—a surplus that was used for accumulation in Europe, USA, and other overseas colonies of European settlement. Apart from India, Indonesia also generated large export surpluses (for a computation, see Bagchi, 1977). Even a country such as Argentina, which apparently received a large amount of foreign investment in the 1880s, began to generate large export surpluses (often amounting to more than a quarter of total exports) from 1894 onwards (Martinez and Lewandowski, 1911, pp. 213–15). Brazil, which already had a large population in 1870, generated an export surplus from 1861 to 1888, with the exception of three years only (see the evidence of J. Beadon to the Herschell Committee, 1893, p. 105). Argentina's monetary policy during the period 1880–1914 has been subjected to detailed analysis, and we know that her ruling oligarchy, consisting primarily of landed magnates, pursued a policy which tended to aggravate the effects of international cycles on the economy (Ford, 1962).

Famines as Costs of Adjustment in the Third World

Despite some investment in the creation of infrastructure catering to international trade in some regions during the period of the Great Depression, the major movements of capital were from the third world countries to the metropolitan centre rather than the other way round During the same period, a very large migration from the European countries to the colonies of settlement was under way and third world surpluses helped finance this movement. Little migration took place from the third world; where there was some migration, as in the case of indentured labourers from India and China to Malaya, Indonesia, Ceylon, Natal, Mauritius, etc., the migrants tended to become the most exploited, and often a partly enslaved stratum of the population in contrast with the European migrants who became at worst free wage-earners in high-wage economies. Contrasts between the development of the first and third worlds extended also to the adjustment mechanism. Whether because of imposition of a silver standard when most advanced capitalist countries moved towards a gold standard together with some attempt at insulation of the economy against international fluctuations, or because of the pursuit of a monetary policy which aggravated the effects of international shocks in the interest of landowners and export-based merchants, or because of the continuing demands of a colonial fiscal system geared towards the steady transfer of a large fraction of the surplus of the country even in the face of a falling exchange, the colonial economies were continually subjected to severe shocks. In the case of densely populated countries such as India and China whose ecologies had adjusted to a different system of exploitation, these shocks took the form of severe famines.

Indian nationalists such as R. C. Dutt (Dutt, 1963) and British liberals such as William Digby attributed the frequency of famines in the last forty years of the nineteenth century directly to the effects of British rule. Dutt regarded British land revenue policy as particularly culpable in this regard. Dutt considered that a Permanent Settlement of the land revenue on the pattern of the Bengal legislation of 1793 would go a long way towards eliminating the danger of famines by improving the staying power of the cultivators. This view was one-sided in that it failed to take account of the whole mechanism of commercial exploitation of India or of the oppression of the cultivators by superior right-holders everywhere in India. But Dutt puts his finger on one of the major reasons for the inflexibility that led to frequent famines, namely the removal of a large part of the produce of India through a tributary fiscal system.

The question may be raised why this period in particular should be so punctuated with famines in India and whether this perspective fits the Chinese situation as well. It is remarkable that the latter half of the nineteenth century opened equally in China and India with the two great revolts of the peasantry and associated superior strata against foreigners and their collaborators. The Taiping and Nien revolts were not simply revolts against the Ch'ing: they were also revolts against the increasing domination of the country by foreigners. The crushing of these two revolts with foreign help involved such an amount of blood-letting that many counties of central China were able to recover to pre-1850 population levels only as late as 1950 (Ho, 1959, pp. 236–47). Through the second Opium War and the crushing of the peasant revolts, China was already 'softened up' for deeper penetration by the colonial powers, while dismemberment of the country which could have led to an exacerbation of inter-imperialist rivalries was avoided. Still, the disorganization of the Ch'ing political order and the impact of foreign economic and political penetration were together responsible for some terrible famines in the last quarter of the nineteenth century. The famine of 1877–8 which struck four provinces of northern China, namely, Shensi, Shansi, Honan, Hopei, and parts of the province of Shantung, was estimated by the Foreign Relief Committee of Tientsin to have cost between nine and thirteen million lives (Ho, 1959, pp. 231–3). The effects of drought were compounded by the breakdown of traditional systems of protection against scarcity and the efforts of a tottering empire to maintain itself through oppressive taxes, and a continually debased monetary system.

In India's case, its government quite deliberately calculated the costs of famine relief adequate for preventing the loss of lives and decided that it would run the risk of losing millions of lives rather than spend the required sum out of the government's Treasury. There was a famine in Bengal in 1873–4, when an unorthodox civil servant, Sir George Campbell, was Lieutenant-Governor of the province. The relief undertaken under his direction was apparently sufficient to prevent the loss of all but a few lives. The Famine Commission of 1880 estimated that if relief had been given during the earlier famines from 1803 to 1873 on the scale of the Bengal famine relief of 1873–4, the total cost would have come to £34 million as against the £4.5 million actually spent. 'The addition of £30 million to the debt of India would have increased the annual expenditure by a million and a half and though it is too much to say that the finances could not have borne the strain, still undoubtedly it would have been very severely felt' (*Report of the Famine Commission* [1880], vol. III, *Famine Histories*, p. 147 quoted in Bhatia, 1967, pp. 86–7). It cannot be claimed that the attitude of the Government of India was inspired by a mistaken dogmatism about balancing the budget, for as we have seen, it was prepared to add fully £50 million to the debt of India as the ransom for the Indian 'mutiny' of 1857. While the Government of India was, under the guidance of such eminent Finance members and governors as Sir Richard Temple or Sir John Strachey, deciding not to spend money on famine relief with the full knowledge that several millions would die as a consequence, it was adding to the public debt of India by constructing financially unprofitable railway lines in North-western India because the latter were supposed to be strategically important in the endemic Russo-British rivalry in Central Asia.

While, on the one hand, the Government of India refused to provide adequate famine relief on the plea of fiscal stringency, it greatly helped to convert scarcities into famines by refusing to interfere in the course of private trade. A test case occurred when Sir George Campbell wanted to have the export of grains prohibited but the Government of India did not sanction his move (for Campbell's views, see Buckland, 1901, chapter 5). The result was that there was often a brisk export trade in food grains while famine was raging in India, and grain moved out of surplus and deficit regions to ports rather than to the areas where it was needed most. The niggardly policy of the Government of India regarding famine relief and the rigid policy about land revenue collection accentuated this problem by depriving the people of purchasing power in years of scarcity. Thus the policy of the Government of India in fiscal and commercial matters must have contributed greatly to the aggravation of the effects of famine, if not to causing them in the first place.

It is interesting to note that while the peasantry and traditional craftsmen were decimated and kept in abject subjection after their mid-century revolts, in India and to a lesser extent in China, a protest movement against colonialism grew up, which had its base mainly among the professional classes. It is probably not too far-fetched to aver that by coercing and killing off the rebellious peasantry through famines and wars, the imperial powers made it possible for the collaborating gentry to turn increasingly against their imperial masters. So even while the metropolitan centre seemed to finally reduce the third world colonies to abject thraldom, the inevitable contradictions of the system were producing the base for the national liberation movements which would sound the death-knell of the old imperial system.

Notes

1. Interestingly enough, the period under discussion also witnessed the growth of Japan into an imperialist and capitalist power. Japan's first colony was not acquired until 1894–5, but her subsequent growth was accompanied by the same exploitation of colonies as had characterized the growth of industrial capitalism in Europe and its overseas offshoots.

2. There were British officials and commentators who perceived that the opening of the whole country to the pull of the external market meant that people in the villages could no longer keep back stocks of food grains for use in the case of scarcity as had been their practice in earlier times. British officials enquiring into the causes of the Deccan riots of 1875 also stressed the harmful effect the increase in the power of moneylenders had on the condition of peasants and their ability to survive an occasional drought. See in this connection, *Report of the Deccan Riots Commission* (1878), *Report of the Famine Commission* (1880), Vol. III, 'Notes by Various Provincial Officers on the Extent of Indebtedness', and Connel, 1885, quoted in Bhatia, 1967, p. 31. But these observations had little effect in altering the general contours of British economic policy in India; the only tangible effect was the passing of some ineffective legislation, imposing curbs on the transfer of land from 'agricultural' to the 'non-agricultural' classes, first in Bombay and then in the Punjab.

3. One of the more curious symptoms of instability is to be found in the freight rates charged on the shipment of rice and wheat from Calcutta to London via the Suez Canal between 1870 and 1885 (O'Conor, 1886, p. 86). Such rates would decline by 58.73 per cent between two years (1876 and 1877) and increase by 222.22 per cent between another two adjacent years (1878 and 1879). Hence although these freight rates fell by 52 per cent between 1870 and 1885, this should not be read as a continuous factor tending to improve terms of trade either way.

4. Throughout the period of the Great Depression and after, India's financial system was subjected to the depredations of foreign

exchange banks which would borrow money within India at times of scarcity, thus aggravating any stringency and withdraw credit from traders when the market for exportables threatened to be slack. While the Indian government had some control over the operations of the Presidency Banks, they had little power over exchange banks, which in fact used all the facilities afforded by the financial operations of the Secretary of State for India without being subject to any of the discipline that central banks in advanced capitalist countries were beginning to exercise on their commercial banks. In this respect, foreign exchange banks operating in colonial countries are true precursors of today's transnational banks.

5. Similarly, figures of 'foreign investment' in the colonies have to be scrutinized to check how much of it represented a real transfer of capital and how much of it was simply a balance sheet of claims, inflated by the monopolistic and political power exercised by foreign investors.

References

Agra Bank, 1975, 'The Agra Bank Limited', *Bankers' Magazine*, January–December.

Atkinson, F. J., 1897, 'Silver Prices in India', *Journal of Royal Statistical Society* (March).

Bagchi, A. K., 1972, 'Some International Foundations of Capitalist Growth and Underdevelopment', *Economic and Political Weekly*, August, Special number.

_____ , 1976, 'De-industrialization in India in the Nineteenth Century: Some Theoretical Implications', *Journal of Development Studies*, January.

_____ , 1977, 'Cost of Economic Growth as viewed from Less Developed Countries'. Discussant's comment presented at the plenary session of the Fifth World Congress of the International Economic Association, Tokyo, August–September (mimeo.).

Bhatia, B. M., 1967, *Famines in India* (Bombay).

Buckland, C. E., 1901, *Bengal under the Lieutenant-Governors*, Vol. I (Delhi).

Connel, A. K., 1885, 'Indian Wheat and Indian Railways', *Journal of the Statistical Society*.

De Cecco, M., 1974, *Money and Empire: The International Gold Standard, 1890–1914* (Oxford).

Desai, A. V., 1968, *Real Wages in Germany, 1871–1913* (Oxford).

Dutt, R. C., 1963, *Economic History of India in the Victorian Age 1837–1900* (Delhi).

Flux, A. W., 1899, 'The Flag and trade: A Summary Review of the Trade of the Chief Colonial Empires', *Journal of the Royal Statistical Society*, September.

Ford, A. G., 1962, *The Gold Standard 1880–1914: Britain and Argentina* (Oxford).

Ghosh, A. K. 1949, *An Analysis of the Indian Price Structure from 1861*, Ph.D. thesis, University of London.

Gold and Silver Commission, 1888, Final Report of the Royal Commission Appointed to inquire into the Recent Changes in the Relative Values of the Precious Metals; with Minutes of Evidence and Appendices (London).

Herschell Committee, 1893, Minutes of Evidence taken before the Committee Appointed to Inquire into the Indian Currency together with an Analysis of the Evidence and Appendices (London).

Ho, Ping-ti, 1959, *Studies on the Population of China, 1368–1953* (Cambridge, Mass.).

An Indian Official, 1878, *A Handbook of Gold and Silver* (London).

Kuznets, S., 1971, *Economic Growth of Nations: Total Output and Production Structure* (Cambridge, Mass.).

Martinez, A. B. and M. Lewandowski, 1911, *The Argentina in the Twentieth Century* (London).

Mitchell, B. R. and P. Deane, 1976, *Abstract of British Historical Statistics* (London).

Morris, M. D., 1974, 'Private Industrial Investment on the Indian Subcontinent 1900–1939: Some Methodological Considerations', *Modern Asian Studies*, October.

Nevill, H. R. (ed.), 1921, *Bara Banki: A Gazetteer*. Vol. 48 of *District Gazetteers of the United Provinces of Agra and Oudh* (Allahabad).

_____, 1923, *Sultanpur: A Gazetteer*. Vol. 46 of: *District Gazetteers of the United Provinces of Agra and Oudh* (Allahabad).

O'Conor, J. E., 1886, *Review of the Trade in India in 1885–86* (Simla).

Reserve Bank of India (RBI), 1954, *Banking and Monetary Statistics of India* (Bombay).

Robertson, J. A., 1908, 'Wages and Prices', in: *Economic,* Vol. 3 of *Imperial Gazetteer of India* (Oxford).

Samuelson, P. A., 1952, 'The Transfer Problem and Transport Costs: The Terms of Trade when Impediments are Absent', *Economic Journal,* June.

_____ , 1954, 'The Transfer Problem and Transport Costs: Analysis of Effects of Trade Impediments', *Economic Journal,* June.

Saul, S. B., 1960, *Studies in British Overseas Trade 1870–1913* (Liverpool).

_____ , 1969, *The Myth of the Great Depression 1873–1896* (London).

Sen, N., 1976, 'Indian's Terms of Trade: 1871–72 to 1892–93', *Economic and Political Weekly,* November.

_____ , 1978, *Fluctuating Exchange Rates and Government Finance in India 1871–72 to 1892–93* (mimeo., unpublished).

Triffin, R., 1969, 'The Myth and Realities of the so-called Gold Standard', in R. Cooper (ed.), *International Finance* (Harmondsworth).

6

Agriculture in Slump: The Peasant Economy of East and North Bengal in the 1930s[*]

Omkar Goswami

This chapter attempts to examine the impact of the Great Depression on the jute growing regions of Bengal.[1] There are three reasons why I have focussed on East and North Bengal rather than on the province as a whole. First, I am more familiar with the eastern and northern region than the western tracts; in any case, the West Bengal districts accounted for less than a third of the total area under cultivation in the province. Second, the eastern and northern tracts specialized in the cultivation of jute, and one would like to examine how the Depression affected a crop which was almost wholly consigned overseas—either directly or as gunny. Finally, it is well known that the western region, with the exception of Midnapur and probably Burdwan, had been going downhill since the end of the nineteenth century; in contrast, the eastern tracts were much more fertile and had witnessed a fair amount of prosperity right up to World War I and even in the 1920s. Hence there was a sharper contrast between

[*] Previously published in the *Indian Economic and Social History Review*, 21, 3 (1984), pp. 335–64.

the pre- and the post-1930 period in the east and in the north than in the west; and, sharp contrasts make good reading.

Prologue: An Overview of the Economy, 1900–1929

There is a great deal of literature on the mushrooming of a bewildering number of intermediate land rights in East Bengal during the nineteenth century, enmeshed in what Tapan Raychaudhuri called 'an incredible maze of criss-cross relationships'.[2] However, one has to check oneself from being carried away by the complexities of intermediate land rights, for, in general, the structure of land rights and that of land use need not belong to the same domain. In East Bengal, the actual land use structure which predated the Raj remained more or less unaffected by the proliferation of intermediate land rights in the nineteenth century. East Bengal villages had, broadly speaking, a three-tier system of land use: a large mass of permanently occupying settled, cash-rent paying *raiyat*s, followed by a lesser number of under-*raiyat*s and, finally sharecroppers or *bargadar*s, who were tenants-at-will. Among the permanently occupying *raiyat*s were some large farmers, or *jotedar*s, who played a major role in village polity. The East Bengal *jotedar*s, however, were neither as ubiquitous nor as powerful as most of their North Bengal counterparts, especially those of Jalpaiguri. This is not to say that there were no inequalities in landholding in East Bengal. Nor does it imply that the categories mentioned were watertight ones: a fully settled, cash-paying occupancy *raiyat* could also double up as a part-time sharecropper, and *bargadar*s frequently had marginal plots of land which they cultivated as settled *raiyat*s. Nevertheless, it would be true to say that the fertility of the eastern districts coupled with the relatively high price of jute during the first fourteen years of the twentieth century, especially after 1904–05, helped to maintain a fairly large body of middle-*raiyat*s free from the bondage of large-scale sharecropping and *jotedari* or other forms of debt peonage.

The North Bengal districts, too, had a similar three-tier system, though here the *jotedar*s were generally quite powerful.

In the districts of Jalpaiguri and Dinajpur, the *jotedars* frequently dispossessed poorer peasants and resettled the land so obtained with sharecroppers who paid half the gross produce as rent. J. A. Milligan, the Settlement Officer of Jalpaiguri, talked of an enormous growth in sharecropping or *barga* tenures between 1905 and 1910 which had resulted in the 'almost entire disappearance of the lower grades of cash paying tenants' and more than 30 per cent of the total settled area in the district was cultivated by sharecroppers under either big *jotedars* or *chukanidars* (smaller *jotedars*).[3] This phenomenon was also prevalent in the Srinagar, Munshiganj, and Raipura *thanas* of the district of Dacca. F. D. Ascoli, while writing his Settlement Report for the period 1910–17, estimated that some 10 per cent of the net area under cultivation was cropped by either ordinary sharecroppers (paying half to a third of the crop as rent) or *dhaki/ thika bargadars* (those who paid a fixed amount in crop, but the amount being greater than the quit rent paid by settled *raiyats*).[4]

In spite of the experiences of two districts in North Bengal and certain areas of Dacca, it can be argued that a growth in sharecropping, either through population pressure or through debt repayment, was more of an exception than a rule in East and North Bengal before World War I. Widespread sharecropping and polarization of holdings through credit mechanisms were unheard of in Tippera (Comilla), Faridpur, Mymensingh, Pabna, Bogra, and most parts of Rangpur. Despite inequalities, the dominant picture was one of relative 'flatness'. This shows up in Table 6.1, which underlines the predominance of permanently settled *raiyats* and the relative unimportance of under-*raiyats* and sharecroppers in the seven major jute growing districts of the province.

Table 6.1, however, also shows that while permanently occupying settled *raiyats* (POSR) formed the backbone of peasant society in East and North Bengal before the 1930s, they had very little land to till. The average area per *raiyati* interest varied between 3.08 acres in Mymensingh and 1.39 in Faridpur and, while a peasant family could have more than one interest, it is unlikely that the total land held by a modal *raiyat* before World

War I was more than 4 acres. In fact, in 1900–1901, the net cultivable area per rural family was a little over 3.25 acres.[5]

Table 6.1 *Proportion of* raiyats, *under-*raiyats, *and proprietors in the major jute districts of Bengal*

District	% of total interests			% of total land			Average area/ Raiyati interest (acres)
	POSR	UR	P	POSR	UR	P	
Dacca	71.7	6.5	14.5	77.7	1.1	8.9	1.59
Mymensingh	74.8	7.5	13.2	71.3	3.3	8.0	3.08
Faridpur	63.0	13.8	7.1	64.6	9.1	2.9	1.39
Tippera	73.7	6.7	2.7	80.8	2.8	3.8	2.03
Rangpur	71.2	12.8	1.2	77.2	6.9	6.8	2.35
Bogra	64.6	17.5	1.6	78.2	6.9	4.6	2.52
Pabna	74.8	10.5	1.5	73.2	4.0	7.4	1.91

Source: Government of Bengal (GOB), *Survey and Settlement Reports,* Dacca, Mymensingh, Faridpur, Tippera, Rangpur, Bogra, and Pabna.

Nevertheless, it can be argued that before World War I, the typical peasant family was not very badly off and experienced a certain amount of prosperity—if this term can at all be used for people cultivating less than 4 acres of land. There are several pointers to this 'prosperity'. Even in districts as highly commercialized as Faridpur, 55 per cent of the peasantry were free from debt;[6] and, while peasants generally took loans to tide over the production cycle, jute and rice prices were high enough for most of them to repay their debts after harvest and still earn a surplus. This element of 'freedom' can be seen from the relative absence of *dadan*—loans taken against standing crop hypothecated at half the market price of the previous season. Ascoli, describing the structures of rural credit in Dacca—another very commercialized district—wrote: 'I doubt if one cultivator in 1,000 is dependent in any way on the *aratdar, bepari* or jute merchant for loans and advances. The experiment has been tried in the district but has been definitely abandoned'.[7] Besides, spurred on by the growing world demand for jute goods, there was a steady increase in the area and output of raw jute; coupled with rising jute and rice prices, this resulted in a growing surplus for the modal peasant family. This was especially true after 1904–05, as can be seen from Table 6.2.

Table 6.2 *Prices and output of raw jute and winter rice and surplus of a 4-acre raiyati family*

Years	P_j	P_{wr}	RO_j	$O_{wr}{}^*$	$RO_j{}^*$	RYJD	Surplus
1900–1901	4.82	3.56	32.47	82.57	28.00	499.13	66 (88)
1901–02	4.40	4.12	36.83	82.66	31.40	523.78	53 (68)
1902–03	4.29	3.83	32.49	84.30	27.54	512.29	52 (69)
1903–04	4.83	3.47	35.79	83.34	27.69	531.56	76 (108)
1904–05	4.95	3.31	35.52	85.07	28.60	495.00	48 (67)
1905–06	5.60	3.79	37.97	84.27	29.95	583.63	107 (137)
1906–07	7.42	5.16	42.19	84.80	32.43	705.49	192 (209)
1907–08	6.88	5.75	42.17	79.24	37.95	774.43	173 (178)
1908–09	5.78	6.00	42.81	74.64	33.01	640.01	118 (120)
1909–10	5.76	5.33	42.45	82.20	32.46	681.70	120 (136)
1910–11	6.10	4.42	33.62	83.30	25.60	592.24	114 (131)
1911–12	7.10	4.83	45.04	84.92	34.29	638.85	150 (163)
1912–13	7.95	5.27	52.14	84.84	34.09	688.74	174 (179)
1913–14	10.38	5.31	47.46	78.90	33.24	812.16	312 (306)

Note: P_j and P_{wr} are prices of jute and winter rice respectively, Rs/maund.

* RO_j is revised output of jute, all India (see Appendix 6.1), million maunds.

* $O_{wr}{}^*$ and $RO_j{}^*$ are output of winter rice and revised output of jute in the major jute growing districts, million maunds.

RYJD is the real gross income in the major jute growing districts, obtained by deflating money income by the wholesale price index computed from Government of India (GOI), *Statistical Abstract of British India*, first issue (Calcutta, 1923) and seventeenth issue (Calcutta, 1942). Measured in Rs million.

Surplus is arrived at by the method outlined in Appendix 6.2. Brackets indicate the magnitude of real surplus. Measured in Rs.

Contd.

Table 6.2 contd.

Sources: For 1900–1912, prices of jute and winter rice (harvest prices) from GOI, K. L. Dutta, 1914, *Report on the Enquiry into the Rise in Prices in India,* Vol. 2 (Calcutta), pp. 136–9. Thereafter from Indian Jute Mills Association (IJMA), 1950, *Report of the Committee 1949*(Calcutta), pp. 116–7 and GOB, 1939, *Report of the Bengal Paddy and Rice Enquiry Committee,* Vol. 1 (Alipore), p. 24.

The data sources of the other columns are given in Appendices 6.1 and 6.2. Wholesale price index is certainly not an ideal deflator, but for this period constructing an appropriate alternative is almost impossible.

Appendices 6.1 and 6.2 outline the methods by which one can arrive at reasonably correct estimates of the area and output of jute as well as the surplus available to a modal raiyati family. Table 6.2 gives the results and underlines the fact that, in spite of inequalities, the 'typical' peasant household enjoyed a reasonable degree of prosperity and a certain kind of economic freedom.

World War I created some disjunctions in the peasant economy of East and North Bengal. The sudden loss of the German and Austro-Hungarian markets as well as severe shortages in shipping led to a slump in raw jute exports and a fall in prices.[8] By September 1914, harvest prices of raw jute had crashed by as much as 33 per cent—and this happened at a time when the cultivators' cash needs were greatest.[9] In response to the high prices of 1911–13, the peasantry had increased the area under jute by almost 13 per cent in the 1914–15 season, and, with a fall in demand, the situation was ideal for a squeeze. Jute traders made no secret of this. The Narainganj Chamber of Commerce, largely a body of jute dealers 'decided to make the best use that it could of this opportunity . . . to permanently reduce the price of jute'.[10] In Rangpur, Marwari merchants refused to buy under instructions from Calcutta;[11] very little trade was being carried out at the Dacca marts, and prices were less than Rs 3 per maund;[12] in Madaripur, an important jute growing area in Faridpur, farm gate prices crashed to Rs 4 per maund—an amount hardly sufficient to recoup cultivating expenses;[13] and, even in the traditionally prosperous district of Mymensingh, 'the condition of the jute market was one of complete stagnation'.[14]

Although raw jute prices picked up during the next two years—thanks to the demand for sandbags in the trenches of the western front—real prices were lower than before. In any case, prices again crashed in 1917–18 and, in general, the real price of raw jute in 1914–18 was 32.4 per cent lower than the 1909–13 average.[15] There was a notable decline in the surplus available to the 'modal' peasant family over this period. While the average surplus between 1909–10 and 1913–14 was Rs 174 and Rs 183 respectively in current and real terms, it was Rs 12 and Rs 9 during the war years.[16] *Dadani* forms of credit started cropping up in areas where they were wholly unknown or extremely rare in the ante-bellum period. By the end of 1916, *dadan* had become an important form of credit in the Narainganj subdivision of Dacca;[17] it was gaining a foothold in Pabna and Rangpur, where the creditors were petty Marwari traders;[18] and, in Mymensingh, too, loans were now being contracted to be repaid in jute at prices less than market rates.[19]

Thankfully, the war years did not permanently scar the peasant economy of East and North Bengal. The great trading boom of the 1920s spilled over to the agrarian sector. With the exception of a short recession in 1921–2 and 1922–3—which reflected a return to peacetime conditions—there was a steady growth in world gunny demand. Gunny exports, at constant prices (1914 = 100), rose from an average of Rs 222.5 million in 1909–13 to Rs 374.4 million in 1927–9.[20] This led to an increase in the acreage under raw jute—at the expense of autumn or *aus* rice—from an average of 2.17 million acres in the major jute districts in 1909–13 to 2.79 million acres in 1927–9; since there was no perceptible growth in productivity, output of raw jute correspondingly increased from 32.55 to 41.88 million maunds.[21] Also, the real income from jute and winter (*aman*) rice cultivation in the major jute growing districts increased from an average of Rs 683 million in 1909–13 to Rs 696 million in the second half of the 1920s.[22]

While the 1920s had the appearance of a boom decade, the picture was not as rosy as in the pre-World War I years. For one, the rate of growth of real gross income from jute and winter rice was less than 2 per cent per annum between 1919–20 and 1929–30, while the ante-bellum rate (that is, for the period 1900–1901 and 1913–14) was 3.9 per cent. Second, the 1920s witnessed growing population pressure on land: between 1921 and 1931 rural population grew by 0.63 per cent per annum, and the growth was greater in the Dacca, Chittagong, and Rajshahi divisions.[23] By 1931, it stood at 46.43 million and, without either an increase in the net area under cultivation or a perceptible growth in cropping intensity, the decline in cultivable area per family (Table 6.3) reflected a fall in agricultural output per rural household.

Table 6.3   *Net cultivable area per rural family, 1911, 1921, 1931 (Acres)*

Districts	1911	1921	1931
All Bengal	3.08	2.80	2.63
Dacca	2.43	2.21	2.15
Mymensingh	3.21	3.02	3.70
Faridpur	2.25	2.73	2.67
Tippera	2.94	2.10	2.08
Rangpur	3.68	3.43	3.39
Bogra	2.77	2.73	2.62
Pabna	2.81	3.32	2.60
Jalpaiguri	5.28	4.05	3.72
Dinajpur	4.78	4.14	3.41
Rajshahi	3.01	3.36	3.30

Sources: GOI, *Census of India 1911*, Vol. 5 (1 and 2); *1921*, Vol. 5 (1 and 2); *1931*, Vol. 5 (1 and 2); and GOB, *Season and Crop Report of Bengal 1909–10 to 1911–12, 1919–20, 1921–2. 1929–30 to 1931–2* (Calcutta, annual).

It would seem, therefore, that because of population pressure, the net cultivable area available to permanently occupying settled *raiyat*s was around 3 acres per family.[24] The other phenomenon that was occurring during the 1920s was the slow growth of sharecropping tenures. As I have mentioned earlier, sharecropping predated the twentieth century. But one ought to make a distinction between the older and newer types of sharecropping—not in terms of its explicit form but of its logic. A classic example of the old barga system is that of Bikrampur thana in the district of Dacca. Here, the majority of tenure holders were Hindu *bhadralok*s, engaged in urban professions and interested not in cultivation but in rental income. They and their widows frequently let out land to sharecroppers and, because of their absenteeism, the *de facto* rents were often lower than what were demanded *de jure*. Such slackness did not exist under the newer *barga* system. The person who now leased out the land was the village *jotedar*, who was not only interested in demanding the full rent, but also had the political and social power within the village to actually collect it. In the new *barga* system, sharecropping was not viewed as the only way in which one could get rental income from land, but as a profitable device for squeezing land-hungry peasants into paying full rent. And, it was the new *barga* system that was coming into the picture in the 1920s. In the eastern subdivisions of Mymensingh—where sharecropping was non-existent in the pre-war years—*bargadari* was on the increase and 'a very large proportion of the *raiyats*. . . now work as *bargadar*s'.[25] In Brahmanbaria, the jute heartland of Comilla 'good farmers (were) being turned into *bargadar*s'.[26]

The growth in sharecropping tenures cannot be quantified for the 1920s, but there are good reasons for believing that this indeed took place. Even before the war, there were many poor cultivating families that had less than 4 acres of land; and the sharp fluctuation in jute prices during World War I and 1921–3 must have led to an increase in their debt burdens. Almost all witnesses appearing before the Bengal Provincial Banking Enquiry Commission spoke of this. In Dinajpur, *jotedar*s and *dadandar*s had become important sources of funds, and their interest rates varied from 40 to 75 per cent.[27] So, too, was the case in Rangpur, where trade and credit were being increasingly taken over by Marwaris[28]—which prompted a local poet to write:

When jute came to this country,
The *paschima* (Marwari) conquered us . . . .
Now, see, they have all the money.

They do not look after the interest of Bengalis.
Those who could not get to eat even chhatu
Now eat *ballam* rice: just think of it!
And the Bengalis do not get Rangoon rice![29]

In Dacca, interest rates on unsecured loans were sometimes
as high as 10 per cent per month, and the district witnessed a
rapid rise in the burden of indebtedness.[30] In Faridpur, the
number of cultivators in debt had increased from 45 per cent of
the rural population in the pre-war years to apparently 80 per
cent in 1929.[31] And, in Mymensingh, the most prosperous of the
jute districts, 'agricultural indebtedness was fast increasing' and
average indebtedness per family was around Rs 100.[32]
Mahalanobis estimated that the average debt burden in eight
jute growing districts in 1928, *exclusive of interest*, was Rs 128 per
cultivating family.[33] If this is corrected for the modal interest
rate—37.5 per cent per annum—then the average debt per rural
family in 1929 was Rs 176, which was considerably greater than
what it was in the pre-war years.

With the exception of two excellent seasons—1924–5 and
1925–6 when jute prices rose to dizzying heights—the average
value of real surplus available to a 4-acre holding permanently
occupying *raiyat* in 1919–29 was around Rs 110 per family, which
was substantially lower than what it was in 1909–13.[34] This and
growing indebtedness went hand-in-glove, and when, for the
poorer peasants, debt reached a point where it could choke off
further advances necessary for the coming production season,
there was little else to do other than transfer a part of the holding
in lieu of debts. Given the general scarcity of, and a growing
demand for land, it is reasonable to expect the *jotedars* to either
directly or indirectly acquire the transferred property and make
the debtor till the same land as a sharecropper at rent assessed
at half the gross produce.

Some contemporaries referred to jute as the root cause of
indebtedness. Abed Ali Mian, a rural poet of Rangpur lamented:

Eto pat dili keno tui chasha?
Ebar pater chashey desh dubali, orey buddhinasha.
Bujhli na tui burar beta,

Abeder katha noiko jhuta,
Khetey hobey pater gora, thik janish mor bhasha.
Monay korechho nibo taka,
Shay asha tor jabey phanka,
Panchiser poya hobey tor, riney porbi thasha.[35]

(Why did you grow so much jute, you peasant?
Now the country is ruined with jute cultivation.
You should have known
That Abed never lies.
Mark my words! You will have to finally eat your jute.
You hoped to make money,
Those hopes will soon be dashed
And you will be neck-deep in debt.)

While Abed's warning had a ring of prophesy, he was being unfair to the cultivators. All said and done, jute was still a profitable cash crop in the 1920s. The profits were not as high as in the pre-war years; population pressure, growing indebtedness, and sharecropping were cutting into the surplus. But, in comparison with the 1930s, the 1920s still allowed some freedom, in spite of other imperatives having entered the system.

The Depression, 1930–1 to 1938–9

The Depression hit the jute industry harder than any other industry in colonial India. Between 1925–9 (average) and 1930–4, export of gunny bag and cloth fell by 13 and 30 per cent respectively in terms of volume; prices of bag and cloth fell by 46 and 45 per cent respectively; and the export of raw jute by volume fell by 20 per cent. Although, in volume terms, gunny output picked up in the period 1935–8—it was, in fact, 15 per cent *more* than the 1925–9 average—prices continued to fall and the 1935–8 prices of gunny bag and cloth were 54 and 51 per cent less than the 1925–9 average (see Table 6.4).

Two features stand out. First, that unlike other Western and most Latin American countries, the Depression did not peter out in the case of jute by 1934–5. While the volume of gunny output and exports in 1935–9 was greater than in 1930–4, prices remained very sluggish—in fact, continued moving downwards. As a result, the value of gunny export was not much greater than in 1930–4 and remained 53 per cent and 24 per cent lower in 1935–9 respectively in current and real terms than what they were in 1925–9. Moreover, world primary product output did not show the kind of sharp fall in volume that plagued the jute industry even in the worst years of the Depression. It is not within the purview of this chapter to explain why this was so. What needs to be pointed out is that jute experienced a volume as well as price fall in 1930–4, while it was largely the latter in the case of other primary products. This shows up in Figure 6.1.[36]

In the very first year of the Depression, raw jute prices crashed from almost Rs 9 to Rs 3–12 per maund—a fall of nearly 60 per cent.[37] Between 1930 and 1934, up-country raw jute prices were, on an average, 57 per cent lower than the 1926–9 levels.[38] The peasants, of course, got less. Firstly, the prices were unweighted twelve-month averages, and these would have been more than the prices that prevailed in the harvest months of August–October. Secondly, as we shall see, the peasants had to bear the brunt of several deductions and allowances, which did not figure in the published prices. Even without such adjustments, the situation was grim enough.

The peasantry suffered not only from a fall in jute prices; winter and autumn rice prices crashed as well, thus knocking the bottom out of other sources of cash income. Table 6.5 tells its own story.

The fall in prices immediately led to a sharp reduction in gross money as well as real income through jute and winter rice cultivation in the districts of East and North Bengal. Money income fell by more than 50 per cent from an average of Rs 978 million in 1926–9 to Rs 486 million in 1930–4; real income fell by 25 per cent over the same period.

Table 6.4   *The jute industry during the 1930s*

Year	Output			Export of				Raw Jute	Prices of	
	000 tons	Rs mill.	Real value (Rs mill.)	Gunny bags (mill.)	Gunny cloth (mill. yds.)	Total gunny	Real value (Rs mill.)	Exports (mill. maunds)	Gunny bags (Rs/100)	Gunny cloth (Rs/100 yds.)
1	2	3	4	5	6	7	8	9	10	11
1925–9 Average	1045	716	483	471.5	1542.2	548.8	371	22.1	47.13	16.13
1930–1	815	334	288	434.1	1272.0	318.9	275	16.9	27.88	8.56
1931–2	795	270	280	388.5	1021.1	219.2	228	15.9	25.94	8.31
1932–3	907	296	318	415.1	1011.7	217.1	238	15.3	24.56	8.75
1933–4	907	304	340	401.6	1052.6	213.8	246	20.4	23.50	9.63
1934–5	968	319	354	423.0	1063.5	214.7	241	20.5	24.88	9.06
% change										
1925–9	(–)	(–)	(–)	(–)	(–)	(–)	(–)	(–)	(–)	(–)
1930–4	16	57	35	13	30	57	34	20	46	45
1935–6	1048	326	358	458.9	1218.3	234.9	258	21.0	21.56	8.38
1936–7	1255	350	385	576.4	1707.9	279.5	307	22.3	20.69	7.88
1937–8	1348	382	375	612.3	1643.1	290.8	285	20.3	20.69	7.13
1938–9	1172	331	348	598.4	1549.7	262.6	276	18.8	24.50	8.25

Contd.

Table 6.4 contd.

Year	Output			Export of				Raw Jute	Prices of	
	000 tons	Rs mill.	Real value (Rs mill.)	Gunny bags (mill.)	Gunny cloth (mill. yds.)	Total gunny	Real value (Rs mill.)	Exports (mill. maunds)	Gunny bags (Rs/100)	Gunny cloth (Rs/100 yds.)
1	2	3	4	5	6	7	8	9	10	11
% change										
1925–9	(+)	(−)	(−)	(+)	(−)	(−)	(−)	(−)	(−)	(−)
1935–8	15	51	24	19	1	53	24	7	54	51

Sources: Columns 2 and 9–11 from IJMA, 1950, *Report of Committee*, pp. 97–101, 114–15 and 116–17. Column 3 from S. Sivasubramonian, 1977, 'Income from the Secondary Sector in India', *IESHR*, Vol. 14, pp. 447–8. Columns 5–7 from GOI, *Annual Statement of Seaborne Trade of British India 1929–30* (Calcutta, 1931) to *1939–40* (Calcutta, 1941). Real prices on the basis of 1914 = 100.

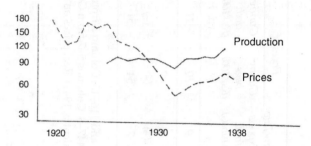

World primary product output, 1929 = 100

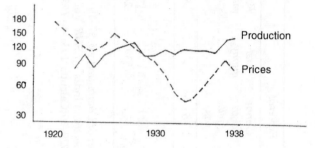

World wheat output, 1929 = 100
Source: League of Nations, 1945, *Economic Instability of the Post-War World* (Geneva), p. 85.

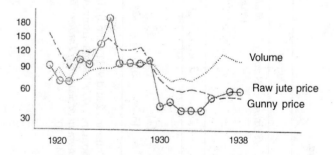

Indian gunny exports, 1929–30 = 100
Source: IJMA, 1950, *Report of Committee*, pp. 114–17.

Fig. 6.1   *Trends in world output and gunny supply, 1920–39*

Table 6.5   *Jute and winter and autumn rice prices, 1926–38 (Rs/maund)*

Years	Jute	Autumn rice	Winter rice
1926–9	8.82 (100)	5.74 (100)	6.83 (100)
1930–1	3.75 (43)	4.11 (72)	6.00 (88)
1931–2	4.25 (48)	2.95 (51)	4.06 (59)
1932–3	3.56 (40)	2.31 (40)	3.31 (48)
1933–4	3.50 (39)	2.04 (36)	2.63 (39)
1934–5	3.56 (40)	2.76 (48)	3.00 (44)
1935–6	4.69 (53)	2.94 (51)	3.25 (48)
1936–7	5.13 (58)	3.06 (53)	3.50 (51)
1937–8	5.19 (59)	3.13 (55)	3.63 (53)

Note: Brackets indicate index numbers.

Jute prices districts	1926 –9	1930 –1	1931 –2	1932 –3	1933 –4	1934 –5	1935 –6	1936 –7	1937 –8
				(Index Numbers)					
Dacca	100	35	40	42	34	37	49	52	52
Mymensingh	100	48	45	42	42	42	67	69	69
Faridpur	100	39	52	47	41	43	66	69	72
Tippera*	100	39	39	39	39	39	59	65	71
Rungpur	100	31	47	31	34	31	31	52	57
Bogra	100	51	51	41	41	41	51	63	63
Pabna	100	36	48	42	42	48	50	64	54
Jalpaiguri	100	35	35	30	28	30	39	47	52

* Tippera figures should be treated sceptically.

Sources: IJMA, 1950, *Report of Committee*, pp. 116–17; *Report of BPREC Committee*, Vol. 1, p. 24 and GOB, *Season and Crop Report of Bengal* (Calcutta, annual) for relevant years.

Table 6.6   *Gross real and money income from jute and winter rice cultivation in the major jute districts, 1926–38 (Rs mill.)*

Years	Money income		Real income	
	Value	Index	Value	Index
1926–9	978	100	672	100
1930–1	668	68	576	86
1931–2	530	54	552	82
1932–3	428	44	470	70
1933–4	380	39	437	65
1934–5	425	43	477	71
1935–6	504	52	553	82
1936–7	496	51	545	81
1937–8	523	53	512	76

Note: Real income is calculated on the basis of wholesale price index, Bengal, 1914 = 100.

Sources: GOB, *Season and Crop Report of Bengal* (Calcutta, annual) for the relevant years. Harvest prices from IJMA, 1950, *Report of Committee*, pp. 116–17; *Report of BPREC*, Vol. 1, p. 24. The method for calculating real income and money income has been given in Appendix 6.1.

These figures, however, hide the number of deductions which were, in the final analysis, passed on to the peasants. At the village level, the first deduction that was charged was *dhalta*—a weight discount to counteract the losses arising out of the allegedly excessive moisture in the jute. Although it was universally recognized that cultivators rarely watered the fibre,[39] *dhalta* was universally applied and was very much a part of the pricing process. It varied according to custom and the relative strength of the peasantry *vis-à-vis* the village level jute pedlar or trader (*faria*): in Mymensingh it was just half a seer per maund (that is, a deduction of only 1.25 per cent), but in Rangpur it was as high as 4 seers per maund (or 10 per cent discount by weight).[40]

A more effective form of shortchanging was carried out through systematic manipulation of weights. The standard maund consisted of 40 seers and each seer was made up of 80 tolas. Yet, in the mid-1930s, there were eleven different jute maunds in East Bengal and nine in North Bengal, varying in weight from 60 to 120 tolas per seer.[41] More often than not, jute bought from the villages—and this accounted for 75 per cent of the crop—was purchased using 84 tolas/seer weight but priced on the basis of the standard maund. This meant that a seller offered 105 true maunds for every 100 false maunds—thus, 5 per cent of the jute sold to the *farias* was offered virtually free, thanks to weight manipulations.[42]

At the secondary up-country markets, too, several deductions were made, whose incidence ultimately fell on the smaller growers. The deductions in terms of quantity were:

(a) *Bachhat,* or further safeguard against weight loss, varying from 3/20 seers/maund in Sirajganj to 2¼ seers/maund in Jiaganj;

(b) *Kabari,* or deductions made for the alleged benefit of the *aratdar's* (up-country merchant, one who has a shed) staff, varying from 5 seers per 100 maunds in Netrakona to 35 in Nayargaon;

(c) *Namuna,* a sampling allowance, quite rare in Bengal, as was

(d) *Pasga,* or deduction against possible mistakes in weighing![43]

The cash deductions were:

(a) *Aratdari,* a commission charged by *aratdars,* usually 2 annas per maund;

(b) *Dalali,* or brokerage fee borne by sellers, which was, when levied, 1½ annas per maund;

(c) *Koyali,* or payment for the alleged benefit of the buyer's weighmen, from ½ pice to 1 anna per maund;

(d) Office expenses, usually at ½ anna per maund;

(e) *Jachandari,* or payment for the benefit of the buyer's assorting staff who graded the jute, usually at 3 pice per maund;

(f) *Britti* or *Iswarbritti,* intended for religious charity, up to ½ anna per maund.[44]

Of course, not all deductions were levied in each and every mart. But, in proportional terms, at Rs 5 per maund, the deductions accounted for 5.3 to 8.6 per cent of the secondary market price which was not a piffling amount as far as the poorer peasants were concerned. Furthermore, it is worth noting that at Rs 5 per maund, the quantity deductions and other specific forms of shortchanging dominated the *ad valorem* deductions. In a scenario of falling and low prices, therefore, the traditional deductions not only affected the level but also the trend of the peasants' surplus. In any case, the picture of the jute economy would not have improved significantly even if we ignored these deductions. The following exercise, carried out under the best possible assumptions, clearly shows that a 3-acre permanently settled, cash rent-paying *raiyat* could not make ends meet in the 1930s.

Revenue from jute and winter rice cultivation in year t is estimated as:

$$R_t = O_{jt} \cdot P_{jt} + \left(O_{wrt} - S\right) \cdot P_{wrt}, \qquad (6.1)$$

where S is the family's subsistence rice needs (here 4 maunds per capita × 5.5 persons). It should be noted that the marketable surplus of winter rice thus computed is a generous oversimplification. In fact, poor peasants sold a large part of their winter rice to meet pressing post-harvest cash needs, and later took paddy loans to tide over their annual subsistence needs. Selling winter rice and consuming inferior Burma rice was a very common feature of East and North Bengal. Thus, a more accurate picture would have been:

$$R_t = O_{jt} \cdot P_{jt} + \left(O_{wrt} - \overline{S}_t\right) \cdot P_{wrt}, \qquad (6.2)$$

where $\overline{S}_t < S$, in general.

Now, another element would enter in the calculation of surplus—the cost of rice bought from the market at retail prices against paddy loans, or:

$$\left(\left(S - \overline{S}_t\right) \cdot p_{rt}^*\right)(1 + i), \qquad (6.3)$$

p_{rt}^* being the retail price of rice.

If $p_{rt}^*> p_{wrt}$ and if $i > 0$, it follows that when a peasant sold a part of his crop and bought it back at retail prices against paddy loans, his cash position at the end of the year would be far worse than what has been assumed in our calculation.

Second, I have reduced the non-rice expenditure of the peasant family by assuming that in a slump it did not buy new clothes, did not spend money on repairs, and kept its social and religious expenditure at the barest minimum.

Third, one has assumed that in the 1930s peasants often did not pay their full rental dues to the *zamindar*s. For instance, between 1929 and 1931—the Depression had just run for two years—default on the March rental *qist* had increased by more than 300 per cent, from Rs 3.91 lakh to Rs 15.91 lakh.[45] I have, accordingly, slashed *raiyati* rent by a third. *Abwab*s have been ignored.

Finally, only to err on the side of safety, I have assumed that even if the 3-acre *raiyati* family incurred a deficit in the income–expenditure account, this would *not* be added on to the principal in the following season. Also, the creditor is assumed to be a person of extremely pleasant disposition, who would continue to loan out the same amount as before, at the same rate of interest (37.5 per cent) without either adding on the defaulted amount or imposing a credit squeeze. According to Mahalanobis, the debt burden in 1929 was Rs 176. Thus, the debt cost would, in this idealized world, be Rs 66 (176 × 0.375) for all times. The other costs are calculated as before (Appendix 6.2).

Even with such generous and wholly unreal assumptions, one sees in Table 6.8 that a permanently occupying, settled, cash rent paying *raiyat* cultivating 3 acres of land—one of the more fortunate people in rural society—simply could not make ends meet throughout the 1930s.

Table 6.7 Deductions and allowances made from the villages to the secondary markets (per 100 maunds)

Districts	Markets	Deductions in quantity (seers/100 maunds)				Valued @Rs5/maund	Cash allowances (Rs/100 maunds)							Total deductions as a % of secondary market price
		A	B	C	D		E	F	G	H	I	J	K	
Mymensingh	Netrokona	50	200	–	5	32.00	3.13	12.50	–	–	1.56	–	1.56	8.6
	Iswarganj	50	160	–	–	26.25	1.98	9.38	–	–	10.52	–	–	8.1
	Mymensingh	50	100	–	–	18.75	1.56	12.50	–	–	4.67	–	1.16	6.7
Dacca	Narsingdi	–150–			25	21.88	–	12.50	4.67	2.0	1.50	–	–	7.3
	Tarpassa	50	200	–	25	34.38	–	–	–	–	12.50	–	1.56	8.2
Faridpur	Charmugaria	200	100	–	–	37.50	–	12.50	–	–	–	–	–	8.5
Rangpur	Saidpur	75	100	–	–	21.88	–	–	1.56	–	–	–	1.04	4.4
Bogra	Jamalganj	150	80	–	–	28.75	–	–	–	–	–	–	1.56	5.3
Pabna	Sirajganj	40	100	15	–	19.38	0.25	12.50	3.13	–	6.5	–	1.04	6.3
Hooghly	Sheoraphuli	50	100	–	–	18.75	3.13	12.50	0.25	–	6.5	0.25	0.25	7.2

Note: A: *Dhalta*; B: Weight manipulation; C: *Bachhat*; D: *Kabari*; E: *Kabari*; F: *Aratdar's* commission; G: *Dadali*; H: *Koyali*; I: Office expenses; J: *Jachandari*; K: *Britti*.

Source: ICJC, 1940, *Report on Marketing and Transport of Jute*, pp. 106–09, Tables XXXV, XXXVI, and LXIV, pp. 223–6.

Table 6.8 *Surplus/Deficit from jute and winter rice cultivation for a 3-acre permanently occupying settled raiyat, after making generous assumptions, 1930–8*

(Rs)

Years	Cash income		Costs (incl. debt cost)	Non-rice subsistence	Surplus
	Jute	Rice			
1930–1	113	72	135	98	– 48
1931–2	128	48	142	81	– 20
1932–3	108	40	109	77	– 38
1933–4	105	32	105	73	– 41
1934–5	105	36	107	75	– 41
1935–6	141	39	109	77	– 6
1936–7	154	39	109	77	7
1937–8	165	42	121	86	0

Sources to, and the method used in getting these numbers are given in Appendix 6.2.

It may be pointed out that, in spite of our assumptions, the situation may well have been better. After all, the *raiyat* did accumulate surplus in the 1920s which could have been spent in lean years. The fact of the matter was that most of the surplus was typically spent on non-income generating activities such as feasts, dowries, greater food expenditure, and better clothing and housing. Many settlement officers observed the growth of tin roofs (in place of thatch) and large expenditures on festivals—which, according to them, epitomized the indigent and feckless nature of Bengali peasants. Such adjectives obscure the simple fact that in many years the *raiyats* simply broke even; if the desire to spend more on consuming goods that they were normally deprived of was considered to be a sign of fecklessness, then the Bengali peasant was a spendthrift. Incidentally, this was also the general reaction towards any signs of higher consumption by former slaves in the American south in the years following their emancipation in 1865.[46] Besides, it can be said that our model is based on extremely kind assumptions. If we allowed for some stocks but simultaneously took into account more realistic assumption, the picture would not be much different from the one above.

Why did these *raiyats* continue cultivating jute and winter rice at such losses? Why did they not switch their cropping pattern to the changing times? The answer is simple as well as tragic. There were no alternative profitable crops. There were at least three reasons why two rice crops were not worth the while in most jute growing areas. First, proportionately less credit was advanced against rice than jute; this was particularly true for autumn rice, which was considered to be an inferior as well as a risky crop. Second, it can be easily shown that, in spite of lower cultivating costs and without incorporating risk, the deficit from *aus* and *aman* rice cultivation would have been even greater. Finally, planting *aus* rice, particularly in the lowlands, was a hazardous venture: the crop was not only exposed to possible floods in August and September, when the stalks were fully mature, but they were also subjected to the menace of water hyacinths which killed the plants. So, the only rational option left to peasants who had no other means of livelihood was to continue cultivating jute and winter rice, not because it was profitable but because it gave greater revenue—and, in the 1930s, cultivation continued due to the compulsive need for cash to keep immiserization at bay for as long as possible.

Once we move away from the unreality of our estimation model to the real world, we can immediately see a sharp growth in the burden of indebtedness. According to Mahalanobis's calculations, the burden of debt, *excluding unpaid debts and interest thereon*, rose by 67 per cent for the whole of Bengal between 1929 and 1934. It must, however, be remembered that Mahalanobis's figures (Table 6.9) are gross underestimates for (i) they did not take into account unpaid loans before 1928–9 and interest thereon, and (ii) they excluded sharecroppers from the picture. Nevertheless, Mahalanobis found that in 1933, when the Depression had not yet worked its way out of the system, 43 per cent of the rural population in Bengal were indebted up to twice their current income and 18 per cent to more than four times their income.[47] Unfortunately, we have no reliable evidence on indebtedness after 1934, but with jute and rice prices being sluggish, it certainly could not have fallen.

Table 6.9   *Indebtedness in rural Bengal, 1929 and 1934*

				(Rs/family)
District	Sample	Indebtedness		Rate of growth (percentage)
		1929	1934	
Bengal	6359	154	257	67
Dacca	549	217	393	81
Faridpur	424	201	298	48
Mymensingh	313	129	275	113
Tippera	345	271	385	42
Rangpur	1043	140	202	44
Bogra	397	153	213	39
Pabna	297	139	228	64
Rajshahi	297	159	261	64

Source: See note 47.

Clearly, such an increase in indebtedness could not exist in a vacuum. This brings out three other aspects of the Depression: the squeeze on rural credit and increasingly inflexible demands for repayment, the shift in the source of credit from the old traditional 'cash-for-cash' *mahajan*s to the 'land for default' *jotedar*s and 'cash against crop' *dadandar*s, and growing fragmentation of landholdings coupled with a sharp rise in *barga* tenures, as tenants desperately tried to face the deepening crisis by selling off parcels of land.

There are no figures, but qualitative evidence certainly points to a sudden credit squeeze within the first couple of years of the Depression. The sharp fall in agricultural income not only cut into peasants' ability to repay but also reduced land values—the asset which was usually held as collateral by the traditional 'cash-for-cash' *mahajan*s. In these circumstances, it was natural for moneylenders to apply a credit squeeze and reframe old debt bonds at higher rates of interest. That the older (Hindu) *mahajans* were definitely making such moves as early as mid-1930 shows up in the evidence of the Kishoreganj riots—a short, bloody uprising that took place in Mymensingh.

Since the rioters were Muslim peasants and the victims largely Hindu families, the disturbance had a distinctly communal tinge. A closer examination shows that the real reasons were largely economic. The Hindu *mahajans* had applied a credit squeeze in June–July 1930 and had rewritten old bonds at higher interest rates. Almost all the 'incidents' followed a definite pattern: Muslim peasants would proceed *en masse* to a moneylender's house and demand the handing over of all debt documents. 'The primary object of the looters was to get hold of money bonds and other documents in the custody of Hindu moneylenders and burn them to pieces.'[48] The object of violence was the *mahajan* and stray Muslim moneylenders were equally affected. Compliance led to nothing beyond the burning of documents; refusal however, 'immediately produced an attack on the house and properties'[49] and, in the event of stiffer resistance, people were killed as well.[50] According to an official note, 1001 houses were looted in the subdivision: all belonged to moneylenders.[51]

Kishoreganj was not a typical peasant response to the Depression. But it serves to highlight the severe impact of a credit squeeze which prompted peasants to leave their standing jute crop and indulge in a brief orgy of violence. Such violence was sporadic but the credit squeeze was continuous and, more often than not, the peasantry, because of their years of subalternity, accepted the higher demands and searched for alternative lines of credit to meet their cultivation needs.

A shift in the source of rural credit along *jotedari* and *dadani* lines had started in the mid-1920s, but accelerated through the 1930s. The older *mahajans*, who had no interest in cultivation and to whom land was only a transferable asset, had become increasingly wary of lending money to cultivators. Matters were made far worse with the passing of the Bengal Agricultural

Debtors Act of 1935. The Act led to the setting up of debt settlement boards across the province. These boards were manned by local *jotedars*—'persons whose literary attainments (did) not go beyond signing their own names'[52]—who treated Hindu *mahajans* as their competitors in the credit market. If the board felt that a cultivator's terms were unfair, it was empowered to unilaterally declare a lower interest rate. If the creditor did not accept the decision, the board could issue a certificate to the debtor which absolved him from paying more than 6 per cent per annum simple interest, and this could not be challenged in a court of law.[53]

The Act, in many ways, signified the growth of *jotedari* power in the countryside—a power that was to play an even more important role in elite as well as local politics with the coming of Fazlul Huq's Krishak Praja Party in 1937. With the passing of the Act, all *mahajani* credit stopped altogether, and the familiar 'cash-for-cash' advances almost disappeared from the countryside. We see this indirectly in the number of money suits in interior courts for arrears of debt. In 1925–9 there were, on an average, 232,846 suits per year; this increased by 47 per cent to an average of 342,812 in 1930–4 and then slumped to 187,054 (a fall of 45 per cent) in 1937–9, when the debt settlement boards effectively came into being.[54] With the chronic need for credit to tide over basic production and consumption requirements, the Act catalysed the withdrawal of the least harmful creditor from the money market—the old 'cash-for-cash' *mahajan*—and cleared the way for a complete domination by the *jotedars* and *dadandars*, who were not considered to be 'moneylenders'.

From the point of view of the cultivators, *dadan* or *jotedari* advances were better than no loans at all. Without advances, however usurious they may be, production could not be carried on; and, if peasants took loans from *jotedars* or *dadandars*, it would be only a matter of time before the disposable surplus of the cultivating family was reduced. *Dadan* prices were, typically, half the prices of the previous season; in other words, *dadan* was profitable as long as the market price did not crash by 50 per cent. This happened only once during the Depression—in 1930–1. No doubt, profits were lower than before, but *dadan* was still profitable. Decline in land prices did not dissuade *jotedar*s from giving loans. In the first place, being farmers, they could not attach a greater amount in case of default. Secondly, with growing population pressure on land, there was no dearth of peasants who would be willing to rent out this land at half the gross produce. While the total value of the surplus extracted from the debtor-cum-sharecropper may have been lower than under normal conditions (the argument can run both ways), the mechanics of loan–indebtedness–appropriation–sharecropping gave *jotedar*s much greater economic and political power over the poorer cultivators.[55]

There is considerable qualitative evidence that points to a sharp rise in *jotedari* and *dadani* loans. In Pabna's Sirajganj subdivision, cultivators were pledging 'a considerable portion of the crop before it [was] harvested' at an implicit interest rate of 2 annas per rupee per month, or 150 per cent per annum, and most *dadandar*s were petty Marwaris.[56] In Tippera, where *dadan* was conspicuously absent before World War I, credit prices were 'fixed at three-quarters or less than the actual market rate'.[57] In Jalpaiguri, an area rife with *jotedar*s, dadan had become the most important source of finance and were executed at '50 per cent below the expected market price'.[58] In Dacca, *dadan* had become so rampant, that there was a term called '*dadan* purchase' in raw jute trade. It seems that in the 1937 season, *dadan* purchase accounted for 60 and 68 per cent of the total raw jute traded in Sirajganj and Narainganj.[59] Even if we treat these figures with scepticism and reduce them by half, they are ominous enough, for it must be a very depressed rural economy that sells 30 to 35 per cent of its leading cash crop at half to three-quarters the market price.

These new forms of credit catalysed the growth in fragmentation of holding sizes and accelerated the development of sharecropping in East and North Bengal. Table 6.10 gives the extent of transfer of permanently occupied *raiyati* holdings during the 1930s in the jute belt.

Table 6.10 *Transfers of raiyati holdings in the 1930s*

District	% of raiyati area transferred	% of transferred area now cultivated by bargadars
Bengal	6.9	31.7
Dacca	4.9	42.7
Mymensingh	5.5	52.2
Faridpur	6.6	20.4
Tippera	4.2	10.5
Rangpur	4.7	38.0
Bogra	3.0	31.4
Pabna	3.8	22.0
Jalpaiguri	9.4	42.2
Dinajpur	3.8	34.8
Rajshahi	3.5	38.1

Source: GOB, 1940, *Report of the Bengal Land Revenue (Flood) Commission*, vol. 1 (Alipore), pp. 120–1.

Arguably, some of the transfers could have been parallel ones, but, in the context of the 1930s, it would seem that net downward mobility would have been the norm. Also, while 6.9 per cent does not look like a very large figure, in absolute terms this translates to 1.6 million acres of cultivated land—which is not a small amount, especially since most of those who were transferring land were small peasants. Besides, many of the transfers took place illegally, particularly after the passing of the Bengal Agricultural Debtors Act and the Bengal Tenancy (Amendment) Act of 1938, and they would not show up in Table 6.10. That the number of transfers were rapidly increasing in the 1930s is also borne out by the data given in the Land Revenue Administration Reports of the period, which have been summarized in Table 6.11.

Table 6.11 does not, of course, say anything about how much of the land changed hands and to whom. But, all the evidence taken together indicates a few things. First, that there is no doubt that land transfers were increasing, and most of the transfers were due to increasing pressure of debt servicing in a period of acute slump. Second, it seems highly unlikely that anything but a very small proportion of the total transfers represented upward economic mobility of small peasants. The deficits incurred by the 3-acre *raiyat*—a relatively better off peasant in the 1930s— precluded such possibilities. Finally, a considerable portion of the transferred area—approximately 500,000 acres of cultivable land—was cultivated by sharecroppers and, given the mechanics of land transfer during the period, it is likely that many peasants who were forced to sell a part of their holdings were recontracted as sharecroppers on what was earlier their own land.

Table 6.11 *Transfers of* raiyati *holdings, 1926–38, under sections of the Bengal Tenancy (Amendment) Act*

Year	Number of transfers	Index number
1926–30 (average)	169,557	100
1930–1	314,494	185
1931–2	311,595	184
1932–3	312,625	184
1933–4	331,560	196
1934–5	393,727	232
1935–6	439,199	259
1936–7	426,027	251
1937–8*	339,732	200
1938–9*	249,491	147

Note: * These figures are more apparent than real. The number of transfers due to money default fell drastically because they were no longer registered after the passing of the Bengal Agricultural Debtors Act and the Bengal Tenancy Amendment Act.

Source: GOB, *Report on the LR Administration of the Presidency of Bengal 1926 to 1938–9.*

With such tendencies manifesting themselves in abundant measure, it is not surprising that the distribution of landholdings became very unequal by the end of the 1930s. In 1937, when the Indian Central Jute Committee was carrying out detailed field investigations, it found that 78.5 and 87.4 per cent of the cultivators in East and North Bengal respectively, produced less than 30 maunds of jute.[60] With an average yield of 15 maunds per acre, this meant that more than 75 per cent of the rural families had less than 2 acres of jute land at their disposal. In other words, their total operational holding, *irrespective of tenurial arrangements*, could not be much more than 2.5 acres. The Bengal Land Revenue Commission (under Francis Floud), while conducting a sample survey of 19,599 rural families in 1939, found that for the whole of the province 46 per cent of the families had less than 2 acres of land while 8.4 per cent had more than 10 acres.[61] Floud's findings are given in Table 6.12.

Table 6.12   *Distribution of landholdings in 1939*

District	% of families with		% of land held by families with	
	Less than 2 acres	*More than 10 acres*	*Less than 2 acres*	*More than 10 acres*
Bengal	46.0	8.4	10.6	38.7
Dacca	62.4	3.5	29.2	13.9
Mymensingh	34.1	6.5	8.8	35.3
Faridpur	81.5	0.6	50.1	15.5
Tippera	63.9	2.9	28.7	11.4
Rangpur	24.6	11.2	3.6	52.6
Bogra	34.5	7.1	8.0	28.0
Pabna	64.1	2.4	26.8	21.3
Jalpaiguri	5.3	20.4	0.6	56.6
Dinajpur	24.2	15.0	3.7	46.5
Rajshahi	31.8	14.6	5.7	42.0

Source: Computed from GOB, 1940, *Floud Commission Report*, Vol. 2 (Alipore), pp. 114–15.

The Floud Commission also attemped to estimate the spread of sharecropping tenures. By 1939, according to the commission, 16 per cent of the rural families of East and North Bengal lived *entirely* as *recorded* sharecroppers.[62] This figure is a gross underestimate. For one thing, when the commission carried out its survey, the Bengal Tenancy (Amendment) Act, 1938, had already been passed and people were expecting further tenancy regulations especially with respect to *bargadars*. In fact, one of the terms of reference of the commission was to look into the status of sharecroppers. In this scenario, many *jotedars* refused to label their sharecroppers as *bargadars* and they were often recorded as *parisramiks* or agricultural labourers.[63] Another reason for underestimating arises from the fact that there were many *raiyati* families with less than 2 acres of land who, to eke out their existence, worked *partly* as sharecroppers—and this was not recorded by the commission. However, if one neglected part-time sharecroppers and treated half of those who were registered by the commission as agricultural labourers as *bargadars*, then sharecroppers would account for 24 per cent of rural families.[64] The number of whole and part-time sharecroppers would be much higher, but we have no way of estimating this for this period.

One can now see the chronological and structural impact of the Depression on East and North Bengal. The fall in prices drastically reduced the gross revenue from jute and winter rice cultivation, and simultaneously increased the debt burden. In the first year, the peasantry attempted to adjust to the slump by reducing the area under jute by nearly 40 per cent, with the fond hope that this would lead to a price revival. When this did not happen—and rice prices collapsed as well—higher debt burden and pressing cash needs forced cultivators to *increase* the area under jute in a desperate attempt to maintain minimum cash revenue in the backdrop of falling income.[65] Since there was no rise in world demand, this kind of peasant response set the stage for a sharper squeeze through the mechanisms of deductions, allowances, *dadan*, and *jotedari* loans. It should be noted that since most of the trade deductions were specific and not *ad valorem*, their incidence was proportionately much greater in an era of depressed prices. Soon the debt burden became high enough for the poorer peasants to sell off a part of their holdings—either legally or outside the court—and take up sharecropping to make ends meet. Every successive dispossession and switch to sharecropping further reduced the surplus of the peasant family, which, in turn, accelerated the movement towards a second round of dispossession. By the time prices started picking up towards the end of the 1930s, it was too late for the great majority of the peasantry.

Population pressure had created great strains on the structure of small peasant cultivation by the end of 1920s. The Depression, with its long-lasting multidimensional effects, destroyed the minimal degree of economic freedom that existed within this structure. In the 1920s, the small peasant economy of East and North Bengal was capable of modest prosperity when prices were high. But the distinction between a good and a bad year was too fine for a family with less than 3 acres, and the equilibrium was so unstable that once it went off the rails into a path of debt-peonage, there was nothing in the system that could pull it back into the break-even state.

The only real gainers were the *jotedars*—not through capitalist farming but through semi-feudal rents. By virtually controlling land and moving into the rural credit vacuum created by the withdrawal of traditional *mahajans*, they swiftly consolidated their power at the expense of *mahajans* and zamindars on the one hand and the poorer peasants on the other. In their methods of appropriation and in their relationship with their subalterns, the *jotedars* were much shrewder than the zamindars. Although a *jotedar* rarely hesitated to attach land in the case of credit default, he was astute enough not to carry out exactions to a point where it cut into the peasant's notion of a morally minimum subsistence. Unlike the zamindar's crude instruments of power— certificate procedure, *abwabs*, and *mahtuts*—the *jotedar* rarely ever threw peasants out of the land and always gave them a status of a *krishak*, however minimal that status may be. From the peasant's point of view, *jotedari* appropriation was charitable for was he not still a peasant and did not the *jotedar* give him food in times of need? Besides, the *jotedars* were Muslims like the peasants themselves, lived much less ostentatiously than the hated Hindu zamindars, stayed in villages and not in cities, and enjoyed a kind of symbiotic relationship with their subalterns—which was the basis for their political power and for the growth of the Krishak Praja Party in the mid-1930s. In spite of being more exploitative in the long run than the relatively ineffective zamindars, *jotedars* succeeded in portraying themselves as fellow *prajas*, and heightened the contradictions between Muslim *raiyats* on the one hand and the Hindu landlords and *mahajans* on the other—contradictions that were to have their expression in the communal violence of the 1940s.

Epilogue

As far as the industry was concerned, World War II wiped off all the gloom of the 1930s and ushered in another period of profits. For the agricultural sector, however, things moved from bad to worse. By 1941–3, land transfers had increased from 439,199 in 1935–6 (see Table 6.11) to over 965,000![66] In 1939, 46 per cent of the rural families had less than 2 acres of land and 25.4 per cent held more than 5 acres.[67] By January 1943, when the famine had just about started in Bengal, 75.6 per cent of the families had less than 2 acres while 8.5 per cent had more than 5 acres of land.[68] By this time, the production possibility frontier for most peasants had shrunk to a point where a sudden shift in relative prices could mean starvation through a failure in exchange entitlements. The price rise that occurred in 1943—from Rs 8.50 per maund of rice in January 1943 to Rs 37 on 20 August[69]—was anything but a minor swing in relative prices. Its upshot was the death of 3 million souls.[70]

It is not my intention to go into the horrors of the great Bengal famine of 1943–4, except to say that the pauperization experienced by the majority of the peasant families during the 1930s made them extremely susceptible to the price rise of the famine year. After the famine, it was found that 36.4 per cent of the rural families *owned no land at all* and lived either as agricultural labourers or sharecroppers; 18 per cent had less than 1 acre of land, including homestead, and, in order to scrape out a subsistence, cultivated at least 0.5 acres in *barga*; 14 per cent had between 1 and 3 acres of land, and they also cultivated, on an average 0.5 acres as *bargadars*.[71] And this downward spiral continued till 1947 and even beyond.

In some instances—such as in the Tebhaga movement in North Bengal—peasants attempted to rebel. But such revolts were infrequent. More often than not, the older *raiyats* dreamt of their pre-World War I days when, after selling their jute, they covered their roofs with tin, dug ponds, and spent money on fireworks and feasts to greet their new daughters-in-law.[72] They also ruefully remembered old Abed Ali Mian's ditty:

> *Beshi pat karo bhairey beshi takar ashey,*
> *Jemon asha temon dash dena pater chashey.*
> *Taka taka majur diya niran kulam kam,*
> *Marwarira ghorey boshey panch taka dei dam.[73]*

(You grow more jute, brothers, with the hope of greater cash,
Costs and debts of jute will make your hopes get dashed.
When you've spent all your money and got the crop off the ground,
Marwari traders, sitting at home, will pay only Rs 5 a maund.)

Appendix 6.1

It is well known that official jute crop acreage was notoriously unreliable during the colonial period—and this was a bone of contention as far as the Indian Jute Mills' Association was concerned. However, one can arrive at an alternative estimate, using the method underlined below:

1. The data on mill consumption of raw jute (Indian mills), mill stock and export are quite accurate. This is available from 1900–1901 and even earlier. From 1906–07, there are data on stocks of raw jute up-country as well as in the Calcutta bazaars. These data are given in GOB, John A. Todd, 1944, *Report on the Working of the Jute Futures and Hessian Futures Markets in Calcutta* (Alipore) and IJMA, 1950, *Report of the Committee 1949* (Calcutta), pp. 97–101.

2. There are no less than nine pieces of evidence spaced between 1907 and 1944 that point to the fact that raw jute yield was more or less constant over the period and in the region of 15 maunds per acre. I have assumed constancy of yield.

3. Now,

   Actual output of raw jute = Indian mill consumption + exports + handloom sector consumption (minimal and given in IJMA, 1949) + change in mill stock + change in Calcutta bazaar stock + change in up-country stock;

   Actual acreage = actual output/15 maunds per acre;

   $$\frac{\text{Actual acreage}}{\text{Government acreage}} = \text{revision factor for the year.}$$

4. I have then assumed that this revision factor is distributed in the same proportion over the major jute growing districts as over the aggregate. Thus,

Actual acreage in jute tract =Government acreage in those districts multiplied by the revision factor for the year.

5. No such revision can be carried out for winter rice. For a critique of one such revision by M. M. Islam, 1978, *Bengal Agriculture*, 1920–46 (Cambridge), see my *Industry, Trade and Peasant Society: The Jute Economy of Eastern India, 1900–1947* (New Delhi, 1991). Thus, income from jute and autumn rice cultivation in the jute tracts (gross income) is revised output of jute multiplied by harvest price plus output of autumn rice multiplied by harvest price. The real gross income is arrived at by deflating this with the wholesale price index for the period.

Appendix 6.2

Estimating farm-level surplus during the period 1900–1947 is an exceedingly difficult exercise and the one we have done must be treated as merely indicative and not one which claims exactitude.

1. In the pre-World War I era, it would be fair to say that the 'modal' permanently occupied settled *raiyat* had around 4 acres of cultivable land. We have assumed that the farmer devoted 3.5 acres for jute cultivation, of which 0.5 acre was kept aside for jute seeds. The remaining 0.5 acre was used for sowing *aman* paddy shoots, which was transplanted across the entire holding after harvesting the jute crop.

2. Yield from jute and winter rice assumed constant at 15 and 11 maunds per acre respectively.

3. Subsistence rice needs estimated at 4 maunds per capita (lower than the jail ration estimate of the period). Family size: 5.18 in the pre-World War I era and 5.5 during the 1930s. Subsistence needs deducted from source.

4. Thus, cash income is

$$A_j \cdot 15 \cdot p_j + A_{wr} \cdot 11 \cdot p_{wr} \qquad (A\ 6.2)$$

5. Debt costs in the pre-World War I period is given only by F. D. Ascoli, in WBSA, GOB, Revenue Dept., Agriculture Branch, F.1-J/15 of 1914, Feb. 1915 Progs 15–32, Ascoli-French, Dacca 22 August 1914. From here, as well as from Jack, 1916, *The Economic Life of a Bengal District*, we have set the initial debt as Rs 50 in the ante-bellum years, assuming that, with pre-war prosperity, the *raiyat* could roll over his debt without affecting the principal, and put the interest at 37.5 per cent per annum (as indicated by both Ascoli, op. cit., and BPBEC, vol. 1).

6. Rent taken as Rs 4 per acre, and *abwabs*, etc. at Rs 5 per year (again Ascoli, op. cit., and *BPBEC*, vol. 1, p. 35).

7. Regarding cultivation, I have assumed:

    (a) ploughing has no cost—done by family labour.

    (b) hiring plough and cattle cost Rs 4 per acre in rice and Rs 8 per acre in the case of jute—the latter requiring two ploughings. These data are for 1914, and are adjusted according to the Wholesale Price Index (WPI) for other years.

    (c) in jute, there is a labour cost for weeding at the rate of Rs 15 per acre in 1914, adjusted according to WPI for other years.

    (d) reaping costs: Rs 5 per acre for jute and Rs 3 per acre for *aman* paddy in 1914, adjusted according to WPI for other years.

    (e) separation of fibre at the rate of Rs 5 for an acre's crop in 1914, adjusted for changes in WPI in other years.

(f) threshing: 1 anna per maund of end product in 1900–1901, adjusted for changes in WPI in subsequent years.

Database for (a)–(f): Ascoli, op. cit., *BPBEC,* vol. 1, p. 35 and N. C. Chaudhury, 1921, *Jute in Bengal,* 2nd ed. (Calcutta).

8. Subsistence expenditure, other than rice included (a) non-rice food expenditure, (b) clothing, (c) repairs and renewals, (d) social and religious ceremonies, and (e) other miscellaneous expenditure. The data for 1929, given in *BPBEC,* vol. 1 pp. 80–1 were used and deflated according to changes in WPI.

9. Surplus = total cash income – total cash expenditure.

10. In this calculus, subsistence has been defined as a peasant family's notion of 'normal consumption,' i.e., the items, and quantities thereof, that the family expects to consume in a normal year. It is made up of two components:

    (a) food, mainly rice, which is subsistence in a strictly classical sense—i.e., without it, the family cannot reproduce its labour power in the following season. It is a biological minimum needed for sustaining the same level of labour in the next cycle.

    (b) other non-food elements. These are more income sensitive in the sense that, in a crisis, they can be reduced. But, it must be stressed that while they can be reduced or eliminated once in a while—as I assumed they were during the Depression—they cannot be eliminated for a long period without adversely affecting future labour power.

11. For World War I, I have assumed the same level of debt as before (i.e., Rs 50) but, in the event of a deficit in the peasant's income-expenditure (as in 1917–18) I have added on this deficit to the principal. Thus, e.g., debt in the beginning of the 1918–19 season is Rs 82 (i.e., Rs 50 + a deficit of Rs 32) and debt cost is Rs 30.75

(Rs 82 × 0.375). A similar assumption has been made for the 1920s.

12. The level of debt for the 1930s has been scaled up from Rs 176 in 1929 (from Mahalanobis, WBSA, GOB, Revenue Dept., L. R. Branch, *Bengal Board of Economic Enquiry*, F.11-R-29 of 1934, nos. 1–3, June 1935, Progs 8–11). Debt costs, therefore, were Rs 66. The rest of the seemingly absurd assumptions, given in the text, were made only to show that even in a seemingly wonderful world, the peasant family having 3 acres of land under permanent *raiyati* tenure just could not make ends meet.

Notes

1. By Bengal I mean what is now West Bengal and Bangladesh, excluding the district of Sylhet.

2. Tapan Raychaudhuri, 1969, 'Permanent Settlement in Operation: Bakarganj District, East Bengal', in R. E. Frykenberg, ed., *Land Control and Social Structure in Indian History* (Wisconsin), p. 163.

3. Government of Bengal (GOB), J. A. Milligan, 1919, *Jalpaiguri Settlement Report 1906–16* (Calcutta), p. 90 and App. 2, pp. ii–iii.

4. GOB, F. D. Ascoli, 1917, *Dacca Settlement Report 1910–17* (Calcutta), pp. 51, 75–6.

5. Government of India (GOI), 1901, *Census of India 1901*, vol. 6(1), pp. 2–4 and GOB, 1901, *Agricultural Statistics of Bengal 1900–1901* (Calcutta), pp. 6, 13.

6. See J. C. Jack, 1916, *The Economic Life of a Bengal District* (Oxford) and also GOB, J. C. Jack, 1916, *Faridpur Settlement Report 1910–14* (Calcutta).

7. West Bengal State Archives (WBSA), GOB, Revenue Dept., Agr. Branch, F.1-J/15 of 1914, Progs 15–32, Ascoli-Kerr, Dacca, 27 April 1914.

8. See Indian Jute Mills Association (IJMA), 1950, *Report of the Committee 1949* (Calcutta), pp. 97–101, 116–17.

9. Ibid., pp. 97–101. Excess supply in 1914–15 was around 8.6 million maunds which was about nineteen times greater than the average between 1909 and 1913.

10. WBSA, GOB, Revenue Dept., Agr. Branch, F.1-J/15 of 1914, Progs 15–32, Birley–French, 17 August 1914.
11. Ibid., Gupta–Rankin, 17 August 1914.
12. Ibid., Progs 19–20, Birley–French, 5 October 1914.
13. Ibid., Woodhead–French, 5 September 1914.
14. Ibid., Spry–French, 11 August 1914.
15. See my Industry, *Trade and Peasant Society: The Jute Economy of Eastern India, 1900–1947* (New Delhi, 1991).
16. Ibid., pp. 135–6, Table IV.2. On the face of it, it seems rather odd that surplus could have fallen so sharply after the boom of 1909–13. It is my contention that not much of the previous stock was kept aside for a rainy day—years of boom had reduced the expectation of slump—and what was, was spent in the first two years, leaving many peasants exposed to the second crash in 1917–18.
17. WBSA, GOB, Revenue Dept., Agr. Branch, F.1-J/5, Sept. 1916, Progs 36–7, note by Kenneth MacLean.
18. Ibid., Progs 33–4, Coll. Rangpur–Comm. Rajshahi Div., 17 September 1916 and Coll. Pabna–Comm. Rajshahi Div., 19 June 1916.
19. Ibid., Woodhead–French, 5 July 1916.
20. See my *Industry, Trade and Peasant Society*.
21. Computed according to the method given in Appendix 6.1, from IJMA, 1950, *Report of Committee*, pp. 99–101 and GOB, *Season and Crop Report of Bengal 1909–10* (Calcutta, 1910) to 1929–30 (Calcutta, 1930).
22. See Appendix 6.1 for the method of computation. Harvest prices of jute and winter rice from IJMA, *1950, Report of Committee*, pp. 116–17 and GOB, 1939, Bengal Paddy and Rice Enquiry Committee (*BPREC*), vol. 1 (Alipore), p. 24 and GOI, K. L. Datta, 1914, *Report on the Enquiry into the Rise of Prices in India*, vol. 2 (Calcutta), pp. 136–9.
23. From GOI, 1901, *Census of India*, vol. 5 (1&2), *1921*, vol. 5 (1&2), *1931*, vol. 5 (1&2).
24. The Bengal Provincial Banking Enquiry Committee put it at 5.21 acres (*BPBEC*, vol. 1, pp. 24–5). This is for the whole province, and takes into account West Bengal where, because of lower fertility and lesser population pressure, average landholdings were bigger. Also, the estimates of 'current fallow' and 'culturable

wasteland other than current fallows' given in *BPBEC* are too high.

25. *BPBEC*, vol. 2 (Calcutta), evidence of Syed Muazzamuddin Hosain, Deputy Collector, Mymensingh, p. 237.

26. Ibid., evidence of B. B. Dutt, p. 534.

27. Ibid., evidences of Furrokh and Goswami, pp. 178, 787–8.

28. Ibid., evidence of Ahmed, pp. 182–3.

29. Abdul Samed Mian, 1921, *Krishak Boka* (Mymensingh), quoted in Partha Chatterjee, 1982, 'Agrarian Relations and Communalism in Bengal, 1926–1935', in Ranajit Guha, ed., *Subaltern Studies*, vol. 1 (Delhi), p. 25.

30. *BPBEC*, vol. 2, evidences of Martin, Basu, and Chatterjee, pp. 190–202.

31. Ibid., evidence of Chatterjee, pp. 211–13.

32. Ibid., evidence of Hosain, pp. 232–7.

33. WBSA, GOB, Revenue Dept., L. R. Branch, *Bengal Board of Economic Enquiry*, F.11-R-29 of 1934, nos. 1–3, June 1935, Progs 8–11.

34. Using the method outlined in Appendix 6.2. For the detailed table, see my *Trade and Peasant Society*.

35. Abed Ali Mian, 1925, *Desh Shanti* (Rangpur).

36. How the Depression affected the industry in Calcutta is given in detail in my 1982 article, 'Collaboration and Conflict: European and Indian Capitalists and the Indian Jute Economy of Bengal, 1919–39', *Indian Economic and Social History Review* (IESHR), vol. 19, no. 2.

37. IJMA, 1950, *Report of Committee*, pp. 116–17.

38. Ibid.

39. See, for instance, WBSA, GOB, Revenue Dept., Agr. Branch, F.1-J of 1906, Progs 45–6, Marr-Comm., Dacca Div., 24 October 1906. Note that this was written during a period of excess demand.

40. Indian Central Jute Committee (ICJC), 1940, *Report on the Marketing and Transport of Jute in India* (Calcutta), pp. 106–07 and GOB, 1934, *Finlow Committee*, vol. 2 (Calcutta), p. 446.

41. ICJC, ibid., pp. 222–4.

42. Ibid., p. 226.

43. Ibid., pp. 106–07.

44. Ibid., pp. 108–09.
45. WBSA, GOB, Commerce Dept., Comm. Branch, F.2E-3, June 1931, Prog B 14, Appendix C, MacPherson, Secy, Board of Rev., Bengal, 27 April 1931.
46. See R. L. Ransom and R. Sutch, 1977, *One Kind of Freedom: The Economic Consequences of Emancipation* (Cambridge), pp. 5–6.
47. WBSA, GOB, Revenue Dept., L. R. *Branch, Bengal Board of Economic Enquiry,* F.11-R-29 of 1934, nos. 1–3, June 1935, Progs 8–11.
48. WBSA, GOB, Home Dept., Political (Conf), F.613/30 of 1930, note by Basak, SDO Kishoreganj, 13 July 1930.
49. Ibid., Cable, Burrows–Secy, GOB, 16 July 1930 and Burrows–Press Officer, GOB, 5 August 1930.
50. Ibid., report of Mackenzie, Superintendent of Police, Mymensingh. When Krishna Kumar Roy, a big *mahajan* attempted to shoot his way out of trouble, the mob waited for the ammunition to run out, and then hacked him and his dependents to pieces. Note by Basak, 13 July 1930 and cable, Burrows–Secy, GOB, 18 July 1930.
51. Ibid., Burrows–Press Officer, GOB, 5 August 1930.
52. GOB, 1938, *Bengal Legislative Council Debates,* Bhupendra Narayan Sinha, 25 January 1938.
53. GOB, 1936, *The Bengal Agricultural Debtors Act 1935* (Alipore), p. 10.
54. GOB, *Report on the Administration of Civil Justice in the Province of Bengal 1925* (Calcutta, 1926) to *1939* (Calcutta, 1940).
55. It could be asked how did sharecroppers survive at all? In the first place, even during the Depression, the *bargadar* had some *raiyati* land, so his deficit would not be as great as that of one who was entirely a sharecropper. Secondly, the *jotedar* would wipe off some of the accumulated debt by adjusting it against the value of land transferred to his account, which would now be tilled by the debtor. Thus, while the peasant's income-generating and surplus-creating capacity would be reduced, so too would the debt burden. Of course, with sluggish prices and a greater rent burden, the long-term trend was towards total immiserization. The process, however, was punctuated by brief plateaux each time a little plot of land was transferred to the creditor.
56. GOB, 1934, *Finlow Committee,* vol. 2, pp. 15, 25 and 67.
57. Ibid., p. 97.

58. Ibid., p. 159.
59. *Hindustan Standard*, 8 October 1937 and *passim*.
60. ICJC, 1940, *Report on Marketing and Transport*, p. 186.
61. GOB, 1940, *Report of the Bengal Land Revenue Commission* (Floud Commission), vol. 2 (Alipore), pp. 114–15.
62. Ibid., p. 117.
63. This method was prevalent even earlier. See Ascoli, 1917 *Dacca Settlement Report 1910–17*, App. xi, p. xxvii.
64. GOB, *Floud Commission*, p. 117.
65. Area under jute:
    1930–1 (adjusted)—2.76 million acres
    1931–2 (adjusted)—1.64 million acres
    1932–3 (adjusted)—2.08 million acres
    1933–4 (adjusted)—2.40 million acres
    1934–5 (adjusted)—2.42 million acres
66. GOB, *Land Revenue Administration Report 1935–36* (Calcutta) to *1942–43* (Calcutta, 1944).
67. GOB, *Floud Commission*, pp. 114–15.
68. P. C. Mahalanobis, et al., 'Sample Survey of the After-effects of the Bengal Famine', *Sankhya*, vol. 7, no. 4, p. 374.
69. GOI, 1945, *Famine Inquiry Commission, Report on Bengal* (New Delhi), pp. 40, 218; and K. C. Ghosh, 1945, *Famines in Bengal* (Calcutta), p. 44.
70. See A. K. Sen, 1981, *Poverty and Famines* (Oxford), Appendix D.
71. GOB, 1946, *Agricultural Statistics by Plot to Plot Enumeration in Bengal*, vol. 1 (Alipore), p. 47.
72. A. F. M. Abdul Hai, 1921, *Adarsha Krishak* (Mymensingh), p. 32, quoted in Partha Chatterjee, 1982, 'Agrarian Relations and Communalism in Bengal', p. 25.
73. Ali Mian, 1925, *Desh Shanti*.

7

Indian Monetary
Vicissitudes: An Interlude*

Marcello de Cecco

The study of the monetary policy of the British Raj is interesting
even if conducted merely for its own sake; it is certainly most
useful as a component of our analysis. As is well known, India
had assumed in the 25 years under discussion (1890–1914) the
role of a protagonist of the international settlements system: her
trade surplus with the rest of the world and her trade deficit
with England allowed the latter to square her international
settlements on current account. This enabled her to use the income
from her overseas investment for further investment abroad,
and to give back to the international monetary system the
liquidity she had absorbed as investment income.

This, however, was not the only reason why India had an
important place in the international monetary system. The
reserves on which the Indian monetary system was based
provided a large *masse de manoeuvre* which British monetary
authorities could use to supplement their own reserves and to
keep London the centre of the international monetary system.
India had played a similar role in the period immediately
preceding, that is, 1873–92, when she had stemmed world

* Previously published in Marcello de Cecco, *Money and Empire: The
International Gold Standard, 1890–1914*, Basil Blackwell, Oxford, 1974, pp.
62–75.

inflation by absorbing huge quantities of silver which would have otherwise glutted the Western markets.

It is a common belief that India was always the silver standard country *par excellence*. This belief, like many others, has been proved to be false. Silver was imposed on India by the British.[1] The East India Company, which ruled India in the first decades of the nineteenth century, chose silver as the standard of value in 1806. In 1816 the Company forced silver rupees into circulation in southern India, displacing the 'golden pagodas' of the Madras Presidency. This policy had a clear aim: to extract gold from circulation at a time when gold production was stationary and demand, especially because of the resumption of cash payments by the Bank of England, was running high.

In 1835 the Government of India declared the silver rupee legal tender in the whole country; silver and gold rupees were coined at a 15:1 parity. Silver did not, however, become the sole standard until 1853, when Lord Dalhousie demonetized gold, forbidding its use for payments to the Treasury. This measure was adopted—at least so available sources state—in order to protect the flow of payments made by the Government of India to the metropolis, at a time when gold prices were sagging as a result of the Californian discoveries. Moreover, in 1862, the Government of India ordered that bank-notes issued by the Presidency Banks be withdrawn from circulation to be replaced by government-issued bank-notes; thereafter, note issues were to be a monopoly of the Indian government. The notes were given a metallic reserve as guarantee, which was called the Paper Currency Reserve.

The monetary history of the British Raj was affected from the beginning by two major opponents: the businessmen (plantation-owners, industrialists, merchants), and the Raj itself. As was to be expected, the former were concerned to see India go, and remain, on a continuously depreciating standard. On the other hand, the Government of India wanted to maintain the country on as strong a monetary standard as possible; its main preoccupation was to appropriate the hard currency needed to cover the Home Charges arising every year. The Home

Charges consisted mainly of interest on debts to England incurred by the Raj, pensions of former Indian civil servants living in England, payments to the War Office for the upkeep of the Indian Army (and of the whole Imperial Army), and purchases of materials in England on the Raj's account, mostly effected through the government stores.

The two opponents' interests therefore conflicted; and from this conflict stemmed most of what may be called Indian monetary policy under the British Raj. However, during the period we are studying, a third interest emerged— the India Office, the branch of British metropolitan administration whose job it was to supervise Indian affairs from London. At its head was the Secretary of State for India, a senior minister in the British Cabinet. Indian monetary policy, then, was the outcome of the interplay of these three separate centres of power.[2] As the period drew toward its close, the power of the India Office grew, and its decisions were the ones that increasingly determined the course of Indian monetary history. In these years, the Office's staff included the best brains of the Civil Services—among them J. M. Keynes and Basil Blackett, men who enjoyed a training in political economy far superior to that experienced by the average British entrepreneur or Indian civil servants. It was the India Office which demonstrated that the gold exchange standard was the monetary system best suited to India's needs. They were fully aware of the part played by the Indian monetary system in keeping both the British and the international monetary systems in equilibrium.[3]

When silver prices began to slump, the conflict of interests that rent the expatriate commercial community and the Raj became more acute. As early as 1875, a report to the British government stressed the need to adopt a gold standard in India. In 1878, the Indian government submitted a proposal to close the mints to silver coinage, in order to induce the rupee to rise to 2 shillings. The proposal was studied by an ad hoc committee but was rejected in 1879. Over the next ten years, the Government of India continually urged Britain to allow her to adopt a gold standard; and in 1886 there was an official request to authorize the closing of Indian mints to silver coinage. But the India Office was adamant. Silver had fallen from 48*d.* to 45*d.* in one year; but in that decade the power of the British commercial community was unchallenged. Exchange stability was therefore unthinkable for the rupee. Continuous currency depreciation—it was authoritatively argued—was the only remedy against worldwide falling prices, the only way of keeping Indian exports competitive in world markets.

After the failure of the official silver price support policy of the United States government and the forced demobilization of the speculative positions of the 'silver corner', silver quotations, as has been noted, crashed. In 1892 the London price had fallen to 39*d.* So the Government of India reiterated its request to reinforce the rupee by closing the Indian mints to silver coinage—as had been done, for the same reason, in Austria-Hungary. The Secretary of State for India decided to submit the proposal to a committee, to which he appointed, among others, Sir Reginald Welby, General Richard Strachey, and Bertram Currie—two financial experts and an 'old India hand'.[4] The committee's report was published on 31 May 1893. Without doubt it is the most lucid pre-Keynesian document on Indian monetary problems. The clarity of its analysis and the honesty of its approach to the problem are remarkable, particularly when compared to the sycophancy of later, similar documents. Seen in the light of the conflict of interests between British merchants and the Raj, it clearly emerges as a document inspired by a 'public' vision of Britain's responsibilities toward India.

The report began by noting, without beating about the bush, that the basic problem with the Indian monetary system stemmed from the fact that:

> The Government of India have yearly to remit a large sum to this country in discharge of their gold obligations. In 1873–4, before the fall [of silver] commenced, the amount remitted was £13,285,678, which at a rate of exchange of $1s.\frac{10}{351}d.$, was represented by RX 14,265,700. During last year [1892–3] the amount remitted was £16,532,215, which, at the average rate of exchange in that year, viz.

$1s.\frac{2}{895}d.$ required payment of RX 26,478,415. If this could have
been remitted at the exchange of 1873-4 it would have needed only
RX 17,751,920. The difference is thus RX 8,726,495 (p. 7).

The Government of India's difficulties were made worse,
the report hastened to add, by the fact that the fall in the exchange
rate had brought protests from the government's own employees,
both civil and military. They received their salaries in rupees,
and asked for compensation for the losses suffered from the
fall. Many of these officials, the report noted, had families to
keep, and children to educate, in England—to whom they had
to send gold. Several private companies had already agreed to
similar requests from their employees. Up to that moment—the
report went on to say—the difference between the value of the
rupee and that of gold had been financed out of increased taxes;
in particular, a tax on salt had been introduced. Thus the weight
of fiscal imposition had been transferred from the shoulders of
one class of Indians to those of another, the poorer class, who
already suffered the greatest from the increases of rupee prices
due to the falling exchange rate. In fact, the report noted, if
price increases were followed by a slower increase of wages,
they would necessarily harm the working classes.

The committee asserted that, if silver kept falling, the
additional rupees needed to remit unchanged amounts of gold
could certainly not be obtained by stiffer taxes. Land-tax rates
were either fixed or could be reviewed only every thirty years.
Income tax (which hit only those incomes above middle-class
level) would need to be doubled to supply the necessary
amount—which would 'produce great discontent amongst those
who are capable of appreciating and criticising the actions of the
Government, and of promoting agitation when they are
prejudicially affected' (p.15). 'Representations that a great
increase of taxation was due to what has been erroneously called
the "tribute" paid to this country would add sensibly to the
danger, and afford an inviting scheme for agitators,' the
committee warned openly (p. 15). Even if a falling exchange rate
for the rupee were to stimulate exports, the committee considered
that this would not benefit India as a whole—although it could

temporarily benefit the entrepreneur at the expense of the labourer since wages rose more slowly than prices. Exports had been no less when the rupee had been stable than when it had fallen. It was also contended that exchange rate stability discouraged British investment from going to India; but this again, said the committee, was contradicted by experience. The committee also recorded the feeling of many that 'by making silver the standard and keeping the Indian mints open to silver the Anglo-Indian Government have attracted to India that depreciating metal, and have thus made India purchase, at a comparatively high cost, an enormous quantity of it which is now of less value than when it was bought' (p. 13).

And it went on to note that since a large part of the savings of Indian peasants were represented by silver trinkets, by closing the mints to that metal, the value of coins in terms of silver trinkets would increase, and the Indian *ryot* would lose much of his savings.

Weighing all the elements that it had found relevant to the controversy, the committee concluded by expressing itself in favour of a closure of the mints to private silver coinage. It supported this proposal by noting that Austria, which had applied comparable measures, had seen her currency fall in the twenty years from 1875 (the year of the closure) to 1892 from 100 to 92.98, while the rupee had, in the same period, fallen from 100 to 67.04.

But while the committee supported such a closure, it qualified its support of the introduction of the gold standard in India by the condition that gold should *not* be introduced into that country's circulation. A gold currency was not a necessary requisite of the gold standard; the experience of many countries showed that clearly. For a country like India, which did not have a well-developed banking system, a gold circulation would have represented a heavy and unnecessary economic sacrifice: the lack of any widespread use of banking cheques would have meant that huge quantity of gold would be required for everyday use.

Having obtained the authoritative support of the committee, the Government of India forged ahead with its plan, and closed the mints to private silver coinage in 1893. American pressure at the Brussells Conference did not succeed in changing this official British policy in India. A small concession to pure gold standard supporters was made in the form of an order to the treasuries in India to accept payment in gold sovereigns at the rate of 15 rupees to 1 sovereign. But, as Keynes later pointed out, the mints' closure had been ordered by law, while the second measure was merely an administrative measure which could be repealed *ad libitem.*

The law of 1895, then, sanctioned the priority of British interest over Anglo-Indian commercial interest. A trend was thus set which would have maintained until 1914; but when gold was discovered in South Africa, Britain again stepped in actively to manipulate Indian monetary affairs. Between 1893 and 1898, the Government of India had carried on with its programme of monetary stabilization. In addition to the already mentioned closure of the mints to private silver, the Indian government had refrained from coining silver rupees itself. The rupee began to rise in terms of sterling; by 1898 it had reached 1*s*. 4*d*. This revaluation caused Anglo-Indian merchants to protest angrily. At the same time, Indian public opinion was in favour of an early introduction of gold into circulation, a measure which was seen as a means to partial liberation from British financial domination. The imperial government appointed another commission,[5] which pronounced in favour of a gold money supply for India. British financial circles, headed by Lord Rothschild, had expressed their approval of such a measure.[6] As has been seen, gold had begun to flow from the Rand to London in ever-increasing quantity, and the possibility that the market might be glutted, and the price may fall, seemed every day to become more real. The Imperial government accepted the commission's proposal, and therefore ordered that sovereign be freely coined in India at a rate of 16 rupees to 1 sovereign. Accordingly, in 1900, Sir Clinton Dawkins, permanent under-secretary to the Treasury, declared that a branch of the Royal Mint would be established at Bombay to coin sovereigns. In the same year, the Gold Standard Reserve was established, which would receive the profits made by the Government of India on

silver rupee coinage and would also serve as a necessary buffer
stock to gold circulation.

Gold circulation was, however, to remain but a pipe dream
in India, at least before 1914. Soon after the British government
had approved its implementation, the Boer War broke out. The
Boer War represented for sterling a real watershed. Confidence
in London, the *sanctum sanctorum* of international finance, began
to falter, which had immediate repercussions for Indian monetary
affairs. As the Bank of England's gold reserve fell to an all-time
low, the decision to introduce gold into Indian circulation began
to look peculiarly ill-timed. Had it been implemented, a
considerable quantity of gold would have flowed to India from
London or elsewhere. It was imperative that the decision be
postponed; so the Treasury and the director of the Royal Mint
engaged in subtle dilatory tactics. Their correspondence with
the India Office on the subject, subsequently published, makes
interesting reading. At the time when Sir Clinton Dawkins had
made his declaration, the Indian government had conducted an
experiment: it had put five million pounds of sovereigns into
circulation in India, following the advice of the 1898 Commission.
This experiment had been carefully monitored by those who
saw the Bank of England reserve falling to a dangerously low
level. On 15 August 1899, the deputy director of the Royal Mint
had already opposed the idea of opening a Bombay branch to
coin gold: he compared the scheme with the mints that had been
opened in Australia, emphasizing that the motive for opening
them was the finding of gold in Australia and they had never
been intended to mint coins for internal use in Australia, but
only for export. Gold production in India being scarcely one-
tenth of what it was in Australia, the reasons that had motivated
the establishment of mints in Australia were not applicable to
India. There was consequently no need to open a mint at
Bombay. The deputy director's opinions were, however,
overruled, and the above-mentioned declaration was made.
Preparations began for the construction of the Bombay mint.
But the deputy director was undeterred; he ordered that
construction work be suspended, as he expressed differences of
opinion with the engineers over the size and location of the Mint

Building. On this subject, a thick file of correspondence between London and Delhi built up in the course of the next year. Then in May 1901, the deputy director, fearing that technical difficulties might at last be overcome, opened fire directly on the validity of the project. He wrote that much had changed in the two years that had elapsed. The gold standard now had a strong foothold in India, so there was no longer any need for the Indian government to press its intention of making gold the main monetary standard. Moreover, India produced less gold than had been expected, and sovereigns freely flowed in from abroad when needed; so the personnel of the proposed Bombay Mint 'would have been kept idle for the greater part of the year, at considerable cost to the Indian Treasury'. But his arguments failed to convince Lord George Hamilton, the Secretary of State for India, who ordered that work on the Mint should continue. In justification, the Treasury reproduced an almost exact replica of its previous arguments. Meanwhile, gold-mine owners in southern India, tired of witnessing this lengthy exercise in inter-departmental prevarication, negotiated long-term contracts with London gold merchants to deliver their produce to that market. When this fact was brought to the attention of the India Office, the latter could only reply by postponing their project indefinitely; the Secretary of State issued an order to that effect in February 1903, without deigning to provide any explanation of his sudden *volte-face*.

The British treasury had thus brilliantly achieved its objectives; at the same time, another event took place which was to make the Indian monetary system rely even more heavily on a gold exchange standard. It will be remembered that a Gold Standard Reserve had been established. By December 1901, it had amassed £3,447,317, of which £2,439,093 in gold was held in India and £1,008,424 in British government stock was held in England (see Table 7.1). At the end of the first quarter of 1902, however, the whole Reserve was transferred to London and invested in British government securities.[7] The British authorities then used it to buttress the fall in the price of Consols resulting from the financial demands of the Boer War.

Table 7.1 Levels, composition, and location of the Indian Gold Standard Reserve (in sterling)

	In England				In India			Total in England and India
	Securities at market values	Cash lent at short notice	Gold held at the Bank of England	Total	Loans and credits	Gold	Silver	
Dec. 1901	1,008,424			1,008,424		2,439,093		3,447,571
Dec. 1902	3,467,372			3,467,372	2,005	260,771		3,730,148
Dec. 1903	3,900,794			3,900,794	295,698	323,417		4,519,909
Dec. 1904	6,951,743	499,605		7,451,347	76,740	200,416		7,728,503
Dec. 1905	9,898,999			9,898,999	97,434	240,000		10,236,433
Dec. 1906	11,910,061			11,910,061	3,520,723		69,540	15,509,324
Dec. 1907	13,208,489	13,810		13,222,299	60,044	263,349	4,000,000	17,545,692
Dec. 1908	5,104,078			5,104,078	1,000,310		11,991,749	18,096,137
Dec. 1909	10,450,141	1,017,192		11,467,333	2,000,344		4,786,734	18,254,411
Dec. 1910	14,513,878	1,437,425		15,951,303			2,534,302	18,485,605
Dec. 1911	15,958,904	973,434		16,932,338			1,934,362	18,886,640
Dec. 1912	15,965,149	1,013,690	250,000	17,228,839			3,745,667	20,974,506

Source: Royal Commission on Indian Finance and Currency, Cmd. 7070, Appendix III, p. 97, HMSO, London, 1913.

This measure marked the beginning of the most interesting phase in the monetary affairs of pre-war British India: the management of Indian financial policy passed into the firm grip of the India Office, which transformed it into a docile instrument of British monetary policy.

It is worth recalling that, from 1900 to 1914, the Indian economy experienced remarkable growth. In 1893–4, Indian exports had been £70,877,900 (see Table 7.2). By 1902–03 they had grown to £85,877,900; and by 1912–13 they had become £164,364,800. Indian visible imports, while doubling in the same period, remained steady at two-thirds of exports. Since the Indian trade surplus had grown so much, it became essential for British governmental and financial circles to make sure it was properly financed. The difficulty lay in making India absorb £40–60 million worth of British financial instruments every year (when Bank of England gold reserves never reached £35 million). As we have shown above, India's foreign trade was structured so that it realized a large deficit with Britain but a large surplus with the rest of the world; it was thus a basic element in the balancing of Britain's international accounts. By preventing India from transforming her annual surplus into gold reserves, the India Office contributed in no small way towards keeping British interest rates lower than would otherwise have been the case. The mechanism worked as follows: in 1902, as seen, the Gold Standard Reserve was changed into British government securities—Treasury Bills, Exchequer Bonds, Consols. This trend continued until 1914. British government securities in the Gold Standard Reserve's portfolio grew from £3.5 million (at market value) in the first quarter of 1902 to £16 million in the first quarter of 1912. In addition, the India Office began to place money from the Gold Standard Reserve, at call and at short notice, with finance houses in the City of London. This began in 1908, when £1,131,223 sterling was so deposited which grew to a maximum of three million in the first quarter of 1910—only to diminish to £1,500,000 sterling in later years. Throughout those fifteen years, the prices of British government securities fell continually, which caused a net capital loss for the Gold Standard Reserve of India. Moreover, the maximum rate of interest on funds lent to the City was

2 per cent.[8] It is valuable to bear in mind that the greater part of those funds was lent to leading banking houses, whose most eminent representatives formed the Financial Committee advising the Secretary of State for India on these very matters; prime commercial paper was held as collateral, as was the practice in Lombard banking. Thus English banks were able to borrow from the India Office at 2 per cent and reinvest on the London market at 3 per cent. But this was not all. The Indian government's broker, a private firm in charge of such transactions, was paid a commission that increased proportionately as these transactions grew in size. During the period in question, the broker amassed revenue to the amount indicated in Table 7.3.

To this mass of money flowing from India to London through the management of the Gold Standard Reserve should be added the money accruing from the permanent Indian surplus. After 1893, the value of the rupee had become stable, mainly as a result of the above-mentioned measures. It became essential to British interests that it did not follow the logic of exchange, and thus increase in value *vis-à-vis* sterling as the trade surplus grew. Several stratagems were devised to prevent it from doing so. First, silver was sold to India, to the tune of £4 million a year for ten years. By putting into circulation rupees of fixed silver content, the Indian government realized the remarkable profits that enabled it to accumulate and invest the Gold Standard Reserve. A good share of the surplus was, despite all efforts by the British, transferred into sovereigns and gold bars, while about 50 per cent was financed by imports of Council Bills—a device which was extensively used by the India Office to keep the rupee on a stable course.[9] It was a system which had been devised previously but which only came into its own during our period. As we have seen, the Indian government was continually obliged to transfer sums to London in gold to pay the Home Charges;[10] they had therefore to find that gold. In order to get it, they sold in the City bills that entitled the buyer to an equivalent sum available, in rupees, in India. These bills were usually bought by importers of Indian products, who used them to make payments in India. However, it was convenient for them to buy bills only when their gold price was lower than the cost of making payments by shipping gold—the alternative method. Initially, the price of Council Bills was determined by their supply, which was in turn strictly limited to the value of the British payments the Government of India had to make. But after the rupee was stabilized, and the Indian trade surplus had begun to grow, that close correlation was broken. Although the Indian government never needed more than £15 million for its British payments in the ten years before 1914, the India Office during the same period sold £241 million worth of Council Bills (if we exclude the fiscal years 1907–08 and 1908–09, when the rate of exchange of the rupee fell following a check in Indian exports owing to the world slump, we find that £220 million worth of Council Bills were sold, against gold requirements of £120 million, which Keynes estimated the Government of India would need over eight years).

This difference between the gold requirements and the actual sales of Council Bills is explained by the India Office's policy of pegging the rupee's exchange rate. Council Bills were sold in weekly auctions at the Bank of England; and the proceeds of those sales were deposited with the Bank, which was also banker to the Government of India. By selling an appropriate quantity of Council Bills, the Secretary of State for India succeeded in preventing the export of gold to that country, since the low price of the bills would make it advantageous to use them for payments in India. The Bank of England, saddled with a host of difficulties depended heavily on the arrangement it had with the government of India, particularly when the latter's account reached huge dimensions after disproportionate sales of Council Bills. The account was therefore eminently stable, and the sums deposited in it could be used by the Bank for ordinary commercial lending, which led to handsome profits. So when the India Office began to lend money to City finance houses, the Bank of England staged what amounted to an open rebellion against the move. The then governor, Mr Cole, harshly criticized it in his evidence to the Royal Commission on Indian Finance and Currency. The decision, he said, played havoc with the Bank's efforts to keep the money markets in equilibrium. Moreover, he added, lending to institutions other than the Bank of England meant a lower revenue for the Government of India;[11] he did not, however, condescend to explain the reasoning behind this claim. The 2 per cent interest rate the India Office received in the City was not the ruling rate, but it was 2 per cent more than could be got from the Bank of England, which paid no interest on deposits.

The management by the India Office of Indian monetary affairs, in the decade before the Great War, generally elicited violent criticism from all sides. As we have seen, the Bank of England openly voiced its dislike. In India, British merchants and industrialists were no less despondent. In a period of prosperity such as India had never known in the recent past, they could not bear the country to be kept in a state of financial underdevelopment just to suit financial interests in the metropolis. At every harvest season, Indian interest rates would shoot up to unbearable levels. Moreover, they opposed what was considered undue government interference in their affairs, especially as far as taxes were concerned. They considered fiscal pressure to be unduly high, in view of the fact that the Indian government's budget was every year in surplus and the country had a trade surplus year after year; in addition to which the government had a substantial credit balance, as shown in Table 7.4. Indian public opinion was equally at odds with India Office monetary policies. They thought it was in contrast with high fiscal pressure; they also realized the advantage, from the point of view of national sovereignty, of a pure gold standard over the gold exchange standard which India had been given. Nor did they understand how it could benefit India to drain her resources in order to send money to a country which invested all over the world. For the Indian bourgeoisie, the gold standard became a nationalistic and anti-imperialistic slogan.[12]

The India Office's conduct of Indian monetary affairs was at the centre of one of the gravest political and financial scandals in English social history. In 1912, the Government of India, through the India Office, secretly bought a very large quantity of silver, using the services of Samuel Montagu & Co., the largest bullion broker in the City. The secrecy of the operation was intended to prevent the speculative price rises that would inevitably have taken place if the Indian government's intention had been made public. But, as Keynes wrote, 'The head of that firm was unfortunately tied by close family links to the Under-Secretary of State for India'. After the scandal exploded, the whole financial policy of the India Office was subjected to violent criticism in the House of Commons, in the press, and in India. Those who had brought the scandal to light were not, perhaps, uninterested in bringing down Lloyd George's reformist Cabinet. The government was compelled to appoint a Royal Commission to inquire into the matter. But their report, published on the eve of war, did not receive much attention; there were graver matters in hand. The report expressed the Commission's unqualified approval of the conduct of the India Office and its warm support of the gold exchange standard as the system best suited to India. The report, and the evidence accompanying it, presented an account of Indian monetary history in minute detail, together with the opinions of a large number of experts. My account of the story has been no more than a reading of those documents in a different light.

Table 7.2 *Balance of payments of India (in sterling, excl. government transactions)*

	1893–4	1894–5	1895–6	1896–7	1897–8	1898–9	1899–1900	1900–1901	1901–02	1902–03
Gross merchandise										
Exports	70,965,100	72,543,300	76,174,900	69,276,300	65,024,800	75,147,600	72,650,800	71,579,300	82,976,600	85,877,900
Imports	49,304,600	46,778,300	46,211,100	47,943,100	46,177,800	45,586,900	47,141,200	50,851,900	54,346,000	52,525,300
Net exports surplus	21,660,500	25,765,000	29,963,800	21,333,100	18,847,000	29,560,700	25,509,600	20,727,400	28,680,600	33,352,600
Export surplus as % of import	44	55	65	44	41	65	54	41	53	64
Financing of surplus										
I British govt. Securities	1,178,200	359,700	–1,149,800	856,100	1,705,300	45,000	414,900	–908,300	1,212,700	1,152,500
Silver, bars and coin	9,172,800	4,250,000	4,400,500	3,905,600	5,622,400	2,648,200	2,379,200	949,100	4,169,800	4,151,000
Gold bars	—	—	—	—	—	1,321,900	978,700	146,500	—	898,900
Total I	10,351,000	4,609,700	3,250,700	4,761,700	7,327,700	4,015,100	3,772,800	187,300	5,382,500	6,702,400
II Imports of Council Bills	9,960,200	15,770,500	18,742,200	15,170,500	9,472,700	18,833,900	18,703,800	18,824,500	18,535,800	18,724,000
Imports of sovereigns	427,500	–3,316,100	1,684,000	1,527,400	3,272,300	3,013,700	5,315,000	4,897,200	3,363,300	5,413,900
Total II	10,387,700	12,454,400	20,426,200	16,697,900	12,745,000	21,897,600	24,018,800	23,721,700	21,899,100	24,137,900

Contd.

Table 7.2 contd.

	1903–04	1904–05	1905–06	1906–07	1907–08	1908–09	1909–10	1910–11	1911–12	1912–13
Gross merchandise:										
Exports	101,973,000	105,000,400	107,806,700	117,713,300	118,240,000	102,020,000	125,253,000	139,921,300	151,896,100	164,364,800
Imports	56,548,900	64,452,200	68,720,000	72,206,700	86,600,000	90,846,700	78,040,000	86,236,000	92,383,200	107,343,900
Net export surplus	45,424,100	40,548,200	39,086,700	45,506,600	31,640,000	21,173,300	47,213,000	53,685,300	59,212,900	57,020,900
Export surplus as % of imports	80	63	57	63	37	26	60	62	64	53
Financing of surplus										
I British govt. securities	996,200	215,500	253,300	–33,300	840,000	533,300	–520,000	1,620,000	706,700	non-disposable
Silver bars and coin	4,476,900	4,625,000	3,346,700	4,460,000	6,686,700	7,973,300	6,246,700	5,738,800	3,528,800	4,382,500
Gold bars	2,428,200	3,498,300	3,413,300	4,906,700	5,133,300	2,273,300	5,240,000	7,610,900	6,712,700	7,280,800
Total I	8,401,300	8,338,800	7,613,300	9,333,400	12,660,000	10,779,900	10,966,700	14,969,700	10,948,200	—
II Imports of Council Bills	23,874,500	24,150,000	31,800,000	33,646,700	15,640,100	5,346,700	27,820,000	26,286,700	26,780,000	25,874,700
Imports of sovereigns	8,457,500	8,577,300	2,886,900	4,953,300	6,643,300	866,700	9,213,300	8,374,900	18,465,500	17,771,600
Total II	32,332,000	32,727,300	34,686,900	38,600,000	22,073,300	6,213,400	37,033,300	34,661,600	42,245,500	43,646,300

Source: Royal Commission on Indian Finance and Currency, *Interim Report*, Cmd. 7070, HMSO, London, 1913.

Table 7.3   Transactions of the Government of India in the London money market and broker's commission expenses

	Treasury balance short-term loans			Deposits with banks			Gold standard reserve short-term loans			Deposits with banks			Total	
	Gross amount	Commission	Net amount	Gross amount	Commission	Net amount	Gross amount	Commission	Net amount	Gross amount	Commission	Net amount	Gross amount	Broker's commission
1893–4	10,293	515	9,778										10,293	515
1894–5	3,373	169	3,204										3,373	169
1895–6	9,650	482	9,168										9,650	482
1896–7	34,435	1,722	32,713										34,435	1,722
1897–8	20,772	1,039	19,733										20,772	1,039
1898–9	30,562	1,528	29,034										30,562	1,528
1899–1900	51,384	2,569	48,815										51,384	2,569
1900–1901	59,114	2,955	56,159										59,114	2,955
1901–02	79,651	3,983	75,668										79,651	3,983
1902–03	145,306	7,266	138,040										145,306	7,266
1903–04	140,038	7,002	133,036										140,038	7,002
1904–05	168,398	8,420	159,978										168,398	8,420
1905–06	218,185	10,909	207,276										218,185	10,909
1906–07	209,656	10,361	199,295										209,656	10,361
1907–08	137,698	6,596	131,102										137,698	6,596
1908–09	49,669	2,432	47,237				1,270	64					50,939	2,496
1909–10	128,163	6,336	121,837	8,236	83		8,550	428		11,640	116		156,679	6,963
1910–11	254,685	12,819	241,866	122,236	1,222		6,380	234		44,844	448		428,145	14,723
1911–12	249,755	6,914	242,841	134,558	1,346		500	15		34,025	340		418,838	8,615
1912–13	280,335	5,908	274,427	98,730	987		18,745	311		21,826	218		419,636	7,424
Total	2,281,122	99,925	2,181,197	363,850	3,638		35,445	1,052		112,335	1,122		2,792,752	105,737

Source: Royal Commission on Indian Finance and Currency, Interim Report, App. xi, p. 318, Cmd. 7070, HMSO, London, 1913.

Table 7.4 *Net credit balance of the Government of India on 31 March*
(excluding the Gold Standard Reserve and taking into account the balance in India
at the £ stg=15 Rupees exchange rate)

	In India	In England
1893	10,181,171	2,268,385
1894	17,043,725	1,300,564
1895	15,019,659	2,503,114
1896	11,000,340	3,393,798
1897	9,249,168	2,832,354
1898	10,654,962	2,534,244
1899	11,177,669	3,145,768
1900	8,425,827	3,330,943
1901	8,767,687	4,091,926
1902	11,880,301	6,693,137
1903	12,081,388	5,767,787
1904	11,702,394	7,294,782
1905	10,597,770	10,262,581
1906	11,494,578	8,436,519
1907	10,026,932	5,606,812
1908	12,851,413	4,607,266
1909	10,235,483	7,983,898
1910	12,295,428	12,799,094
1911	13,566,922	16,696,990
1912	12,279,689	18,390,013
1913	19,543,900	8,372,900

Source: Royal Commission on Indian Finance and Currency, *Interim Report*,
App. II, p. 74, Cmd. 7070, HMSO, London, 1913.

Notes

1. On the establishment of the silver standard in India, see, 1915,
   S. V. Doraiswami's perceptive book *Indian Finance, Currency and
   Banking* (Mylapore), pp. 1–20.
2. And contemporary observers, from the Indian Currency
   Committee of 1895 to Alfred Marshall, saw it in these terms. The
   evidence given by Marshall to the Gold and Silver Commission,

and to the Indian Currency Committee of 1898, is particularly noteworthy. On the second occasion, Marshall clearly identified the conflicting interests of the Indian government and of the exporters.

3. See J. M. Keynes, 1913, *Indian Currency and Finance* (London), and Basil Blackett's unpublished memorandum in the Public Record Office (Treasury Files T. 170/19).

4. *Report of the Committee Appointed to Inquire into the Indian Currency*, HMSO, London, 1893. It is generally known as the 'Herschell Committee' as Lord Herschell, the Lord Chancellor, was its chairman.

5. The Indian Currency Committee, appointed in 1898 under Fowler's chairmanship.

6. In his evidence to the committee, Alfred Marshall also expressed his approval, although with the inevitable qualifications which always accompanied his utterances. He considered that a *stable* monetary standard favoured the expansion of trade, and made it clear that exporters were certainly favoured by progressive depreciation, but exports were not necessarily encouraged (op. cit., p. 301). He also declared himself against the introduction of gold into Indian circulation. He clearly understood that the majority of the countries which had gone on the gold standard had already transformed it into a gold exchange standard, by buying foreign short-term securities to build a first line of defence around their gold reserves (op. cit., p. 303).

7. Marshall stated: 'When one country invests into another country's securities, I call that lending to the other country' (op. cit., p. 316).

8. This fact emerges from the interesting evidence given by M. de Webb, President of the Karachi Chamber of Commerce, to the Royal Commission on Indian Finance and Currency: Cmd. 7070, HMSO, London, 1913, Appendix xxi, p. 550 ff. De Webb, an English *piednoir*, was interested in an independent Indian monetary system; being himself an entrepreneur in India, he consequently thought that an independent monetary system would allow him to borrow money in India at less prohibitive interest rates. He also considered the high taxation rate imposed by the Indian government to be totally unjustified, in view of its ability to show a budget surplus every year.

Since 1908, de Webb maintained that London merchant bankers and stockbrokers had borrowed very high sums from the India

Office. He gave a detailed list of borrowers and the sums they had borrowed; the idea was—so de Webb considered—to establish permanent credit lines at short-term interest rates. He also gave a detailed list of joint-stock banks which had borrowed from the Indian government at rates lower than the market rates.

De Webb's evidence reveals the tendency towards independence that was developing among the British in India, just as it had done in the Dominions. On that tendency, see also S. B. Saul, 1960, *Studies in British Overseas Trade, 1870–1914* (Liverpool).

9. On the mechanism of Council Bill transactions, the classic is Keynes, 1913, *Indian Currency and Finance,* p. 102 ff, which was largely duplicated in the *Final Report* of the Royal Commission on Indian Finance and Currency.

10. The Home Charges had experienced a considerable increase in value. As regards their legitimacy, it is amusing to read Marshall's evidence to the Indian Currency Committee of 1898. Marshall maintained that India had found in British rule a cheaper form of government than any other she could have: 'Were it an expensive Government,' he stated, ' I think our presence in India would not be justifiable' (op. cit., p. 291). It should also be remembered, he continued, that 'For instance, we export to India a great number of prime young men. If their value were capitalised, as it would be if they were slaves, it would be several thousands of pounds apiece. We bring them back afterwards, if they come back at all, more or less shrivelled and worn out. Those are vast unreckoned exports. India complains she sends us a tribute of goods for which we have given no return. We have given a return for many of them in the shape of men in the prime of life, who on the whole, I think are very cheap for the purpose' (op. cit., pp. 312–13).

11. See the evidence given by Cole, Governor of the Bank of England, to the Royal Commission on Indian Finance and Currency, and Blackett's previously mentioned unpublished memorandum.

12. For an expression of this state of mind, see Doraiswami, 1915, *Indian Finance, Currency and Banking;* and also S. K. Sarma, 1911, *Indian Monetary Problems* (Madras). It is interesting to note that at the time of the great depreciation of silver, Indian 'responsible public opinion'—to use the words of the Herschell Committee— had passionately fought for the free coinage of silver. For further information on Indian monetary affairs, and for other views

than those expressed here, see D. Tripathi, 1966, 'The Silver Question: India and America', *Journal of Indian History;* K. N. Chaudhuri, 1968, 'India's International Economy in the Nineteenth Century: A Historical Survey', *Modern Asian Studies* (reprinted as chapter 2 in this volume); and D. Rothermund, 1970, 'An Aspect of the Monetary Policy of British Imperialism', *Indian Economic and Social History Review.*

8

Britain and the Indian
Currency Crisis, 1930–2*

B. R. Tomlinson

The early 1930s were crucial years in the development of the
imperial relationship between Britain and India. Previous
accounts of the period have seen this in predominantly political
terms and have concentrated on the narrow process of
constitutional reform that culminated in the 1935 Government
of India Act.[1] The origins of this Act are certainly an important
subject, but one that cannot be properly understood without a
wider knowledge of the priorities and concerns of British policy-
makers for India and the Empire over a wide range of issues.
Part of the larger context needed for such a study can be seen
through an analysis of the causes, course, and consequences of
the Indian currency crisis of 1930–2.

Many aspects of the relationship between Britain and India
were altered by the Great Depression of the early 1930s and its
political consequences. For example, as has been pointed out,

* Previously published in the *Economic History Review,* Second Series, 32, 1
 (February 1979), pp. 88–99. The research on which this article is based has
 been supported by grants from Trinity College, Cambridge, and the Social
 Science Research Council. Earlier versions of this article were given as
 seminar papers at the Institute of Commonwealth Studies, London, in
 November 1975 and at the Delhi School of Economics in August 1976. I am
 grateful to all the members of these seminars, and especially to Professor
 L. S. Pressnell, Professor I. M. Drummond, Dr Susan Howson, and Dr John
 Toye for their help and encouragement.

this period was one in which the attitude of British policy-makers towards the problem of maintaining sales of Lancashire cotton goods in India underwent a fundamental change, with the carrot of bilateral consultation being substituted for the stick of imperial command.[2] It was also the period in which important questions about the financial relationship between Britain and India and the monetary link between sterling and the rupee were at last dragged into the open although, in the event, they were then dodged rather than faced squarely.

The decision of the British government in September 1931 to take sterling off the gold standard and to impose a sterling standard on the rupee was momentous in itself. It is also important as illustrative of one important aspect of the imperial relationship. The year 1931 was the occasion for one of the last acts of naked aggression, so beloved for propaganda purposes by Indian nationalists, by the British government against the government of India. Despite the protests and threatened resignations of the Viceroy and the whole of his Executive Council, Whitehall imposed a harsh budget and a rigid monetary policy on India. These events seemed to support nationalist accusations that Indian monetary policy was designed solely to advance the interests of Britain, and that London's claims to be about to confer greater autonomy on the Government of India in a new constitutional settlement were transparently false. They also gave rise to new indictments—that the rupee was being manipulated to prop up sterling and to expropriate the gold of the Indian peasant for the Bank of England.

This chapter investigates the policies and actions of the British and Indian governments during the currency crisis of 1930–2 in an attempt to separate fact from fiction on these points. A close analysis of the episode will also help to throw light on the underlying purpose of British rule in India, a purpose which had to be maintained in any new constitutional settlement. Further, the story of British policy in the Indian currency crisis of the early 1930s will illuminate aspects of Britain's relationship with areas of the empire/commonwealth at a time when a distinct sterling area was beginning to emerge from the wreckage of the revivalist free-trade Empire of the 1920s.

I

The Indian currency crisis of 1930–2 was a crisis of confidence in the rupee. Political uncertainly and economic depression stimulated a flight of capital from India and a decline in the market for her export staples, thus putting increasing pressure on the established exchange rate of Re 1 = 1s. 6d. The impact on the exchange rate of the world depression in commodity prices, which turned the terms of trade against India, sapped its balance-of-payments surplus in commodities and depressed internal prices, was aggravated by the British government's advertised policy of introducing sweeping reforms in the structure of central government. The mere mention of such reforms caused concern to overseas holders of rupees because, it was widely believed, the transfer of control over monetary policy to an Indian minister responsible to an elected central assembly (a likely result of a new Government of India Act) would lead to a deliberate devaluation of the rupee to 1s. 4d. at best and a generally inflationary monetary policy which might well push the ratio lower still.

The problem which faced the Indian currency authorities in 1930 and 1931 was how to relieve the pressure on the rupee exchange rate, either by restoring confidence in the future management of Indian monetary affairs, or by devaluing to increase the competitiveness of Indian goods in world markets and to counteract the impact of Depression on the internal economy. Neither of these alternatives was practicable without support from London, for it was the British government that would decide the shape of future constitutional reforms and because India's foreign currency reserves were not adequate to defend a policy of deliberate devaluation without extra help from the Bank of England or the British Treasury.

By 1930 the British government had certainly become concerned about the Indian currency crisis. But the priorities of London-based policy-makers were not necessarily the same as those of their counterparts in New Delhi. So far as London was concerned, the central problem of the Indian currency crisis was ensuring the payment of the government of India's obligations in the United Kingdom, especially of the interest on the Indian sterling public debt and of the Home Charges (the cost of the upkeep of the India Office and the pay, pensions, leave allowances, and training costs of Indian military and civilian service personnel).

The government of India's sterling debt of over £350 million, and its Home Charges of approximately £30 million a year, had to be serviced and paid from revenue raised in India in rupees and then converted into sterling and remitted to London. The government of India was the largest dealer on the Indian foreign-exchange market. To meet its obligations in London, the government of India needed to secure an adequate income in India and to purchase enough sterling remittance with rupees thus raised. If sufficient revenue were not forthcoming, the government of India had to borrow in India, or the Secretary of State for India had to borrow in London, to make ends meet. If, for any reason, the government of India could not purchase enough remittance, there were a number of options open. Gold or silver could be shipped from the official reserves and sold in London. The secretary of state could borrow on the London market. A proportion of the Indian currency reserves was held in London in sterling and transfers from the government of India to the Secretary of State could be made through them by cancelling currency notes in India, thus creating a surplus in the London currency reserves which could be used as revenue.

None of these alternatives to normal remittance was looked on with much favour. Excessive borrowing by the secretary of state was thought to be prejudicial to India's credit-rating abroad. Shipping gold from the reserves in India was never a practicable proposition, since Indian commercial and political opinion was united in a desire to build up the gold reserves in anticipation of India's moving from her gold-bullion standard to a full gold-standard system. Silver could be shipped at an acceptable political cost, but the world demand was small. Remitting through the reserves was a certain way of transferring cash from India to London, and was used extensively,[3] but it was expensive both politically and financially. Many Indian businessmen and politicians were convinced that the rupee was overvalued[4] and each time the government contracted the currency in India to release sterling from the reserves in London, it faced a storm of protest. Furthermore, contracting the money supply in India tended to lower prices and raise interest rates, and this in turn could impose a strain on the budgets of central and provincial governments.

II

The winter of 1929–30 was a time of political ferment in India, culminating in December 1929 with the announcement by the leaders of the Indian National Congress of their decision to launch a full-scale agitation against British rule, using currency depreciation, sterling-debt repudiation, and the penalizing of British commercial and financial interests as a major plank in their campaign platform. These events, in conjunction with the depression in the Indian economy, led to a considerable, although unquantifiable, flow of capital out of India.

In normal years an influx of long-term capital was an important factor in balancing India's international account and in providing remittance for the government. Even more important in creating a demand for rupees, and hence in providing sterling remittance for the government of India, was the practice of the foreign exchange banks, which financed almost all of India's international trade, of transferring short-term funds to India during the trading season. This seasonal flow had been augmented, in the late 1920s, by the import of short-term foreign capital for investment in government rupee debt, following the Government of India's deliberate policy of increasing the interest rates on its Treasury bills to attract new sources of finance from overseas. From 1927 onwards this policy had some success, but its result was that when, in 1930, the head offices of the exchange banks became frightened by the deteriorating political situation and began to put pressure on their Indian branches to run down their balances and to obtain immediate cover for every transfer of funds to India, and when other holders of short-term rupee funds also started to withdraw their investments, the flight of capital put both government remittance and the funding of the rupee floating debt in jeopardy.[5]

By 1930 it was clear that the rupee ratio was at risk. Refusing to buy below the lower gold point of $1s. 5\frac{7}{8}d.$ per rupee, the government of India managed to purchase only £15 million worth of remittance between April 1929 and March 1930, and in the next fiscal year it had to sell £300,000 more sterling than it was able to buy. The Secretary of State's commitments in London of £64 million over these two years could only be met by remittance through the currency reserves, running down the home treasury balances, and borrowing in London.[6]

To meet this exchange crisis, the government of India had a number of devices for controlling the supply of currency and credit in India. Weakness in the exchange and failure in remittance were thought to result from inflated, non-competitive prices in India and a surplus of loose money available for currency speculation. Low interest rates in India also meant that those who needed rupees to purchase India's exports found it cheaper to obtain these by borrowing in India than by selling sterling to the government at the fixed exchange rate. The solution was to contract the money supply by remitting through the currency reserves, to issue Treasury bills to mop up floating capital, or to raise the Imperial Bank of India's rate for advances. All these expedients, or any combination of them, would, it was thought, inhibit speculation and, by forcing down Indian prices and raising credit rates, ensure a boost in exports, bring out remittance, and strengthen the exchange.

Unfortunately, the reality of 1930–2 did not match up to the diagnosis implicit in this approach. The technical remedies available to the monetary authorities were designed only to correct imbalances in the internal economy stemming from financial causes, while the origins of the crisis of 1930 were to be found, as the government of India frequently pointed out, in the world economy and the political situation. And even without these special circumstances, the policies available to the Indian monetary authorities were not very effective for shoring up the exchange rate. The absence of a central bank hampered all attempts to manage the Indian economy. Currency contraction tended to be an inefficient way of lowering prices, for it was the accepted policy of the Imperial Bank of India to make advances freely on treasury bills. Thus, when the government issued such bills to finance a contraction of the currency, it was, at the same time, creating sources of credit which would counteract the contraction. It was also extremely difficult for the Indian authorities to devise policies to hold short-term funds in the country. The exchange banks kept a large proportion of their Indian reserves in the form of treasury bills so that, if they wanted funds to remit home, all that they had to do was to cash in these bills on maturity. This, in turn, would create an acute short-term funding problem for the Government of India.

There was one further major difficulty with a policy of contraction as far as the government of India was concerned. Deflation of the domestic economy affected the customs duties, income-tax returns, and land revenue on which central and provincial governments depended for their revenue, and also made it difficult to raise extra money in long- or short-term loans. The only way out of a severe budgetary crisis was to inflate the currency, by the government of India issuing treasury bills to the Paper Currency Reserve and the Controller of Currency paying for these by printing extra notes 'covered' by the increase in securities in the reserve. This device, which an earlier Secretary of the Finance Department had called to 'reach for the morphia syringe',[7] was thought prejudicial to public confidence in the convertibility of the paper currency and was seen to be inflationary. By nullifying the effects of deflation, it further put the rupee exchange at risk.

Despite misgivings, Indian Finance Department officials tackled the currency crisis with the resources they possessed. During 1930 and the early months of 1931, goaded by constant demands from the India Office, the monetary authorities contracted the currency tighter and tighter, and even encouraged the Imperial Bank to impose conditions on the uses to which its advances could be put.[8] Even so, by May 1931 it was clear that the breaking-point had been reached. The Secretary of State was in urgent need of funds, but there seemed to be no way of getting money to him. The rupee was at $1s.5\frac{13}{16}d.$ and no remittance would come out unless it were forced up by another $\frac{1}{8}d.$; a sterling loan in London had just failed and another could not be tried until conditions were more stable. The India Office suggested yet more contraction, but as the government of India pointed out, there were no resources left to effect this and such a policy would increase agrarian distress in India and thus, perhaps, wreck the fragile truce with the nationalists concluded a month earlier.

The Indian authorities were convinced that it was now time to abandon ineffectual technical remedies and to attack the root cause of the problem—the loss of confidence caused by political uncertainty and the world depression in the price of primary produce. Since India's new constitution was being made in London, only the British government could repair the situation. The government of India suggested that the British government should provide a drawing credit for India of £50 million to ease the budgetary problems of the Secretary of State and to show that 'they are prepared to back India financially while the constitutional changes are being considered and initiated'.[9] In early September the Indian Finance Member, George Schuster, suggested a still more radical solution. Using credit from the Bank of England he now proposed to ease the strain on the rupee, raise Indian prices, give a boost to exports, and placate nationalist opinion by devaluing to $1s. 4d.$[10]

In London, the India Office officials were well aware of the effect of political uncertainty on government remittance, but found it easier to diagnose the problem than to cure it. The political considerations were delicate. The confidence of foreign holders of rupees could be restored by providing wide-ranging safeguards over the control of monetary policy in the new Indian constitution, but to insist on these would prejudice the success of the round-table conferences with Indian leaders and might well swell support for nationalist agitations. On the other hand, accommodating Indian opinion by devaluing the rupee would have even more serious consequences. It was thought likely in London that the rupee, once devalued, would sink to near its bullion value of 8d. Such a collapse in the exchange rate would disturb the whole pattern of India's foreign trade and internal economic life and, most importantly, would greatly increase the rupee costs of the government of India's sterling obligations. The central government budget was already in deficit and revenue was hard to increase during a time of depression and currency instability. The only way that the Indian government would be able to meet its internal commitments would be by inflating the currency, which would push the exchange rate lower still. Default on India's sterling debt would be the inevitable result.[11]

During 1930 and early 1931, India Office officials wriggled on the horns of this dilemma. Soothing words were used to salve the wounds. In January 1930 the start of the nationalist campaign of civil disobedience caused a collapse in the price of government of India sterling loan stock on sale on the London market. In consultation with the Treasury, the India Office published an open letter which made it clear that, while India's sterling debt was in no sense guaranteed by Britain, the British government had 'no intention of allowing a state of affairs to arise in India in which repudiation of debt could become a practicable possibility'.[12] A year later, when the Prime Minister was drafting his speech for the end of the first round-table conference, India Office officials, again in alliance with the Treasury, successfully put pressure on MacDonald and Wedgwood Benn (the Secretary of State for India) to specify that essential safeguards would have to be written into any scheme of constitutional reform to ensure that India continued to meet its sterling commitments.[13]

Both these statements of intent increased investment in India's sterling public debt and, by making it possible for the Secretary of State to raise more of his requirements on the London market, eased the remittance problems of the government of India. Yet this did not provide a satisfactory permanent resolution of the larger issues. By May 1931 it was clear to the India Office, as it was to the government of India, that a crisis point had been reached and that some unequivocal decision would have to be made. When the Indian idea of a £50 million drawing credit was sent to them (the amount was shortly afterwards raised to £100 million) the India Office officials took it up with enthusiasm and succeeded in getting the Finance Sub-Committee of the Cabinet Committee on India to agree to it.[14]

This was going too far for the Treasury, however, and, when the proposal came up to the full Cabinet Committee for ratification, the Chancellor of the Exchequer stepped in to bar the way. The Treasury had always refused to consider any proposal for alleviating India's difficulties by 'transferring the burden, even contingently, on to the shoulders of the British taxpayer'[15] and now protested that the 'absurd' proposal for a drawing credit would, in the end, leave the British Exchequer liable for all of India's obligations in London and for all of Australia's as well.[16] In preference to this, the Treasury suggested either abandoning any plans for constitutional reform or else devaluing the rupee without any support or British commitment.[17]

The India Office, as we have already seen, regarded an unsupported devaluation as the shortest road to ruin. In late June 1931, the whole issue was thrashed out in the Cabinet India Committee. The Chancellor still firmly opposed any plan for a drawing credit and urged devaluation in preference to any firm commitment by the British government, but the majority, including the Prime Minister, supported the India Office in finding the consequences of devaluation too horrible to be contemplated and so a compromise was patched up—the British government would make a vague, general statement of support for Indian finance.[18] This was announced by the Prime Minister in the House of Commons on 26 June:

> It will not be possible to introduce the proposed constitutional changes if financial stability is not assured and His Majesty's Government are determined not to allow a state of affairs to arise which might jeopardise the financial stability and good government of India for which the Secretary of State is at present responsible. They have, therefore, decided that, should the need arise, they will apply to Parliament for the authority necessary to enable them to

give financial support under suitable conditions to the Government
of India for the purpose of maintaining the credit of the country.[19]

The India Office had to pay dearly for even this statement.
The Treasury officials hoped that the Prime Minister's
announcement would restore confidence without ever having
to be backed by action, and they insisted that a rigidly
deflationary budget and monetary policy be imposed on India,
and that the Secretary of State's reserves be used to the full,
before Parliament could even be asked to provide assistance.[20]

The Treasury's commitment to the Prime Minister's statement
was always less than wholehearted[21] and it was never decided
what form British assistance might take in practice. Nor was the
statement itself effective in restoring the confidence of holders
of rupees—by August 1931 the flow of capital out of India was
as heavy as ever and the prospects for a new sterling loan were
nil.[22] But the statement did have one vitally important result.
After the end of June 1931, the Treasury officials became
convinced that the exchequer would be unable to avoid providing
compensation for British investors in India's sterling public debt
should the Government of India ever default.[23] Thus, when the
crucial decision about the rupee link to sterling was made in
September 1931, the Treasury now fully supported the India
Office line that no risks could be taken with the rupee ratio.

The drain of capital out of India, and the consequent pressure
on the rupee, began again in August. From January to June, the
Indian authorities had paid out almost £3 million to support the
exchange; in August the 1s. 6d. rate cost a further £4 million, and
in the first three weeks of September a further £5 million.[24] The
Secretary of State's commitments until November could be met
by floating sterling India bills, for which there was still a market,
but between then and March 1932 he would need an estimated
£30 million income (most of it to cover a debt repayment in
January). It did not seem likely that any remittance would be
available, the total currency reserves that could be used were
only £46.8 million (£30 million of them in India) and the home
treasury balances stood at £5.7 million.[25] A new crisis had arisen
and yet, despite the decisions of the previous months, the India

Office reacted to it in the traditional way. The government of India was forced to introduce a deflationary emergency budget and the India Office began to demand that gold be shipped from the Indian currency reserves to London.

September 1931 was, of course, a period of monetary crisis in Britain as well as in India. At the heart of sterling's problems was thought to lie the lack of foreign confidence caused by illiquidity in London, the low reserves of the Bank of England, and the large amounts of British money tied up in short-term loans to poor creditors. In regard to India, the opinion of the British government was now that a falling rupee and a defaulting government would bring the pound and the Empire's financial reputation crashing down with them.[26]

On 19 September it was decided to take sterling off the gold standard. A committee drawn from the India Office and the Treasury recommended that the rupee should also leave gold and should be settled on a sterling standard at the 1s. 6d. ratio.[27] To prevent argument, this decision was announced in London before it was cabled to the government of India. Angered by this treatment, the whole of the Viceroy's Executive Council threatened to resign, but were dissuaded by an unprecedented appeal from London for imperial solidarity. This appeal was touching, but it did not contain any concessions.[28]

III

The action taken by British policy-makers in September 1931 was not intended to solve the problems of Indian finance, and even less to mitigate the strains caused by the Great Depression on the Indian economy. As has been seen, officials at the Treasury and the India Office were concerned to prevent the situation from becoming much worse, rather than with trying to improve it in any way. And yet their policy, by creating a premium in the sterling price of gold, did provide a way out of the impasse.

With sterling and the rupee depreciated, it was now possible to sell gold in London at a considerable profit, and large amounts of commodity gold began to be exported from India. Between September 1931 and March 1932, Rs 629 million worth of gold left private hoards in India and was sold in London. In 1932–3 a further Rs 672 million worth was exported, and in 1933–4 another Rs 592 million worth. The flow continued for the rest of the decade—between September 1931 and March 1939 India's net exports of gold totalled Rs 3072 million (£230.97 million) worth, although this was still over Rs 1200 million worth less than India's total net gold imports in the period 1921–9.[29]

The question of where this gold came from is a vexed one. Gold was the preferred savings medium of the vast bulk of the Indian population. The mechanisms of the new gold export trade, like those of the traditional gold import trade, are not yet properly understood. It is not yet possible to assess to what extent the bullion exports were the result of agriculturists being compelled to liquidate their savings to pay rent and revenue, or more voluntary decisions to take advantage of the rise in the rupee price of gold. It is also not yet possible to estimate the impact of the new liquidity in the Indian economy, resulting from the sale of so much gold, on internal economic development during the rest of the 1930s.

The gold exports effectively solved the problems of Indian currency and finance, strengthening India's balance-of-payments surplus on private account and, in 1932–3, giving it a visible balance-of-payments surplus with Britain for the first time in the twentieth century. The gold trade also provided the government of India with adequate remittance to meet all its commitments in London, allowed the monetary authorities to expand the currency by over Rs 500 million in the second half of 1931–2, and put gold on the London market for the Bank of England to buy in sterling and use to pay back Britain's own obligations to the United States and France.

The outflow of gold from India was so opportune, coming at just the right time and in just the right manner for both the government of India and the British government, that it is tempting to assume that British policy towards India had been designed to ensure that it took place. However, there is no evidence whatsoever to suggest that this was the case. Neither before, nor immediately after, the break with the gold standard did anyone in London or New Delhi anticipate what would happen. As late as the end of November 1931, when gold was already being shipped from India, the government of India, the India Office, the Treasury, and the Bank of England were gloomily contemplating what fresh emergency measures would be necessary to obtain the sterling needed to meet the maturity of £15 million worth of India bonds in January 1932.[30] Officials in India and London greeted the gold exports with delight and relief, but still caused themselves needless worry by consistently underestimating the volume and the length of the flow. As the Government of India Finance Department put it in early 1933, the gold exports were 'a purely accidental condition the continuance of which for any length of time cannot be relied upon. *This is so well known that it need not be dealt with at any length'*.[31] Ironically, the gold exports, vitally important as they were, were unplanned and unexpected.[32]

So far as Whitehall was concerned, the Indian currency crisis had been resolved by 1932. Constitutional reforms could now be introduced safely, provided only that the confidence of foreign holders of rupees was buttressed by rigid financial safeguards and an insistence on the established ratio. The important safeguards laid down in the new Government of India Act were discretionary powers for the Governor-General over budgetary and monetary policy, and the establishment of a non-political Reserve Bank to act as a central bank in India.

Government of India officials were less happy with this stress on safeguards, but were eventually forced to accept a Government of India Act and a Reserve Bank of India Act based on these principles. The Indian authorities also continued to be unhappy about the solution that London had now found to the larger problems of Indian currency. To the Indian Finance Department, linking the rupee to sterling at the old ratio was, at best, a necessary evil and was only justifiable as a permanent solution if the British government were to direct its monetary policy towards raising sterling prices. The depreciation of sterling from its old rate had boosted Indian prices to some extent by 1932, but the future was still uncertain. Since they were now tightly bound to sterling, Indian officials looked to an imperial solution. From September 1931 until the Ottawa Conference of July 1932, the government of India added its voice to the swelling dominion chorus urging that sterling policy should be based on the requirements of the Empire as a whole.[33]

These appeals fell on deaf ears. By the spring of 1932 British policy-makers were prepared to accept that a sterling area was the best medium-term solution to Britain's international monetary problems and were prepared to concede that sterling's natural level lay some way below the exchange rate imposed in 1925. But the Treasury was not willing to see sterling devalue too far, for this would depress the returns on British overseas investments, thus damaging the balance of payments, and, by sapping foreign confidence, would create problems in the repayment of debts and the rehabilitation of London as a world financial centre.[34]

The hopes of the government of India that the Ottawa discussions might lead to the establishment of a sterling bloc in which all the participants would have a voice in the making of currency and credit policy[35] were quickly dashed as it became clear that sterling policy was going to be decided in Britain's interests, and that these were not necessarily the same as that of the Empire. At the Ottawa conference, the only concession that Neville Chamberlain was prepared to make was the general expression of a wish to see sterling prices rise, and a promise that British short-term credit policy would be directed to this end. It was alleged that the chancellor might have gone further than this had he not received a series of telegrams from the Bank of England warning about renewed American speculation against the pound, and that what he did say went further than the Treasury representative at the conference had wished to go.[36] The Government of India was now forced to recognize that the British government was not prepared to risk its own perceived interests in order to help the Indian economy.

IV

The devaluation of sterling and the rupee in 1931, London's cheap-money policy, and the British government's other monetary and non-monetary measures aimed at raising world commodity prices undoubtedly helped India to recover from the Great Depression. But the way in which India had been treated during the currency crisis of 1930–2 did little to still Indian official and non-official criticisms of London. The government of India had been arguing that India's interests required the rupee to be devalued more than British interests required sterling to be devalued against other major currency blocs. Devaluing the rupee by 12 per cent against sterling in the summer of 1931 might not have helped the Indian economy very much, but such an action could well have helped to improve relations between Indian business and political opinion and the British bureaucracy and, by promoting the economic development and political tranquillity of India, have brought lasting benefits to Britain itself. As it was, currency policy, which in 1931 Schuster had called 'the worst cause of discord in recent years',[37] remained a contentious issue in the relationship between Britain and India until 1947.

It is interesting to compare British policy towards the Indian currency crisis with events elsewhere in the empire/ commonwealth. The impact of the Depression in Australia was very similar to the Indian case. Here, too, the collapse of primary-produce prices and large sterling debts in London caused an acute economic, budgetary, and monetary crisis. Yet the Australians were able to use a much more flexible policy. In 1930–1 the Australian pound was devalued by 25 per cent against sterling, although this was the result of unchecked market forces, not of a deliberate policy by the Commonwealth government or the Commonwealth Bank. The Treasury and the Bank of England were worried by this, but did no more than offer advice and, in 1932, a drawing credit of £3 million to boost Australia's London reserves and so prevent a further collapse in the exchange.[38] New Zealand also devalued, and also received a Bank of England credit of £3 million to allow it to meet its London commitments.[39]

The major difference between the antipodean and the Indian cases seems to have been simply that the British government had formal powers of control over the government of India that did not exist elsewhere. It is also true that, because Australia and New Zealand sent a higher percentage of their exports to Britain, and because there were no major outflows of British capital from these countries, their sterling position was never as desperate as was India's and the credits required were much smaller. Further, even a slightly suspect Australian or New Zealand government was thought to be more trustworthy, and creditworthy, than a future Indian administration containing a Finance Member fully responsible to an elected central legislature.

British policy during the Indian currency crisis of 1930–2 revealed an interesting and important point about the nature of British interest in India during what can be called the geriatric years of the Raj. The events of 1930–2 demonstrated that the British government did have a substantial financial stake in India, and that any future scheme of constitutional reform would have to be modified to ensure that this stake was maintained. Yet these same events also revealed that this stake was short term and defensive, not positive or dynamic. It was, in fact, an overwhelming concern to ensure that the British taxpayer did not have to foot the bill for India's debt repayments and pension obligations. When the Treasury discovered, in June 1931, that the British exchequer would be unable to avoid covering the debts of a defaulting India, one door to radical constitutional advance was closed. It was not to be reopened until 1945, when India had replaced its sterling debt of £350 million with sterling balances of almost four times as much.

Notes

1. See, for example, R. J. Moore, 1974, *The Crisis of Indian Unity, 1917–40* (Oxford), and idem., 1970, 'The Making of India's Paper Federation, 1927–35', in C. H. Philips and M. D. Wainwright, eds, *The Partition of India: Policies and Perspectives, 1935–47*, pp. 54–78. P. S. Gupta, 1975, *Imperialism and the British Labour*

Movement, 1914–64, pp. 216–23, deals with commercial and financial policy in 1930 and 1931, but the book's exclusive concern with Labour governments limits its usefulness to historians of India. For my analysis of the constitutional question, see B. R. Tomlinson, 1976, *The Indian National Congress and the Raj, 1929–42* (London), ch. I.

2. I. M. Drummond, 1972, *British Economic Policy and the Empire, 1919–39* (London), pp. 130–40.

3. Between April 1929 and March 1932, over £35 million, about one-third of the Secretary of State's total requirements, was remitted in this way.

4. For a convenient statement of this view, see Purshotamdas Thakurdas's minute of dissent to the *Report of the Royal Commission on Indian Currency and Finance* (Cmd. 2687, 1926).

5. On the movement of short-term funds, see Government of India Finance Department (henceforth GOIFD), file 13 (x) F, 1927 (National Archives of India), and India Office Finance Department (henceforth IOFD), file L/F/6/1169, 1930, no. 7459 (India Office Records). There is also some evidence that Indians were exporting capital during this period.

6. 'The sterling and gold resources of government and the problem of remittance' memorandum by George Schuster dated 30 October 1939 [*sic*], Treasury Papers (henceforth T), 160/519 F.12471/05/4 (P.R.O.).

7. D.O. Officiating Secretary Finance Department to Officiating Controller of Currency, no. 2410-F, 5 September 1919, GOIFD. Proceedings Accounts and Finance Branch nos. 33–55A, April 1920.

8. GOIFD files I (2) F, 1930, I (8) F, 1931.

9. Government of India (Finance Department) to Secretary of State, no. 1299-S, 9 May 1931, GOIFD, I (8) F, 1931.

10. 'Note on finance and currency' by George Schuster, sent as private and personal telegram (8 September 1931), Viceroy to Secretary of State, Templewood Papers, vol. 11, bdl. 2 (India Office Records). The idea of devaluation had been in Schuster's mind for some time. In September 1930 he had suggested to Montagu Norman that the idea should at least be considered, but had received no encouragement whatever. See Schuster to Lord Irwin, 9 October 1930, Halifix Papers, vol. II (India Office Records).

11. For the clearest statement of this view, see the memorandum by C. H. Kisch, 'The effect on Indian economy and credit of collapse of the rupee exchange' (18 September 1931), IOFD, L/F/6/1183, 1931, no. 6444.

12. See correspondence in T160/472 F.11879 and IOFD, L/F/7/ 792, coll. 81/55. The quoted formula comes from an open letter from A. Hirtzel (Under-Secretary of State) to Mr Holloway, 21 January 1930.

13. See correspondence in T160/399 F.12471, annex I, pt. II. The safeguards delineated were those suggested by the Federal Structure Sub-Committee of the round-table conference—a non-political reserve bank and special powers for the Governor-General over budgetary and monetary policy.

14. Cabinet Office Papers (henceforth CAB) 27/471; BDG (31) 6, 19 June 1931 (P.R.O.).

15. F. W. Leith-Ross to Findlater Stewart, 1 January 1931, in IOFD, L/F/7/2396, coll. 381/4.

16. Note by Leith-Ross, 4 June 1931, in T160/400 F. 12471/03/1.

17. Note by Richard Hopkins, 10 June 1931, and unsigned note, 13 June 1931, T160/400 F.12471/03/1.

18. CAB 27/470; BDG (31) 7, 25 June 1931; note by Hopkins, 24 June 1931, T160/400 F.12471/03/2.

19. Hansard (Commons), 1930–1, CCLIV, coll. 769.

20. Secretary of State to Government of India (Finance Department), no. 2041, 7 July 1931, IOFD, L/F/6/1180, 1931, no. 5952.

21. In September 1931 Findlater Stewart of the India Office was informed that the Prime Minister 'does not want to close the door to an escape from the guarantee'.–Note for Stewart by H. A. Rumbold, 14 September 1931, IOFD, L/F/7/897, coll. 107.

22. See Controller of Currency to Government of India Finance Department, no. B&R 1567, 8 September 1931, GOIFD, 1 (8) F, 1931.

23. See CAB 24/224; CP232 (31) and note by Leith-Ross, 28 September 1931, T160/474 F. 12471/06/1.

24. Unsigned, undated note, T160/400 F. 12471/04.

25. CAB 24/224; CP232 (31).

26. See CAB 24/224; CP243 (31). Interestingly enough, the Prime Minister's personal file on the last stages of the sterling crisis (Premier's Office Papers, 1/97) contains copies of the monthly

balance sheets and estimates of the India Office for the summer and autumn of 1931.

27. CAB 23/68; 62 (31) 8, 22 September 1931; Secretary of State to government of India (Finance Department), no. 2576, 20 September 1931; no. 2803, 23 September 1931, GOIFD, 1 (10) F, 1931.

28. The government of India accepted a sterling standard for the rupee, but wanted an extra devaluation for the Indian currency. The Treasury scotched this move by declaring that the June guarantee was conditional on the 1*s*. 6*d*. rate.

29. A. K. Banerji, 1963, *India's Balance of Payments, 1921–2 to 1938–9* (London), table IV.

30. See T160/400 F.12471/04; IOFD, L/F/6/1180, 1931, no. 6060, private and personal telegrams Secretary of State to Viceroy, 21 October 1931, 28 October 1931, 19 November 1931, and ditto, Viceroy to Secretary of State, 30 October 1931, 11 November 1931, 24 November 1931, Templewood Papers, vol. II.

31. Government of India Memorandum on Federal Finance, sent with Finance Department despatch, 15 May 1933, GOIFD, 14 (4) B, 1933, para. 12. Italics not in original.

32. This is not as surprising as it may seem at first sight. On previous occasions when the rupee exchange had fallen against gold prices (as in 1922–3), no significant exports had taken place.

33. Government of India (Finance Department) to Secretary of State, no. 2475-S, 3 October 1931, no. 746, 9 March 1932, no. 2745-S, 10 November 1931, IOFD, L/F/7/561, coll. 45/15. Some of the Secretary of State's financial advisers now supported the Government of India—a memorandum of 8 March 1932 by Reginald Mant and Henry Strakosch (ibid.) even argued that, since India's gold exports had greatly benefited Britain, the Treasury should look kindly on India's wishes for sterling policy.

34. See papers in T175/56, T175/57, pts. 1–2 (especially the various drafts of the Treasury memorandum of 8 March 1932 for the Cabinet Committee on Currency Questions), T172/1768, T175/1775, T168/48.

35. Notes by H. Denning and George Schuster, 16–17 May 1932, GOIFD, 17 (36) F, 1932.

36. 'Confidential report on the discussion of monetary and financial questions at the Imperial Economic Conference, Ottawa, 1932',

by Henry Strakosch and George Schuster, 23 September 1932, IOFD, L/F/9/13.

37. George Schuster to Henry Strakosch, 5 October 1931, Templewood Papers, vol. 8.

38. See L. F. Giblin, 1951, *The Growth of a Central Bank: The Development of the Commonwealth Bank of Australia, 1924–45* (Melbourne), pp. 74–8, 126–9, 136–50.

39. See R. S. Sayers, 1976, *The Bank of England, 1891–1944* (Cambridge), II, 449.

9

The Depression*

G. Balachandran

Already important features of the contemporary global macro-economy in the aftermath of World War I and during the 1920s, both India's counter-cyclical role in the world economy and Britain's determination to manipulate it as a means of easing her own financial problems intensified in the course of the inter-war Depression. With the onset of the slump and the decline in American overseas lending, Britain's external financial problems grew severe enough to force her off the gold standard in September 1931, and sterling was never to return to its traditional parity with gold. But thereafter, Britain adopted relatively unorthodox exchange rate and monetary policies to counter the slump at home. Enabling her to accumulate large reserves of gold whilst following 'cheap money' policies was the dramatic outflow of large quantities of gold, among other places, from India where orthodox deflationary policies reinforced the impact of the Depression. As incomes declined, Indian households were forced to liquidate their savings held in the form of precious metals to meet fixed obligations or finance consumption. With price differentials too funnelling precious metals abroad, India, no longer a 'bottomless sink', yielded up nearly £250 million (net) of gold between 1931 and 1939. British policy-makers felt vindicated by the outcome but, thanks to gold being released on a smaller scale elsewhere and increasing output from the mines,

* Previously published in G. Balachandran, *John Bullion's Empire: Britain's Gold Problem and the India between the Wars,* Curzon Press, Surrey, 1996.

were soon saddled with a greater supply of the metal than they and the American monetary authorities could together handle. Fearing runaway inflation and for gold's future monetary role, officials in London began now to consider steps to *reduce* supplies or *increase* the demand for the metal. For several months in the late 1930s until the American economy went into recession and war became more imminent, Britain's policy-makers prayed for Indian gold exports to cease and for her gold appetite to revive!

The relatively benign impact of the Depression upon the Indian economy masks the considerable intersectoral shifts and dislocations which marked these years. Although accounts of the Depression in India usually take note of her large exports of gold, there is insufficient appreciation of their origins in agrarian distress; or of the manner in which dissaving and gold exports from India, both of which might have been checked through appropriate policy, helped the metropolitan economy manage its own recovery in the slump. However, this chapter does not purport to be a general or comprehensive account of the Depression in India. Severe as its impact was at this time, nor was the particular aspect of the policy regime it discusses peculiar to the 1930s. But the Depression was, first and foremost, an *international* occurrence. Therefore, and despite the small size of India's foreign trade sector in her overall economy, our understanding of economic developments in the colony during this decade might be usefully enhanced if they were restored to the wider multilateral context whence the slump arose and its impact transmitted across the world.

The next section presents a brief background discussion of Britain's external liquidity context during the early years of the Depression as it concerns us, and her policy-makers' growing apprehensions of a 'gold shortage'. The third and fourth sections respectively sketch the impact of the Depression on the Indian external account, and the official policies of the period. The following section deals with India's large gold exports after September 1931 and documents British efforts to encourage the flow. The sixth section has a brief discussion of the effect of gold exports on the Indian economy, while the seventh recounts the emerging official approach to the threat of a gold deluge in 1937.

'Gold Shortage' and the Sterling Crisis

During the 1920s Britain and most of industrial Europe looked
to the United States to support economic growth by keeping
interest rates low and increasing overseas lending. The USA was
indeed the major international lender during the ten years
following the Armistice;[1] and the 'fragile economic equilibrium'
of the second half of the decade 'rested squarely on [US]
lending'.[2]

American overseas lending began to decline from mid-1928.
After reaching a peak of $1050 million in the first half of that
year, it fell to about $450 million each in the second half of 1928
and in the first half of 1929. It fell further to $229 million in the
second half of 1929. Europe, in particular, was badly affected by
the decline, managing in 1929 to attract less than a quarter of the
preceding year's capital inflow.[3] The redistribution of world gold
reserves set in train by American overseas lending was also
reversed, with the US gold stock beginning to rise from mid-
1928 after having declined for nearly three years.[4] Though
overall, the creditor countries' share of the world's gold reserves
increased by 5 percentage points each year in 1929 and 1930,
only the USA and France gained any gold during these years,
almost equally splitting Europe's total gold gains over the
preceding four years.[5]

Lower American lending adversely affected Britain's external
finances. Thanks to a weak current account, even her restricted
overseas lending during the 1920s led to Britain running up short-
term debts to foreign countries.[6] 'As a rule' before 1914, the
Bank of England's gold reserves and Britain's liquid and short-
term claims on foreigners were believed 'at least (to) equal (or
exceed)' her short-term liabilities.[7] Whether or not this was true
before the war, recognition grew during the 1920s that Britain
was following unsound banking practices—borrowing short to
lend long. Moreover the Bank of France, which bought sterling
to limit the franc's appreciation in 1926–7, and private French
speculators held a significant share of these short-term debts,
the former's short-term claims on Britain alone nearly equalling

the Bank of England's gold reserves. As became evident before long, this pattern of distribution of Britain's external liabilities was a major recipe for sterling instabililty.[8] Restoring a healthier look to the maturity structures of Britain's external assets and liabilities required a stable economic and financial climate. But the worldwide decline in economic activity from the second half of 1928, growing defaults on overseas debts as Latin American primary producers faced falling trade and capital receipts, and the introduction of exchange controls in central Europe combined sharply to upset Britain's external account at the same time as the resulting international financial uncertainty increased short-term capital outflows from London. Consequently, the Bank of England's gold reserves, which peaked at nearly £174 million in September 1928, fell to less than £131 million in October 1929; and although they rose during 1930 and for some part of 1931 thanks to reserve liquidation by primary product exporters and to capital fleeing the continent, British gold losses resumed in mid-1931.[9]

It is not necessary to discuss sterling's fall from gold at any length, since a substantial body of work exists on various aspects of the subject.[10] Apart from fundamental macroeconomic imbalances and the limited, on–off character of international cooperation, sterling's plight during 1929–31 was worsened by deep domestic political and policy divisions within Britain, particularly over the priority to be attached to external stability when nearly a fifth of her workforce was unemployed. Hence, domestic credit and expenditure policies excited great controversy, and even as Montagu Norman, the governor of the Bank of England, joined his American and French counterparts to urge economies or the merits of tight money upon his own government in order to stabilize the frail British currency, British Treasury officials were remonstrating in Paris against French gold withdrawals.[11] As one Treasury official noted, though London was willing to supply gold, yet 'the situation here over unemployment and prices is so acute . . . that we cannot be indifferent to operations which have the indirect effect of putting a further strain on the market'.[12] The Treasury also ignored French advice to put up the bank rate because, in Frederick Leith-Ross's words, 'to propose dearer money in London (was) to suggest decapitation as a cure for a toothache'.[13] Even at the height of the run on its reserves following the collapse of the Austrian *Credit Anstalt,* the Bank of England could secure Treasury consent for a bank rate increase only after much argument concerning the instrument's ability to retain funds in London.[14] In addition, the sharp cutbacks in public expenditure, mainly unemployment payments, needed to reassure foreign investors and stabilize sterling proved difficult to achieve despite a split in the ruling Labour party and the formation of a National Government committed to defending the gold standard.[15] With foreign hopes evaporating of gold losses forcing greater fiscal discipline on Britain, the run on London balances proved unstoppable when they resumed in July–August 1931, and sterling had to be taken off the gold standard and gold payments suspended over 19–21 September 1931.

As the world economy went into a slump, and particularly as the deflation required to preserve sterling on the gold standard grew more prolonged, British policy-makers began openly to express the view that 'maldistribution' of the world's monetary gold reserves was the chief source of the crisis. Offering a respectable front for Britain's bullionist inter-war agenda, the 'gold shortage' view guided the activities of several prominent British academics, bankers, and public officials since the early 1920s, and served as the basis for Britain's monetary reform initiatives at the Genoa conference. British officials remained nervous about both the shorter- and the longer-term aspects of the gold problem through the middle years of the decade, and not surprisingly as the Depression worsened, the 'gold shortage' school began to emerge into the open.

It was largely at the prodding of British protagonists of the gold shortage view that the Financial Committee of the League of Nations constituted a Gold Delegation in 1928 to investigate the problem. Apart from Montagu Norman's advisor Henry Strakosch, who was its most active member, the committee included, among others, Reginald Mant, who had recently retired from the India office, O. M. W. Sprague, an American economist who acted occasionally as Norman's advisor, and the Swedish economist Gustav Cassell. Unable to shake off suspicions that the exercise was a major British conspiracy directed against France and the USA, Norman and the Bank of England were forced to disclaim any interest in the delegation's activities.[16] But not only had the argument that 'maldistribution' of gold was the chief cause of the world's economic problems gained new converts, it was also firmly in the public domain: bullionism was now, as it were, out of the closet. As R. V. Nind Hokins, who stepped into Otto Niemeyer's shoes in 1927 after the latter left Whitehall for the Bank of England, noted in the course of preparing material for the Macmillan Committee, the

> general problem of prices, apart from the drop following the US slump, is mainly a world central banking problem. An aggregate standard of gold reserves in excess of gold supply means a perpetual inconclusive struggle for more gold in each country. US and France from different angles have especially acquired more than their share. The British (reserve) . . . is an extremely moderate sum given population and wealth and international market.[17]

The influential Royal Institute of International Affairs (Chatham House) organized a series of discussions on the distribution of international reserves attended by leading British government officials and their advisers. The views conveyed by several official witnesses, including Niemeyer and Norman, to the Macmillan Committee—in particular the description of the inter-war gold standard as a 'competitive scramble for gold'—also suggest the influence of the gold shortage school.[18]

The Macmillan Committee's report also endorsed the gold shortage view, and attributed the slump to the 'illiquidity' of the world economy caused by 'international lending power' shifting away from Britain.[19] Such views were widely held in Britain's official circles through the next two decades, and dictated British proposals not only at the 1933 London conference but also at Bretton Woods more than a decade later.[20] It is against the background of such perceptions and of Britain's failure to persuade the United States and France to sustain a coordinated redistribution of the world's gold reserves that one must examine British–Indian macro-policies during these years and the effect they had of forcing India to finance reserve needs at the 'centre'.

But first, a discussion of the Depression primarily as it affected India's external sector.

The Depression and India's External Sector

During 1923–6, the Indian trade surplus reached unprecedented levels, peaking at Rs 1189 million in 1925–6. But the following year it fell to nearly a third, before rising to about Rs 500 million in 1927–8. However attenuated the impact on India of the global boom of 1928–9, her exports continued to rise, and as imports fell slightly, the trade surplus too rose during the year. Further, thanks to reduced gold imports which offset a large increase in interest and dividend outflows, India also ran a lower current account deficit during the year (see Table 9.1).

Yet even in 1928–9, India's external account was showing definite signs of strain. Trade remittances still did not cover external obligations which had to be met out of fresh loans and transfers from the Paper Currency Reserve.[21] The medium-term portents were also none too happy, with a bunching of maturities, mainly of loans floated during 1921–3 to finance sterling obligations under the managed float regime, about to occur in the next two years.[22] When the Depression intervened, therefore, India too depended on a steadily expanding world economy to meet her external obligations in a non-deflationary manner.

Expectedly, India's foreign trade was the first to be affected in the Depression, her trade surplus declining steadily from 1929–30 until 1932–3, when exports bottomed out at about 40 per cent of the 1928–9 level. Imports hit the floor at Rs 1360 million in 1933–4, down from about Rs 3000 million in 1928–9.[23] But with the exception of 1932–3, India maintained a trade surplus throughout the 1930s. With her gold imports falling further, India's current account deficit too continued to decline through 1929–30. In 1930–1, however, the trade surplus dropped by more than gold imports and service outflows together, and the current account deficit increased sharply. Even so, the 1930–1 deficit was only about a tenth of India's commodity exports during the year. This was not much higher than the 1927–8 proportion, and indeed lower than the 1926–7 proportion of nearly 15 per cent. Hence, though perhaps unsustainable in the circumstances, India's current account position did not quite call for panic measures.

Table 9.1   *Indian current account, 1926–7 to 1937–8*

Year	Commodity exports	Commodity imports	Interest and dividend	Other services	Net gold exports	Current account balance
1926–7	3320	2969	–194	–298	–347	–488
1927–8	3529	3016	–181	–314	–347	–329
1928–9	3663	2998	–325	–312	–212	–183
1929–30	3404	2867	–316	–180	–142	–100
1930–1	2442	2071	–336	–159	–128	–251
1931–2	1740	1518	–348	–179	580	275
1932–3	1460	1515	–344	–162	655	95
1933–4	1635	1364	–339	–122	571	380
1934–5	1707	1594	–325	–139	525	174
1935–6	1821	1628	–320	–160	374	88
1936–7	2175	1608	–324	–183	278	338
1937–8	2050	2050	–302	–181	163	–320

Note: All figures in nearest Rs million; (–) signifies net imports.

Source: 'Government of India's Estimates . . . submitted to the League of Nations', in A. K. Banerji, 1963, *India's Balance of Payments, Estimates of Current and Capital Accounts from 1921–22 to 1938–9* (London), pp. 236–7.

These, rather than Banerji's own more methodical estimates, are used here since the latter are available only from 1921–2; Banerji also does not report short-term capital movements separately.

The most severe effects of the Depression were, however, felt on the capital account (see Table 9.2). It is evident that with net long-term capital inflows declining, short-term inflows financed almost the whole of the current account deficit in 1928–9. Thanks to increased official borrowings, long-term inflows picked up during the next three years, but from 1929–30 the volatility of short-term funds became a major source of concern. Net short-term capital inflows of Rs 179 million in 1928–9 became

net outflows of Rs 33 million in 1929–30, Rs 181 million in 1930–
1, and Rs 393 million in 1931–2. Short-term outflows grew smaller
thereafter, but by now net long-term flows had turned negative
as the colonial government suspended overseas borrowing and
moved instead to reduce India's external debt. Enabling India
to afford the luxury of debt reduction (and overseas lending) in
the Depression, when other non-industrialized countries were
responding to reduced capital inflows by defaulting on their
external obligations, were her large gold exports (see Table 9.1).

Table 9.2   *India's capital account, 1926–7 to 1937–8*

Year	Long-term inflows	Long-term outflows	Short-term inflows	Short-term outflows	Net inflows
1926–7	407	92	107	3	488
1927–8	182	35	248	66	329
1928–9	145	140	179	–	184
1929–30	204	71	41	74	100
1930–1	484	52	–	181	251
1931–2	358	240	–	393	–275
1932–3	128	193	52	82	–95
1933–4	254	496	–	96	–312
1934–5	37	124	–	106	–192
1935–6	n.a.	n.a.	n.a.	n.a.	–121
1936–7	n.a.	n.a.	n.a.	n.a.	–333
1937–8	n.a.	n.a.	n.a.	n.a.	53

Note: All figures in nearest Rs million rupees; (–) indicates net outflows.
Source: Same as Table 9.1.

As pointed out earlier, Indian gold imports began to decline
from longer-term trend levels in 1928–9, and continued doing
so through the next two years.[24] However, from the middle of
1931 India emerged as a net exporter of gold. These exports
lasted until the end of the decade, and totalled over £250 million.
Although gold exports by her were not unknown, India's gold
exports during the 1930s were unprecedented in size and

duration. These exports enabled India to run a current account surplus until 1936–7, discharge a part of her foreign debt, and lend abroad. Given the conditions of the world economy and Britain's external liquidity position, Indian gold exports functioned as a useful variable, and contemporaries welcomed them as the most powerful expansionary influence globally, and in particular, on the British economy.[25]

The Policy Response and Constraints

Scholars familiar with the 1930s would recognize that the outflow of short-term capital was not peculiar to India.[26] In addition to depressed trading conditions, higher interest rates in New York and other leading financial centres, and the climate of financial uncertainty worldwide, short-term rupee holdings were affected also by the run on sterling. As sterling, to which the rupee was anchored, weakened against the dollar and the franc, the flight from the rupee may actually have reflected a flight from the sterling area. A run on Indian reserves due to an attack on sterling had been foreseen in 1925 and it was to this that Osborne Smith, General Manager of the Imperial Bank of India, attributed the rupee's weakness.[27] The small amounts of gold India exported in January 1931, bypassing London and going directly to Paris, also supports this view. In the same month, a British cabinet memorandum admitted that capital was fleeing the sterling area, and by August 1931 it was becoming clear that even British firms were leaving sterling for 'dollars, francs and guilders'.[28]

Officials in Delhi were aware that the flight from the rupee might owe to global conditions, in particular the volatility that had beset even the developed capital markets. Whitehall too conceded privately that short-term outflows were partly, at least, due to factors originating outside India.[29] British–Indian businessmen, notably Sir Thomas Catto and exchange bankers, attributed the outflows to a number of factors, including the Wall Street boom, the 'disorganized' world economy, and Indian inroads into British positions, especially in jute, tea, and sugar.[30] Yet, publicly, officials in Delhi and London preferred to attribute

the rupee's weakness almost entirely to nationalist agitation and
the prospect of political reforms in India.[31]

Undoubtedly, political agitation in the form of the Civil
Disobedience Movement, and nationalist threats to repudiate
India's sterling debts and devalue the rupee were important
features of this period. In addition, during these years,
negotiations were underway on a new constitutional scheme for
India, central to which was the idea of a federal arrangement
balancing the greater powers allowed to the government in New
Delhi. Although these reforms were thought to be 'the best way
. . . of maintaining British influence' in India, they were caught
up in factional squabbles within the Conservative party, while
even those sympathetic to them were concerned about
safeguarding British interests in the proposed dispensation.[32]
With alternative political and constitutional arrangements being
actively deliberated in Round Table Conferences or select
committees, it would have been natural for investors and
businessmen to take them into account. Moreover, frequent
government warnings regarding the financial consequences of
Indian political reforms may have been self-fulfilling in some
degree. For example, the speeches of Samuel Hoare, the Secretary
of State for India and member of a leading family of City
bankers, could not have been better calculated to spread alarm
among investors about the colony's credit situation.[33]

On the other hand, the bureaucracies in Delhi and London
had good reasons of their own to play up political factors. While
the Government of India used them to resist London's pressure
to deflate, officials in London found them handy to avoid
transferring control over monetary affairs to Delhi.[34] Further,
whatever the advantages of studying the 'official mind', insight
into the decisions of businessmen is not one of them, and there
is little evidence of observers in the main *business* centres regarding
politics as a major factor in the weak rupee. Sir Thomas, no friend
of nationalist politicians, explicitly ruled politics out, and the
communications from the currency controllers, who were in
direct day-to-day touch with the exchange markets in Bombay
and Culcutta, contain hardly any reference at all to political
uncertainty depressing the rupee.[35] Montagu Norman too thought

financial factors were responsible for the run on the rupee.[36] It is also worth noting, in passing, that short-term capital outflows were not uncontrollably large in 1935 when political reforms were finally implemented in India, because by now, Britain's capital account had grown much stronger.

As capital outflows grew, the Indian monetary authorities could have imposed restrictions on them as several Latin American countries did.[37] Some Indian government officials proposed restrictive measures, but Whitehall and the Bank of England would have nothing to do with them until September 1931. Maintaining India's uninterrupted repatriation of short-term balances was as vital for London as the servicing of her sterling obligations, and other objectives were subordinated to these.[38] In fact, India's ability to meet her external obligations and the state of the market for rupees were the only criteria Whitehall officials used to measure the colony's recovery in the Depression.[39] Monetary and fiscal policies were oriented towards the former, and towards the financing of short-term outflows.

The factors determining London's financial priorities in India have already been anticipated. At a time of weakness on her current account, transfers from the colony grew in importance.[40] Besides, unable any longer to adequately regulate short-term fund movements between the major money centres, the London bank rate now depended upon the free flow of capital from the Empire. Above all, however, with Britain's short-term position unravelling and capital flows turning more volatile, the signals which an Indian capital account embargo sent to sterling holders would have been little short of catastrophic. As the India Office admitted to the Government of India after swearing it to 'utmost secrecy', 'sterling and rupee are intimately connected and . . . collapse of one might bring down the other . . . .'[41]

With short-term capital outflows gaining momentum, the exchange rate controversy, never far from the surface, revived, as Indian politicians and businessmen once again made it a focus of agitation. Officials in Delhi and some advisers to the India Office such as F. C. Goodenough favoured the rupee's devaluation.[42] But not surprisingly in the background of exchange rate policies adopted in the 1920s, and despite the Royal Commission on Indian Currency and Finance (better known as the Hilton-Young Commission, 1926) having recommended the step in the event of world prices falling, the India Office refused steadfastly to concede a parity change. The arguments its officials used to justify their stand were diverse and contradictory, and merit separate attention. Yet they are worth summarizing in a few lines.[43]

London officials apprehended a rupee devaluation to affect British exports to India, but this was not the crucial argument against it. An internal India Office memorandum warned that besides damaging the interests of British exporters, rupee devaluation would 'profoundly shock' international trade and, rather than reassuring the markets, accelerate the fight from the rupee. At a more general level, the India Office adopted one of two positions. Its argument that devaluation would not improve the economic situation was based on a model of a fully monetized economy in which offsetting adjustments to exchange rate changes were universal and instantaneous. But the India Office presented a different and more realistic model to the League of Nations. According to this model, less than a third of the transactions in India were mediated through the market and about two-thirds of the marketed farm output went to settle fixed debt and revenue obligations. Other payments, including wages, were made in kind. The India Office did not extend this model to conclude, as its critics more logically did, that the sluggish adjustment to an external shock implicit in it made a devaluation more, rather than less, necessary. At a meeting with India Office advisers, Indian businessmen and politicians argued (using a similar model) that devaluation would leave the large majority of rural Indian households better off. At this time, the India Office not only rejected this argument, but embellished its own model of a fully monetized economy with a wage-bargaining process in which agricultural labourers (paid in cash) sought to protect their real wages in an inflationary environment![44]

The Bank of England was also cold to the idea of rupee devaluation. Norman consulted M. M. S. Gubbay on the effects of a rupee devaluation; and interestingly, Gubbay's memorandum, unlike those prepared by the India Office, explicitly dealt with gold flows to India, and suggested that a devaluation might increase them.[45]

With devaluation rejected, the authorities were now left with the option of borrowing abroad to strengthen reserves, and enforcing further contraction in India. Even in 1928, Norman had been unhappy about India issuing loans in London when he was attempting informally to regulate British overseas lending, and saw the colony's need for sterling loans as evidence of its government's failure to contract credit.[46] Despite Norman's reservations, the Indian government borrowed £31 million in three issues between May 1930 and February 1931. But its credit in London suffered a major blow in May 1931 when nearly two-thirds of another loan issue for £10 million had to be retained by the underwriters.[47] Hence the pressure grew to intensify contraction, Norman seeking 'money famine' in India 'to frighten bears of exchange . . . .'[48] Following contractionary policies, gross currency circulation in India fell from Rs 1867 million in September 1929 to Rs 1487 million in September 1931 (Table 9.3), while for all but four months during this period (when it was 5 per cent), the Imperial Bank rate remained at or above 6 per cent;[49] and by the end of 1930, even Norman's hand-picked head of the Imperial Bank of India was forced to protest London's demands.[50] The Depression also affected the government's budgetary position. Actual revenues fell short of estimates by about Rs 110 million in 1930–1, and with actual expenditure exceeding estimates, the year's accounts yielded a deficit of Rs 115 million. Although duties on many goods were increased in the 1931–2 budget and in the emergency budget of September 1931, this year too ended with a deficit of similar magnitude.[51]

In addition, there were two further problems. As budget deficits grew, the Imperial Bank found greater difficulty in hiking the bank rate since it affected the government's loan programme adversely. The Imperial Bank's efforts to tighten the market were often neutralized by banks discounting short-term government paper—a practice the former could not discourage without damaging the market for these securities. Secondly, as already noted, the Depression and the government's pro-cyclical policies adversely affected incomes and forced Indian households to sell their gold holdings in order to settle dues and debts and finance consumption. As early as July 1929, there were reports from Hyderabad (Deccan) of substantial sales of precious metals by the public, and though silver dominated in the early months, significant quantities of gold were also released.[52] According to the Amritsar agent of the Imperial Bank of India, by July 1930, low grain prices had led to 'reverse gold business' even in the more prosperous agricultural regions, with farmers trying to sell ornaments and jewellers forcing down prices by refusing to buy.[53] By January 1931, some 1600 ounces of gold ('mostly in the form of jewellery') were arriving every day in Bombay from up-country centres. Much of this gold ended up in the government's coffers since the *bazaar* price of gold was lower than the official price, and by early 1931, monthly gold flows into the mint amounted to nearly £1 million.[54] These gold receipts increased the potential resources available to the government to defend the rupee, but threatened, more immediately, to undo the monetary contraction effected so far.

Table 9.3   *Gross coin and note circulation, quarterly, 1929–34*

Year	March	June	September	December
1929	–	1877	1867	1794
1930	1772	1637	1715	1613
1931	1608	1525	1587	1793
1932	1781	1708	1757	1748
1933	1769	1765	1797	1781
1932	1772	1808	1851	1839

Note: All figures in nearest Rs million.

Source: Government of India, *Report of the Controller of Currency*, different years.

The process and the seemingly spontaneous manner whereby gold sales by India's private sector made up for reserve losses in intervention, invites comparison with the 1920 stabilization episode. In 1919–20, a non-deflationary solution to her currency crisis depended on India receiving adequate amounts of gold or silver against her large sterling reserves. At this time London, seeking to ease Britain's already severe financial problems, revalued the rupee to deflate the Indian economy and force households to liquidate their savings in the form of precious metals, so that the colony's currency system would be stabilized without gold or silver imports.[55]

A converse of the above process was at work during 1930–1, as reserves were being depleted in London, and accumulating in India. The logical course now, in terms of the counter-cyclical 1919–20 precedent, would have been to devalue the rupee to improve India's trade position and reverse capital outflows, and expand currency to reduce official metallic reserves in the colony.[56] But in both periods, Britain forced deflationary policies upon India, with this difference that they were counter-cyclical in the former case and pro-cyclical in the latter. In other words, with Britain again confronted with a financial crisis, the onus of adjustment again fell on Indian households which were once more forced to liquidate their assets to finance consumption or settle debts in the face of falling incomes. In the process, the Indian households again financed a transfer of liquid resources to Britain.

Gold Exports and Sterling Policy

As early as July 1929, when early reports arrived of gold sales in Hyderabad, officials at the Bank of England sensed that unusual developments were afoot in the Indian gold market. Hearing of the Hyderabad sales from the governor of the Imperial Bank of India, Niemeyer at the Bank of England was 'most interested to know' whether 'India [was] at last beginning to be less of a treasure hoarder'.[57] In the following months, the Bank of England closely followed gold arrivals in Bombay;[58] and as the run on sterling accelerated, Bank officials began to look towards Indian gold exports to ease their plight. With intervention to defend the rupee also leading to a sizeable decline in India's gold standard reserve in London and her government's currency offices inundated by gold, Whitehall too, for its part, began urging Delhi to export gold to Britain.[59]

In 1931, the Bank of England had good reasons for looking to additional supplies of gold from within the Empire to tide over a difficult summer. Apart from financing the drain of short-term balances from London, larger gold arrivals would have helped the Bank resolve its differences with the Treasury over allowing the drains to affect money supply in Britain. Through much of July 1931, the Bank of England was negotiating with the Federal Reserve Bank of New York and the Bank of France for credits to meet the outflow of short-term funds from London. One of the conditions attached to these credit lines obliged the Bank of England to export gold 'in amounts sufficient to liquidate (the loan) at maturity', if necessary by replacing the gold backing domestic currency, with government securities.[60] The Treasury generally supported the latter course to minimize the domestic deflationary impact of gold losses. Although the Bank of England was itself no novice at conducting open-market operations to offset the effects of gold losses on the money supply, its officials were convinced that carried 'beyond a certain point', such adjustments encouraged short-term outflows.[61] With widening differences on monetary policy between the Treasury and the Bank of England, gold receipts from India offered the possibility of reconciling the former's distaste for monetary contraction with the latter's desire for effective intervention to arrest the run on sterling.

Hence official gold exports from India acquired an importance which, though not disproportional to their potential size, was certainly not commensurate with the size of the first shipments her government appeared likely to make. So much so, during these difficult days, the Bank obtained private intelligence from shipping companies about the booking of official and non-official gold cargoes from India.[62] After the American and French credit lines were established, the Bank came under increasing pressure from the New York Federal Reserve to 'let some gold go' alongside using the credit. As reserve losses mounted and London's crisis worsened, senior

Bank of England officials were looking, barely days before being forced off the gold standard, towards 'substantial' gold arrivals from India to relieve sterling.[63]

In the event, India did not export much gold until sterling went off gold in September 1931 and Whitehall decided, without consulting officials in Delhi and to their great consternation, to peg the rupee to sterling at the existing parity.[64] As sterling, and alongside it the rupee, depreciated, the price of gold expressed in these two currencies rose. In addition, the metal's price in London was higher than in India, leading to the export of large quantities of privately held gold from India after September 1931 (see Table 9.1).[65] In 1931–2 Indian gold exports (about £45 million) almost matched that of South Africa. They equalled 85 per cent of South Africa's growing exports by value in 1932–3, 70 per cent in 1933–4, 64 per cent in 1934–5, 38 per cent in 1935–6, 25 per cent in 1936–7, and 16 per cent in 1937–8. Set against India's earlier imports of 15 per cent to 30 per cent of the world's gold output, even the outflows of the last two years are remarkable.[66]

While, undoubtedly, movements in gold prices stimulated these exports, there was another part to this process which should not be overlooked. It was noted above that the Indian public began selling gold at least two years before its price began rising in September 1931. These could only have represented distress sales. Some gold was exported even in December 1930, and India became a net exporter of the metal from the second quarter of 1931.[67] Indian commodity prices continued to fall until early 1933, returning durably to March 1931 levels only in 1937 (see Table 9.5). Hence, as some officials at the Bank of England recognized, there is no reason to suppose that distress sales ceased after September 1931.[68] Besides, as Rothermund has stressed, higher gold prices encouraged moneylenders to collect their debts in gold.[69] In general, however, officials in London and Delhi insisted that profits motivated gold sales and refused publicly to concede that destitution may equally have been at work.

Some gold sales would doubtless have taken place, whatever the domestic policies adopted. But the absence of measures to mitigate the Depression's impact on producers' incomes ensured a steady outflow of gold saved up in better years. In the event, with Indian macro-policies determinedly pro-cyclical in the slump, the gold releases of the Depression years were the logical sequel to policy whose aim was to check India's demand for gold in the more expansionary 1920s. When the world went into a slump in the 1930s, India became an exporter of gold, and an expansionary influence globally. Thus, India fulfilled Keynes's prescription of her role in the international economy, and his prophecy.

It is not surprising, in the circumstances, that Indian gold exports were a major cause for celebration in Whitehall and in the City. To those in London entrusted with the charge of Indian finances, these exports were especially welcome. The rupee was easily stabilized, and funds began flowing back to India by the end of October 1931. By January 1932 Whitehall was confident enough about these trends to discharge a £15 million loan that fell due that month. Now, at long last, officials handling Indian finances had something to cheer, and the surge of gold and the resulting improvement in the colony's external accounts and credit led to an outburst of self-congratulation. Viceroy Willingdon exulted that

> for the first time in . . . history owing to the economic situation, Indians are disgorging gold . . . . We have sent . . . to London in the past 2 or 3 months . . . 25,000,000 sterling and I hope the process will continue . . .![70]

The India Office claimed to have wrought a 'miracle' in the habits of the 'East', and in a boastful note, the Secretary of State claimed credit for the development. The British cabinet congratulated him for the 'accomplish(ment)'.[71]

The help which Indian gold exports provided to Britain's balance of payments and to sterling soon became evident. Earlier, officials at the Bank of England had considered offering 'long-dated gold bonds' to persuade the 'more pro-British [Indian] Princes to let us look after part of their gold for them', since 'even a small percentage' of India's net gold imports during 1900–1930 (£400 million according to Bank of England estimates) 'would be sufficient to repay the Bank of France credit.'[72] But the flow of gold from India soon relieved the Bank of England from having to resort to such desperate measures, and enabled it to meet the maturing debt.[73] As Neville Chamberlain, Britain's Chancellor of the Exchequer, noted the

> astonishing gold mine we have discovered in India has put us in a clover. The French can take their balances away without our flinching. We can accumulate credits for the repayment of our £80m loan and we can safely lower the bank rate. So there is great rejoicing in the City . . . .[74]

Besides discovering that its immediate problem of finding resources to pay off French and American credits was no longer as daunting, the Bank also recognized that the 'change of habits' in India '. . . will prove of great practical significance in the future when the question of supplies of Gold in relation to requirements again becomes of urgent practical importance'.[75]

Not surprisingly therefore, policy-makers in London wanted to see Indian gold exports continue without interruption. In January 1932 the Treasury opposed lifting capital account controls in India to which it had earlier taken objection, because it 'may diminish the export of gold which is at present the only legal method of exporting capital from India. The export of gold has been very useful for the sterling.'[76] London also refused, despite the Indian government's continuing budgetary problems, to allow a tax on gold exports because, as Niemeyer at the Bank of England put it, 'one of the great needs' of the day was to 'discourage hoarding', and the

> more gold can be loosened . . . in India . . . or elsewhere . . . and sent to a place where it will . . . tend to come into the hands of monetary authorities, the better for everyone including India.[77]

For the same reason, suggestions that the Indian government intervene in the local gold market or buy gold to strengthen the reserves of the proposed Reserve Bank were turned down.[78]

Besides, policy-makers in London were not entirely willing to wait upon events in India, and were quite prepared to determine them. Within weeks of India beginning to export gold, the Bank of England took steps to stimulate the outflow and direct it towards London by instructing the Hongkong and

Shanghai Banking Corporation (HSBC) to 'obtain a good percentage of all [gold] shipments' from Bombay on its behalf. The Hongkong Bank was also asked to provide 'easy facilities' for financing gold shipments, with the Bank of England itself offering to secure the necessary rupee funds through the Indian government. Following protests by other firms that it was 'monopolizing' gold purchases, the Bank advised the HSBC to lower its profile and limit its share to around 40 per cent of each shipment. The 'main objective at this stage', the Bank of England told the Hongkong Bank, 'is to ensure a continuance of outflow of gold from India'.[79] Norman confided to the governor of the New York Federal Reserve, his desire to 'gradually accumulate some gold, . . . from India', and the Bank's Bombay operations continued for much of the 1930s.[80]

As British officials recognized the link between sterling's depreciation against gold and Indian exports of the metal, they also learnt to manage sterling in a manner as to sustain these exports. The availability of gold from India, in turn, enabled smoother management of sterling in a climate marked by impending or actual competitive depreciation of rival currencies.

By December 1931, Treasury officials were privately ruling out a large increase in the sterling parity of about $3.40 unless world prices rose. Hence rather than allow speculative short-term inflows to push up sterling, officials decided to buy gold and strive rapidly to reduce the bank rate. If lower bank rates, easier credit, and exchange intervention 'do not cure the inflow, it will be necessary to let the pound respond in some degree. But I should keep any rise slow', an official noted.[81] The most important device for managing sterling·during these years was the Exchange Equalization Account (EEA), set up explicitly to 'keep *down* the pound'.[82] Enabling intervention in the gold and foreign exchange markets, the EEA allowed Britain to insulate her economy from speculative capital flows and preserve the cheap money conditions considered necessary for domestic recovery.

Indian gold exports played a noteworthy part in enabling the EEA to operate. Although Britain's capital account began to improve after she left the gold standard, London continued to face unpredictable outflows until early 1933 when the dollar came under attack, and when exchange uncertainty once again gripped the major money markets.[83] Hence the British authorities were unable to buy gold or foreign exchange without weakening sterling more than they desired to, and Indian gold exports came handy in this respect. For example in February 1932, the Bank of England managed to avoid a fall in sterling while it bought dollars and francs, thanks, among other reasons, to gold flows from India which accounted for two-thirds of Britain's total receipts of the metal during the month. With

> ... any diminution in supply (of gold) ... it would be by no means so easy to continue heavy ... purchase ... (of foreign exchange) ....
> Our store of gold is low . . . (and if we) should fail to purchase sufficient exchange [needed to repay loans and steady sterling in the autumn] it would be necessary to draw further on our gold reserves.[84]

Continued gold arrivals from India sustained sterling through seasonal drains the following autumn. Falling reserves and low interest rates caused a greater weakening of sterling than the British authorities wished to see. But '. . . Indian gold still . . . comes in at a substantial rate. We continue to get the advantage of it, and it is a material help at this difficult season of the year'.[85]

Britain's capital account no doubt improved after 1933. Yet gold receipts from India remained a key factor in the management of sterling. In spring that year, the Treasury, expecting widespread currency instability, greatly expanded the EEA, and began substituting gold in place of its holdings of foreign exchange. With the British demand for gold rising, Bank of England officials wondered whether London should not announce gold buying prices from time to time in a way as to 'afford a channel for the flow of gold from India'.[86] In the event, the extreme step was not taken. Yet, as Table 9.4 shows, additions to the account after 1933 were almost entirely in the form of gold. Clearly, had gold from India not been available, Britain would have been much more vulnerable to competitive American depreciation, and the EEA would have lost its teeth. Thus, regardless of the strength of Britain's capital account, sterling management continued to depend on greater gold availability.

Table 9.4   *Official British holdings of gold and foreign exchange, half-yearly, 1931–8*

Holdings as on	Foreign exchange	Gold	Holdings as on	Foreign exchange	Gold
30 Sept. 1931	12	167	27 Mar. 1935	−1	430
30 Mar. 1932	84	157	25 Sept. 1935	−2	497
30 Sept. 1932	26	226	25 Mar. 1936	0	522
31 Mar. 1933	48	314	30 Sept. 1936	−1	639
27 Sept. 1933	20	339	31 Mar. 1937	−10	716
27 Mar. 1934	0	422	30 Sept. 1937	8	820
25 Sept. 1934	−2	414	31 Mar. 1938	−2	835

Note: Amounts in £ million; 0 indicates holdings less than £ 0.5 million.

Source: Howson, 1980, *Sterling's Managed Float: The Operations of the Exchange Equalization Account, 1932–9*, Princeton Studies (Princeton), p. 62.

Hence the need to promote Indian gold exports became an important factor in the management of sterling during this period. In instructing the Hongkong and Shanghai Banking Corporation to stimulate gold exports from India and secure 'around 40 per cent' of each shipment of the metal by 'giving competition' to other purchasers, the Bank of England revealed a flexible attitude towards the sterling price of gold.[87] Subsequently, the principle of flexing sterling in order to increase gold exports from India appears to have become quite general. As officials in London saw it, the EEA's

> tendency is to draw out gold from hoards here and in India as has been seen in recent months. This results in an addition to gold stocks available for monetary purposes in the longer run . . . .[88]

Opposing a rise in sterling or its stabilization, Frederick Phillips, the chief Treasury adviser argued that the

> . . . most desired objective is a general rise in world . . . prices and . . . the most single powerful force to that end at the moment is the flow

of gold from India . . . that flows depends . . . on the depreciation of
the rupee, that is the depreciation of the sterling.

He added that at $3.60 or $3.70, gold exports from India would
not be checked, but at $3.90 they could cease. 'A rise in the sterling
would have a deadening effect [on Indian gold exports] which
would be most unfortunate . . . .'[89]

Gold Exports and the Indian Economy

While a major objective guiding sterling policy in the early years
of the float was to encourage gold releases from India yet, neither
the low sterling nor the liquidation and export of private stocks
of the metal helped raise Indian prices. As Table 9.5 shows, Indian
prices did not bottom out until March–April 1933, returning
durably to the September 1931 level only in the middle of 1935
and to the 1914 level (though not yet to the pre-Depression level)
in March 1937.

The impact of India's gold exports on her external financial
position is easy to follow. In the main, sterling receipts from
gold sales were used to reduce India's foreign debt and replenish
exchange reserves in London.[90] But their effects on the domestic
economy can do with more research. In recent years attention
has been drawn to the relatively benign macro-effects of the
Depression on the Indian economy; according to both
Sivasubramonian and Heston, real per capita incomes fell by less
than 3 per cent over five years (from about Rs 171 in 1930 to Rs
166 in 1935), and it is likely that gold dissaving and exports helped
cushion the overall impact of the slump.[91] Attention has also been
drawn to the rise in the deposits of commercial banks and post-
office savings banks during the Depression.[92] This increase is no
doubt significant, but since banks and post offices were located
overwhelmingly in cities and towns, perhaps more as an indicator
of changing urban asset holding habits or of worsening
distribution of incomes and wealth, than as that of general
prosperity. Note that deposits of rural cooperative banks did
not rise.[93]

Table 9.5   *Calcutta index of wholesale prices, 1929–37*

Year/ Month	1929	1930	1931	1932	1933	1934	1935	1936	1937
Jan.	145	131	98	97	88	90	94	92	98
Feb.	144	126	99	97	86	89	90	91	98
Mar.	143	125	100	94	82	88	87	91	100
Apr.	140	123	98	92	84	89	88	92	103
May	139	121	97	89	87	90	91	90	103
Jun.	138	116	93	86	89	90	91	90	102
Jul.	142	115	93	87	91	89	91	91	104
Aug.	143	114	92	91	89	88	89	90	105
Sep.	143	111	91	91	88	89	89	91	104
Oct.	140	107	96	91	88	89	93	93	104
Nov.	137	103	97	90	88	88	92	93	103
Dec.	134	100	98	88	89	88	93	94	101
Ann. av.	141	116	96	91	87	89	91	91	102

Note: All 1914=100.

Source: *Statistical Abstracts for British India,* 1937–8, p. 385; the index averaged 145 in 1928, with a peak of 146 (April, July, and November) and a trough of 142 (September).

Although few detailed studies are available, the Depression appears on the whole to have been a grim event for the large majority of people in rural areas from whom the bulk of the gold is said to have originated, and on whose behalf the British authorities claimed to be framing their policies. Commercialized segments of agriculture such as jute may have done worse than others, but elsewhere too the Depression extracted its price. The burden of rural indebtedness, in particular, became more crushing. According to Goldsmith, the nominal value of agricultural debt increased from Rs 11,500 million in 1929 to Rs 18,000 million in 1939. The rural debt–income ratio also doubled. A quarter of the farmer's income went towards debt servicing in 1939, as against an eighth in 1929. In the economy as a whole, not surprisingly, there was net dissaving.[94]

London officials were however interested only in the state of India's external account and oblivious to other indicators. In January 1932 Norman's advisor, Charles Addis warned the Bank of England that India's gold exports were leading to currency expansion which might combine with low interest rates to cause a rise in her internal prices.[95] In 1932, the Indian government attempted to impress upon Whitehall the need for policies to stimulate the economies of the sterling area. Rejecting Delhi's contention that India might otherwise be unable to meet her external liabilities after gold exports dried up, a Treasury official noted on the margin of the Indian government's memorandum, '430 million (ounces) of gold absorbed in last 70 years, 55 million (ounces) so far exported'.[96] Earlier, George Schuster, the Indian Finance Member, had urged Britain to keep primary producers' interests in mind whilst managing sterling. The official reply was non-committal, but privately the Treasury reaction was: '. . . the (Indian) tail can't expect to wag the Bulldog'.[97]

Whitehall's perspective on the necessary constituents of an Indian recovery had not changed even two years later. In July 1934 Strakosch expressed concern about the weakness of India's economic recovery, and suggested that sterling be so managed as to promote expansion in India and elsewhere in the Empire. Disregarding the price evidence, a Treasury official responded that he did not

> attach much weight to Strakosch's views as to the desperate plight of India; Cecil Kisch finance official at the India office tells me the financial position is greatly improved, and there is no doubt that India is getting through the crisis better than . . . any other country.[98]

A Gold Glut?

The counterfactual can be an interesting tool in economic history. Were it possible to use it here, the following might seem an obvious question to ask: had she faced the opposite kind of a financial problem, that is an excess supply of gold pushing up the costs of stabilizing it or threatening runaway inflation, might

Britain have wished to see Indians revert to their habit of 'hoarding' gold? Fortunately, there is no need to invent this counterfactual because a similar situation arose in real life.

Once the early shock passed, officials at the British Treasury came to value the ability a floating sterling gave them, of pursuing domestic stability without paying much heed to the external account.[99] They also resolved that a return to fixed exchange rates and the gold standard should not take place ahead of a sizeable increase in Britain's share of the world's gold reserves; until, that is, she had a 'gold basis larger than that required by any other country'. As a Treasury official put it,

> ... however inconvenient [it] ... may be when we are ... advocating economy in the use of gold, we have to face the fact that we could not risk going back to a ... gold standard without a larger share of the gold supply of the world ... .[100]

But within four years, the avalanche of gold pouring into Britain's reserves forced her officials to reconsider the issue. This section briefly recounts their response to this qualitatively new crisis.

Britain's efforts to accumulate gold during the 1930s were largely successful. As Table 9.4 shows, her gold holdings more than doubled between September 1933 and March 1938, rising also in relation to her imports and external liabilities (see Table 9.6).[101] Meanwhile, as commodity prices and world trade volumes stagnated, monetary gold reserves rose both in real terms and in relation to world trade. Britain's Economic Advisory Council (EAC) estimated that the gold value of world trade in 1936 was only 40 per cent of the 1929 level while the share of annual gold output going into official reserves had risen from 33 per cent to 125 per cent over the same period.[102]

This unusual situation now exercised British policy-makers. As the EAC pointed out, the accumulation of gold in New York and London 'was an embarrassment'.[103] Regretting that the minor central banks no longer held gold reserves, the council expressed fear that the burden to Britain and the USA of purchasing gold 'might eventually become intolerable, if the ... output of gold remains at its present level, still more if it increased'.[104] The balance of payments of the sterling area depended on gold exports, but if the USA decided to reduce her gold burden, Britain too would have to follow. Whatever the course of action adopted, it would have serious implications for Britain, global stability, and the future of gold as a monetary metal.[105]

Table 9.6 *British gold and foreign exchange reserves as proportion of net external liabilities and imports*

	As proportion			As proportion	
Year	(1) of net external liabilities	(2) of imports	Year	(1) of net external liabilities	(2) of imports
1931	51	18	1935	82	68
1932	53	27	1936	98	90
1933	69	38	1937	102	87
1934	71	60	1938	105	73

Source: Howson, 1980, *Sterling's Managed Float,* pp. 53–4.

Treasury officials expressed similar sentiments. They feared gold following in the wake of silver as excessive gold supplies damaged the metal's monetary role. A 'gold buyers' strike . . . (was) a real imminent danger', but if increased gold supplies must not lead to uncontrolled inflation, 'other means of absorbing gold must be found or developed', supplies checked, or its price gradually reduced. Central banks could absorb gold, but those that could afford it already had all the gold they wanted. The 'industrial arts and Eastern hoarders' were another prospect, but the high price was inhibiting demand from these quarters, and hastening release of the metal. After considering possible ways of easing the flood and highlighting the need for coordinating policy with the USA, an official recognized that the problem would not be resolved quickly or easily. Even though undecided as to the means of achieving it, he was nevertheless very clear about the desired outcome. Policy, he concluded, should aim to '*stimulate consumption for industrial purposes and . . . check or reverse the flow of gold from the East*'.[106]

The gold glut continued to be debated in Britain and the USA through much of 1937. But the indications were that an Anglo-American agreement to relieve the glut would be as difficult to achieve now as a coordinated solution to the opposite problem had been a decade earlier. However, before the position could become serious enough to force Britain's economic policy-makers to consider influencing macro- and reserve-policies in the 'east' in order, now, to increase gold absorption there, the issue was taken out of their hands by the American economy going into recession, and by the evolving political situation in Europe. London's gold stocks ceased to grow as rapidly after the autumn of 1937, and as war grew more imminent, short-term drains from London resumed. The Bank of England also resumed buying gold in Bombay through the newly-formed Reserve Bank of India, both to steady sterling and to build a war chest.[107] Assuring the governor of the Bank of England that India still possessed large quantities of gold, the governor of the Reserve Bank of India pointed out that

> the net decrease . . . (in Indian gold stocks) since 1931 has been barely sufficient to cancel the increase during the preceding seven years, and the total amount of gold in India at the end of 1937 is . . . approximately the same as it was at the end of 1923.[108]

Conclusion

The evidence that Britain regarded private Indian reserves of gold as an important counter-cyclical device during the Depression is inescapable. Britain's objective during the Depression (and more generally during the entire inter-war period) of a redistribution of the world's monetary gold reserves could have been achieved through a combination of domestic adjustment and US-induced global expansion. But the former was a contentious issue at home, while the USA was yet to grow into the global financial role that World War I thrust upon it. Britain's dependence during the 1920s on global expansion had compelled her to try and restrict the flow of gold to India which accompanied and checked a world boom. When the world went into a slump in 1929, she turned her attention towards the potential which India's private reserves of gold held as an external source of world expansion along the lines Keynes had anticipated. The behaviour of these reserves, far from being entirely spontaneous, was to a large extent assisted and encouraged by policy.

Thus apart from the primary effects of the Depression, macro-policy (anti-cyclical during the relatively expansionary 1920s but pro-cyclical during the 1930s) ensured that private Indian reserves would be liquidated to finance consumption or settle debts. Before 1931 this gold accumulated almost wholly in the Indian portion of the gold standard reserve. In other words, the Indian householder made up for reserve losses sustained in exchange intervention in a manner that would have pleasantly surprised even the most convinced advocates of a 'pure' gold standard. The pressure that was then mounted on the Indian government to export this gold to London should therefore be seen as the second of the two-part process by which India was expected to relieve Britain's problems in a fixed exchange-rate regime.

When sterling went off the gold standard in September 1931, the process, though not the underlying dynamics, changed. The pressure on the rupee eased and defensive intervention was no longer necessary. But distress gold sales continued in India, while sterling depreciation stimulated private exports of the metal. Thereafter, sterling policy was driven by the need to ensure the continuation of these exports. Thanks to private reserve liquidation and increased production of the metal during the Depression, Britain was only too successful in increasing her gold reserves. So much so, that by 1937, the problem plaguing her was no longer one of 'gold shortage' and deflation. Rather, the problem was a potentially inflationary gold glut, to eliminate which British officials began to pray for the revival of the very tendency they had earlier tried so hard to check, that is, India's large demand for gold. By now the latter, far from being alarming, had become positively alluring. The wheel had come full circle.

Notes

1. A. Fishlow, 1986, 'Lessons from the Past: Capital Markets during the 19th Century and the Inter-war Period', in M. Kahler, ed., *The Politics of International Debt* (Ithaca), p. 72.

2. B. J. Eichengreen, 1992, *Golden Fetters: The Gold Standard and the Great Depression* (New York), pp. 223–4.

3. B. J. Eichengreen and R. Portes, 1987, 'The Anatomy of Financial Crises', in A. K. Swoboda and R. Portes, eds, *Threats to International Financial Stability* (Cambridge), p. 15; for the rest of the world, the corresponding proportion was 80 per cent, falling to 50 per cent when Canada is excluded; also Eichengreen, 1992, *Golden Fetters*, pp. 226–7.

4. L. V. Chandler, 1971, *American Monetary Policy, 1928–41* (Washington), p. 35.

5. Committee on Finance and Industry (Macmillan Committee), 1931, *Report*, para. 311, 140–3; the other 'creditor' countries were Britain, Belgium, Holland, Switzerland, and Sweden.

6. D. H. Aldcroft, 1977, *From Versailles to Wall Street, 1919–1929* (London), p. 242; L. S. Presswell, 1978, '1925: The Burden of the Sterling', *Economic History Review*, 2nd Series, vol. 31, pp. 82–3, 88; Eichengreen and Portes, 1987, 'Anatomy of Financial Crises', p. 15; on Britain's lending checks, see J. M. Atkin, 1977, *British Overseas Investment, 1918–1931* (New York); R. S. Sayers, 1976, *The Bank of England 1891–1944*, vol. 3 (Cambridge), app. 30, pp. 288–91; also India Office Library and Records, London (IOLR), L/F/6/1033, f. 5837, Board of Trade Advisory Council, 'Trade Outlook and Foreign Loans', A.C. 119, 'Written Observations of Members of Council', April 1925.

7. Macmillan Committee, 1931, *Report*, para. 351; A. I. Bloomifield, 1959, *Monetary Policy under the International Gold Standard:1880–1914* (New York), p. 42 for a dissenting view.

8. Macmillan Committee, 1931, *Report*, paras. 301, 351–2; R. Triffin, 1960, *Gold and the Dollar Crisis* (New Haven), p. 66; K. Mouré, 1991, *Managing the Franc Poincaré: Economic Understanding and Political Constraint in French Monetary Policy* (Cambridge), ch. 2; J. Kooker, 1976, 'French Financial Diplomacy: the Inter-War Years', in B. Rowland, ed., *Balance of Power or Hegemony: The Inter-War Monetary System* (New York); A. Cairncross and B. J. Eichengreen, 1983, *Sterling in Decline: The Devaluations of 1931, 1949 and 1967* (Oxford), pp. 51–2; also see P. B. Kenen, 1963,

Reserve Asset Preferences and the Stability of the Gold Exchange Standard, Princeton Studies (Princeton) on the relationship between the distribution of the foreign short-term liabilities of the key-currency centre, and the stability of the key currency.

9. P. Fearon, 1979, *The Origins and Nature of the Great Slump, 1929–1932* (London), p. 51; B. Eichengreen, 1992, 'The Origins and Nature of the Great 'Slump Revisited', *Economic History Review*, 2nd series, vol. 45, p. 229; Eichengreen, 1992, *Golden Fetters*, pp. 280–1; Macmillan Committee, 1931, *Report*, paras. 165–6, and app. II.

10. Among the more recent studies, see Eichengreen, 1992, *Golden Fetters*, D. B. Kunz, 1987, *The Battle for Britain's Gold Standard* (London), R.W.D. Boyce, 1987, *British Capitalism at the Crossroads, 1919–1932: A Study in Politics, Economics and International Relations* (Cambridge), and P. Williamson, 1992, *National Crisis and National Government: British Politics, the Economy and Empire, 1926–1932* (Cambridge).

11. A. Boyle, 1967, *Montagu Norman* (London), p. 153; Boyce, 1987, *British Capitalism at the Crossroads*, pp. 196–7; Mouré, 1991, *Managing the Franc Poincaré*, pp. 49–65.

12. Public Record Office, London (PRO), T160/430, f. 12317/1. Leith-Ross to Waley, 30 May 1930; Britain liquidated a secret dollar reserve of $50 million and sought in other ways to minimize the deflationary effects of gold outflows; see Leith-Ross's note, 17 Nov. 1930; H. Clay, 1957, *Lord Norman* (London), pp. 254–5; Sayers, 1976, *Bank of England*, vol. 1, pp. 231–3.

13. PRO, T160/430 f. 12317/2, 'Gold Movements: Points for Discussion with the French Treasury', Leith-Ross's memorandum, 12 Feb. 1931; also see Mouré, 1987, *Managing the Franc Poincaré*, pp. 63–4.

14. Churchill College Archives, Cambridge (CCA), Hawtrey Papers, Htry 1/47, 'Bank Rate and the Crisis', Hawtrey's memorandum, 1 Aug. 1931; Macmillan Committee, 1931, *Report*, para. 351: by August 1931 even British firms were fleeing sterling; see PRO, Cab. 24/219, C.P. 3(31), 'The Financial Situation'; PREM 1/97, Reading to Prime Minister, 10 Sept. 1931; S. K. Howson, 1975, *Domestic Monetary Management in Britain, 1919–1939* (Cambridge), p. 70; Boyce, 1987, *British Capitalism at the Crossroads*, p. 340.

15. P. Williamson, 1984, 'A "Banker's Ramp"? Financiers and the British Political Crisis of August 1931', *English Historical Review*, vol. 99.

16. Sayers, 1976, *Bank of England,* vol. 1, pp. 347–50; Boyce, 1987, *British Capitalism at the Crossroads,* pp. 288–91; Bank of England, London (BOE), G14/313, Committee of Treasury, 30 Nov. and 7 Dec. 1927, 13 June 1928, 3 Sept., 10 Sept., 22 Oct. and 4 Nov. 1930; Norman's note, 1 March 1930; Treasury note, 2 March 1930; Moreau to Norman, 28 Dec. 1928 and 8 Jan. 1929; Norman to Lubbock, 2 Feb. 1929, to Harrison, 29 Aug. and 6 Sept. 1930; to Young, 6 Sept. 1930; Young to Norman, 4 Sept. 1930; Harrison to Norman, 4 Sept. 1930; 'League Inquiry into the Stabilization of Gold', by Siepmann, 26 Nov. 1928; on the delegation's report, see Eichengreen, 1992, *Golden Fetters,* pp. 198–201.

17. PRO, T170/46, 'Gold Standard Rationalization: Notes', undated; T160/430, f. 12317/1, Hawtrey to Hopkins, 10 Dec. 1930; Boyce, 1987, *British Capitalism at the Crossroads,* pp. 290–1.

18. Royal Institute of International Affairs, 1931, *The International Gold Problem* (Oxford); Clay, 1957, *Lord Norman,* p. 246; I. M. Drummonol, 1981, *Floating Pound and the Sterling Area, 1931–39* (Cambridge), pp. 128–33; D. E. Moggridge, 1989, 'The Gold Standard and National Financial Policies, 1913–39', in P. Mathias and S. Pollard, eds, *Cambridge Economic* History of Europe, vol. VIII: *The Industrial Economies: The Development of Economic and Social Policies* (Cambridge), pp. 291–5; Macmillan Committee, QQ. 6724–5.

19. Macmillan Committee, 1931, *Report,* paras. 140–50, 185, 240.

20. Drummond, 1981, *Floating Pound and the Sterling Area,* p. 139; J. M. K. Keynes, 'Proposals for an International Clearing Union', in D. E. Moggridge and E. Johnson, eds, 1971–80, *Collected Writings,* vol. xxv (London) (hereafter *JMK xxv* etc.), pp. 72–7, 93–4; Armand van Dormael, 1978, *Bretton Woods: Birth of a Monetary System* (London); Marcello De Cecco, 1979, 'Origins of the Post-war Payments System', *Cambridge Journal of Economics,* vol. 3, pp. 49–61.

21. IOLR, L/F/5/100, Finance Department Statistics, pp. 205–06; L/F/6/1191, f. 2784, 'Statistical Note on Indian Finance'; colln. 107, L/F/7/897, Western India Liberal Association to Secretary of State, 13 March 1931; National Archives of India, New Delhi (NAI), Government of India, Finance Department (GOIFD), f. no. 5(I)-F-1928, particularly the Controller of Currency's telegram, 13 Aug. 1928.

22. IOLR, L/F/5/100, Finance Department Statistics, pp. 117–19; L/F/5/101, p. 119. See *John Bullion's Empire,* chapter 5.

23. Not unexpectedly, since she was predominantly an exporter of primary products, the terms of trade also moved against India; see K. N. Chaudhuri, 1982, 'Foreign Trade and the Balance of Payments c. 1757–1947', in Dharma Kumar and M. Desai, eds, *Cambridge Economic History of India*, vol. 2 (Cambridge), p. 840.

24. Federal Reserve Bank of New York (FRBNY), C252, Case to Crane, 4 Nov. 1928, for an early assessment of lower Indian gold imports.

25. PRO, T175/57, part 2, Phillips's memoranda, 27–9 Feb.; letter to Henderson, 26 Feb. 1932; *JMK xxi*, pp. 70–2; *JMK ix*, p. 353; BOE, OV 48/9, 'Factors Influencing the Movement in Gold Prices', by Per Jacobsson, 12 March 1932; OV 48/10, 'The Future of the Gold Standard', also by Per Jacobsson, April 1934, p. 24.

26. Moggridge, 1989, 'Gold Standard', p. 313; C. F. Diaz-Alejandro, 1982, 'Latin America in Depression, 1929–39', in Mark Gersovitz, Carlos F. Diaz-Alejandro, Gustav Ranis, and Mark R. Rosenzweig, eds., 1982, *The Theory and Experience of Economic Development: Essays in Honour of Sir William Arthur Lewis* (London); Fishlow, 1986, 'Lessons from the Past'; also see the essays in R. Thorp, ed.,1984, *Latin America in the 1930s: The Role of the Periphery in the World Crisis* (London).

27. CCA, Hawtrey Papers, 1/3/2, Hawtrey to Balckett, 16 Oct. 1925; Nehru Memorial Museum and Archives, New Delhi (NMMA), Purushottamdas Thakurdas Papers (PT Papers), f. 105, Smith to Thakurdas, 20 Nov. 1930; *JMK xvi*, pp. 7–8; as the rupee was effectively on a sterling standard and sterling remittances were the cheapest means of moving funds from India, rupee holders buying dollars or francs had first to buy sterling. Hence a weak sterling also meant a weak rupee.

28. PRO, PREM 1/97, Reading to Prime Minister, 10 Sept. 1931; Howson,1975, *Domestic Monetary Management*, p.70; Boyce,1987, *British Capitalism at the Crossroads*, p. 340.

29. IOLR, I/F/6/1180, f. 6060, Viceroy to Secretary of State, 16 Sept. 1931; L/F/5/189, Stewart to Lord Chancellor, 21 Aug. 1931.

30. NAI, GOIFD, f. 5(2)-F-1929, conference with exchange bankers, 27 Nov. 1929; f. no. 1(2)-F-1930, Lindsay to Trade Commissioner on a conversation with Sir Thomas, 8 April 1930; O. Goswami, 1985, 'Then Came the Marwaris': Some Aspects of the Changes in the Pattern of Industrial Control in Eastern India', *Indian Economic and Social History Review*, vol. 22.

31. IOLR, L/F/7/474, f. 22, colln. 43, Viceroy to Secretary of State, 9 &10 May 1931.

32. See C. Bridge, 1986, *Holding India to the Empire: The British Conservative Party and the 1935 Constitution* (Delhi), chs. 3–4 for a good account of these developments; the quote is from p. 153; also see S. Sarkar, 1983, *Modern India, 1885–1947* (Delhi), ch. 6.

33. Samuel Hoare, 1935, *Speeches by the Secretary of State for India* (London), p. 10; R. Kapadia, 1988, 'The Bombay Business Community and Economic Policy-Making, 1917–37', M.A. Dissertation, University of Pennsylvania, p. 18.

34. Citing political instability, Delhi pleaded for a stand-by credit of £100 million; London rejected the plea, but undertook to guarantee Indian debts in the new regime; see PRO, T160/400 f. 12471/03/1–2 and IOLR, L/F/6/1177 f. 3693; this episode is discussed in B. R. Tomlinson, 1979, 'Britain and the Indian Currency Crisis 1930–2' (chapter 8 in this volume), *Economic History Review*, 2nd series, vol. 32 and Drummond, 1981, *Floating Pound and the Sterling Area*; London's refusal to grant 'monetary autonomy' to India is discussed in Balachandran, 1996, *John Bullion's Empire*, ch. 8.

35. NAI, GOIFD, f. no. 1(2)-F-1930; Lindsay to Trade Commissioner, 8 April 1930, quoting Sir Thomas; the views of the currency controllers are in 1-(2)-F-1930, and 1-8(F)-1931, parts 1 and 2.

36. FRBNY, Harrison Papers 3115.2, note of telephone conversation with Norman, 11 June 1931.

37. See Note 25.

38. BOE, OV 9/17, Denning to Kisch, 5 March 1930; Kisch to Niemeyer, 22 March; reply, 24 March 1930; Niemeyer to Schuster, 22 April 1930.

39. PRO, T177/12, Phillips to Hopkins, 20 July 1934.

40. PRO, T172/1756, Treasury memorandum, 'The Balance of Payments', n.d. but summer of 1931; more generally, Eichengreen, 1992, *Golden Fetters*, p. 280.

41. IOLR, L/F/5/189, Secretary of State to Viceroy, 10 Sept. 1931.

42. BOE, OV 9/17, pt. 2, 'Mr. Goodenough's visit', Niemeyer's note, 8 Jan. 1930; G1/411, McWatters's memorandum, 2 Aug. 1930; G14/96, Committee of Treasury, 26 Nov. 1930.

43. Summary based on IOLR, L/F/5/189, Kisch's 'The Exchange Question', 24 Nov. 1930; L/F/6/1183 f. 6444, Hoare's note, 30 Aug.; Kisch's 'The Effect on the Indian Economy and Credit of a

Collapse of the Rupee Exchange', 18 Sept. 1931; L/F/6/1201 f. 1291, League of Nations, Monetary and Economic Conference, provisional minutes, 10 Jan. 1933; L/F/5/189, appendix, 'The Ratio Controversy' in Stewart to the Lord Chancellor, 21 Aug. 1931.

44. IOLR, L/F/6/1183 f. 6619, meeting on financial questions, 16 Oct. 1931, p. 34.
45. BOE, G14/96, Committee of Treasury, 26 Nov. 1930; Gubbay to Shaw, 1 Dec. 1930; a former currency official in India Gubbay now headed the P&O Banking Corporation.
46. BOE, OV/17, Schuster to Niemeyer, 15 Jan. 1928; Clay, 1957, *Lord Norman*, p. 368.
47. IOLR, L/F/5/102, Finance Department Statistics, pp. 51-2.
48. IOLR, L/F/6/1177, f. 3693, Norman to Kisch, 5 May 1931, who agreed in advance on the wording of the letter–BOE, ADM 20/20, Norman's diary, 5 May; OV/56/51, memoranda by Kershaw and Catterns, 4 May and 28 May 1931; G14/96, Norman's report to the Committee of Treasury, 10–11 June 1931; IOLR, L/F/6/1175, f. 2222, Secretary of State to Viceroy, 18 April 1931.
49. Reserve Bank of India, 1953, *Banking and Monetary Statistics of India* (Bombay), p. 693.
50. NMMA, PT Papers, Smith to Thakurdas, 27 Nov. 1930; BOE, OV/9/17, Smith to Strakosch, 2 Dec. 1930; also see NAI, GOIFD, f. no. 5(2)-F-1929, Smith to Controller of Currency, 8 Feb. 1929; and Sanjiva Row's notes, 6 Feb. and 9 Feb. 1929.
51. *East India Finance and Accounts*, HMSO, London, various years.
52. BOE, OV/9/17, Niemeyer to Smith, 10 July 1929; reply, 22 Aug. 1929.
53. NAI, GOIFD, f. no. 1(8)-F-1931, part 1, Dawson to the Manager, Imperial Bank of India, Lahore, 30 March 1931.
54. IOLR, L/F/6/1172 f. 37, P &O Bank to Kisch, 1 Jan. 1931; Viceroy to Secretary of State, 1 April 1931 in L/F/6/1175 f. 2222; 24 April 1931 in colln. 43, L/F/7/474 f. 22; 20 Jan. 1932 in L/F/6/1188; G. Schuster, 1979, *Private Work and Public Causes: A Personal Record* (Cardiff), p. 115; NAI, GOIFD, f. no. 1(8)-F-1931-1, Kelly's letters, 25 Mar., 25 April, and 30 May 1931.
55. The 1920 stabilization episode is discussed in Balachandran, *John Bullion's Empire*, ch. 4.
56. For empirical evidence that such measures worked in the 1930s, see B. Eichengreen and J. S. Sachs, 1985, 'Exchange Rates and

Economic Recovery in the 1930s', *Journal of Economic History*, vol. 45, and J. M. Campa, 1990, 'Exchange Rates and Economic Recovery in the 1930s: An Extension to Latin America', *Journal of Economic History*, vol. 50.

57. BOE, OV/9/17, Niemeyer to Smith, 10 July 1929; reply, 22 Aug. 1929; also see Notes 52 and 53.

58. BOE, OV/9/17, Niemeyer's note on Fisher's 'India', 4 April 1930; BOE, OV 56/1, 'Gold' by Catterns, 15 April 1931.

59. Reserve Bank of India, *Banking and Monetary Statistics*, p. 668 for reserve figures; IOLR, colln. 43, f 22, L/F/7/474, Viceroy to Secretary of State, 24 April, 13 July, 31 Aug. 1931; Secretary of State to Viceroy, 28 April, 6 May 1931; Baxter's note, 26 Aug. 1931; Secretary of State to Viceroy, 28 Aug., 10 Sept. and 17 Sept. 1931; L/F/6/1175, f. 2222, 'Notes on Viceroy's telegram of 24 April 1931' and minute by Kisch, 4 May 1931; L/F/6/1178, f. 4247, Secretary of State to Viceroy, 30 June 1931.

60. FRBNY, Harrison Papers, 3117.1, telephonic talks with E. M. Harvey, Deputy Governor, Bank of England, 30 July and 3 Aug. 1931; Sayers, 1976, *Bank of England*, vol. 3, app. 22, pp. 257–61; George Harrison was Strong's successor as Governor of the New York Federal Reserve.

61. Sayers, 1976, *Bank of England*, vol. 1, pp. 309–13; Macmillan Committee, Minutes of Evidence, QQ. 340–53.

62. BOE, OV 56/1, P&O telegram from Bombay, 21 Aug. 1931.

63. FRBNY, Harrison Papers, 3117.1 telephone conversation with Harvey, 17 Sept. 1931; Bank of England files are silent on this subject, and even routine reports to the Committee of Treasury are available only with large blanks; also see Sayers, 1976, *Bank of England*, vol. 1, p. 259; and vol. 2, pp. 626–39.

64. The relevant exchanges are in IOLR, colln. 43, f. 22, L/F/7/474, L/F/6/1181, f. 6195; L/F/6/1180, f. 6060; PRO, T160 400/ F12471, annex 7; for accounts of this episode, see Tomlinson, 1979, 'Britain and the Indian Currency Crisis'; Drummond, 1981, *Floating Pound and the Sterling Area*, pp. 41–3; George Schuster, the Indian Finance Member, believed that London delayed news about sterling to present him with a *fait accompli*; see Schuster, 1979, *Private Work and Public Causes*, pp. 112–5.

65. For an idea of the price differentials during 1931–2, see D. Rothermund, 1992, *India in the Great Depression, 1929–1939* (New Delhi), pp. 48–9; and Drummond, 1981, *Floating Pound and the Sterling Area*, p. 48.

66. L. Katzen, 1964, *Gold and the South African Economy* (Amsterdam), pp. 18–9, 40–1, and 60–1; South Africa produced about 60 per cent of the world's gold.

67. IOLR, L/F/5/102, Finance Department Statistics, p. 9.

68. BOE, OV 56/1, Strakosch to Kershaw, 24 Dec. 1931; EID 3/194, 'Exports of Gold from India', 23 Dec. 1931; OV 56/3, 'India: Gold and Silver', 12 July 1937, both by Kershaw; FRBNY, C261, Osborne (Bank of England) to Crane, 13 Jan. 1932.

69. Rothermund, D., 1988, *An Economic History of India: From Precolonial Times to 1986* (London), pp. 104–05; as an All India Congress Committee pamphlet put it, it was 'deplorable' that people had to live off their savings; that they obtained higher prices for it was 'a mitigation of their misfortune'; *Indian Currency and Exchange*, Congress Golden Jubilee Brochure no. 11 (Allahabad, 1935), p. 30.

70. University Library, Cambridge (ULC), Baldwin 105, Willingdon to Baldwin, 17 Jan. 1932.

71. CCA, Grigg Papers 2/20, Stewart to Grigg, 19 Oct. 1934; PRO, T160/400, f. 12471, annex 7, 'The Repayment of an Indian Loan: An Incident in the History of Whitehall Control', C.P.23(32), 15 Jan. 1932, and cabinet resolution, 20 Jan. 1932.

72. BOE, OV 56/1, note by Catterns, 2 Oct. 1931.

73. The *Economist*, the *Investors' Chronicle*, both 30 Jan. 1932.

74. Chamberlain's letter to his sister, quoted in Bridge, 1986, *Holding India to the Empire*, pp. 73–4.

75. BOE, EID 3/194, Kershaw's 'Exports of Gold from India', 23 Dec. 1931; FRBNY, Harrison Papers, 3115.3, telephonic talk with Norman, 10 Feb. 1932.

76. PRO, T160/400, f. 12471, annex 7, Robinson's note, 21 Sept. 1931; f. 12471/06/2, Waley's minute; Leith-Ross to Kershaw, both 22 Jan. 1932; also see T160/474, f. 12471/06/2, Kisch to Leith Ross, 25 Jan. 1932; Hopkins to Leith-Ross, 26 Jan. 1932.

77. BOE, G1/411, Niemeyer's note, 31 May 1934; Grigg to Norman, 21 May 1934; 'An export tax on Indian gold', separate memoranda by Kershaw and Niemeyer, and by Taylor, both 17 May 1934.

78. BOE, G1/308, copy of Indian government telegram, 18 March 1933 and Kershaw's undated note; NAI, GOIFD, f. no. 2(18)-F-1932, Lala Jagdish Prasad's speech; also see f. no. 1(11)-F-1933.

79. BOE, C43/279, H.S.B.C. cables, J. K. Hutton, (London) to H. D. C. Jones (Bombay), 21 & 22 Jan. 1932; Jones to Hutton, 8 & 9 Feb. 1932; Hutton to F. B. Rickett (Bombay) 13 May 1932; F. H. H. King, 1988, *History of the Hongkong and Shanghai Bank*, 3 vols. (Cambridge), vol. 3, pp. 195–6; National Archives and Records Administration, Washington, D. C. (NARA), GB 120, American consul's despatch from Bombay, 23 Jan. 1933.

80. FRBNY, Harrison Papers, 3117.2, telephone conversation with Norman, 16 June 1932; BOE., C43/279, 'Intervention in the Bombay Bullion Market', by Catterns, 29 Nov. 1935; also C43/259; NARA, GB 120, US Consular's reports, 13 Feb. and 5 Sept. 1933; Treasury Dept., Haas to Secretary Morgenthau, 15 Dec. 1936; RG 59, box 6238, 845.51/185, American Consul's report, 29 Mar. 1939; 845.51/192, Chandler to Murphy, 6 Feb. 1939; US Consul's despatch, 2 Aug., 12 Aug., and 27 Sept. 1939; and 15 Nov. 1939 in box 6240, 845.5151/97; also see R. A. C. Parker, 1983, 'The Pound Sterling, the American Treasury and British Preparations for War, 1938–1939', *English Historical Review*, vol. 98.

81. PRO, T175/57, Hopkins's 'Note on Mr. Keynes's memorandum of 16 November', 16 Dec. 1931; T175/57, Phillips's memorandum, 5 March 1932; S. K. Howson and D. Winch, 1977, *The Economic Advisory Council, 1930–39* (Cambridge), pp. 104–05.

82. 'We cannot however put it quite as bluntly as that . . .'; PRO, T175/57, 'Exchange Equalilzation Account Proposals', Hopkins's note, 6 April 1932, emphasis in original; Howson 1975, *Domestic Monetary Management*; S. K. Howson, 1980, *Sterling's Managed Float: The Operations of the Exchange Equalization Account, 1932–39*, Princeton Studies (Princeton); Sayers, *Bank of England*, vol. 3, app. 24, pp. 266–9.

83. Howson, 1975, *Domestic Monetary Management*, p. 102; for balance of payments data, see Pressnell, 1978, 'Burden of Sterling', p. 88.

84. PRO, T175/57, Phillips's memorandum, 'The Present Position of the Pound', n.d., but Feb. 1932; also see Committee on Financial Questions, 'Report on Sterling Policy', March 1932, in Howson and Winch, 1977, *Economic Advisory Council*, pp. 254–63, paras. 3–4.

85. PRO, T175/70, note to the Chancellor, 15 Oct. 1932; T172/2082, memorandum, 21 Jan. 1933, both by Hopkins.

86. BOE, C43/139, 'Exchange Control', 20 April 1933; also see Kershaw's memorandum, 21 April 1933.

87. See Note 79; but by October 1932 the Bank was more willing than the Treasury to stabilize sterling, but exchange policy had come firmly under the latter's control; BOE, C43/139, 'The Foreign Demand for the Return of the United Kingdom to Gold', memorandum on Bank-Treasury conference, 29 Oct. 1932.

88. BOE, C43/22, Phillips to Hambro, 23 May 1932 and Hambro's undated reply; FRBNY, C261, Osborne to Crane, 13 Jan. 1932.

89. R. O., T175/57, part 2, Phillips's memorandum, 27–9 Feb.; letter to Henderson, 26 Feb. 1932; see Howson and Winch, 1977, *Economic Advisory Council*, pp. 104–05 on the significance of this memorandum.

90. Reserve Bank of India, *Banking and Monetary Statistics*, pp. 881 and 668 respectively.

91. O. Goswami, 1986, 'The Depression, 1930–1935: Its effects on India and Indonesia', *Itinerario*, vol. 10, pp. 164–5; for easily accessible national income estimates, see A. Heston, 1982, 'National Income', in Dharma Kumar and M. Desai, eds, *Cambridge Economic History of India*, vol. 2 (Cambridge), and R. W. Goldsmith, 1983, *The Financial Development of India, 1860–1977* (Delhi), p. 69.

92. B. R. Tomlinson, 1979, *The Political Economy of the Raj, 1914–1947: The Economics of Decolonization in India* (London), p. 38.

93. Goldsmith, 1983, *Financial Development of India*, pp. 126–8.

94. Goldsmith, 1983, *Financial Development of India*, pp. 126–8; O. Goswami, 1984, 'Agriculture in the Slump: the Peasant Economy of East and North Bengal in the 1930s', *Indian Economic and Social History Review*, vol. 21, pp. 347–58 (reprinted as chapter 6 in this volume); C. J. Baker, 1984, *The Indian Rural Economy, 1880–1955: The Tamilnad Countryside* (Delhi), pp. 577–8; U. Patnaik, 1991, 'Food Availability and Famine: A Longer View', *Journal of Peasant Studies*, vol. 19, pp. 8–11; more generally, see Rothermund, 1992, *India in the Great Depression*.

95. BOE, OV 56/51, note by Catterns, 14 Jan. 1932, of a meeting with Addis.

96. PRO, T177/8, 'Memorandum on Effects of the Fall in Prices', June 1932, and Phillips's pencilled comment.

97. PRO, T160/474, f. 12471/06/2, Viceroy to Secretary of State, 9 March 1932; Treasury to India Office, 23 March 1932; Leith-Ross's remarks on Waley's note, 5 March 1932; BOE, G1/308, Viceroy's telegram, 18 April 1932, and memorandum; Delhi's

views are in NAI, GOIFD, f. no. 17(36)-F-1932, Denning's note, 14 April; memorandum, 16 April 1932; Viceroy's telegrams, 15, 16, & 18 April, and 20 & 28 May 1932; Warren's note, 16 May 1932; Schuster's note, 17 May 1932; and memorandum 'India and the Management of the Pound Sterling'; 17(71)-F-1933, speeches of Schuster and Strakosch at the Ottawa Conference; Taylor's note, 31 May 1933; Drummond, 1981, *Floating Pound and the Sterling Area*, pp. 23–7.

98. PRO, T177/12, Phillips to Hopkins, 20 July 1934.

99. Howson and Winch, 1977, *Economic Advisory Council*, pp. 100–105.

100. PRO, T175/17, part 2, Hopkins's note, 30 March on 'Exchange Equalization Accounts' by Phillips, 27 March 1933; T172/1775, Phillips's and Ferguson's briefs for the Chancellor, 7 March 1934.

101. Other Western central banks also gained gold; PRO, T177/39, Phillips to Per Jacobson, 28 Aug.; reply 3 Sept. 1937.

102. PRO, T160/77, f. 15583, Committee on Economic Information (CEI), 23rd Report, Oct. 1937, part 2, 'International Trade, the Price Level and the Gold Problem', para. 52, table 24; Howson and Winch, 1977, *Economic Advisory Council*, pp. 145–7.

103. CEI, 23rd Report, para. 45 (iv).

104. CEI, 23rd Report, paras. 54–5.

105. CEI, 23rd Report, paras. 73–6; also see BOE, ADM 22/14 and C43/141.

106. PRO, T175/94 part 1, 'The Present and Future of Gold' by Phillips, italics supplied; BOE, OV 48/11, 'Gold Price', memorandum by Catterns, 9 June 1937.

107. Parker, 1983, 'The Pound Sterling', pp. 275–6.

108. BOE, OV 56/86, Taylor to Norman, 17 Aug. 1938; also see Drummond, 1981, *Floating Pound and the Sterling Area*, pp. 224–48; Howson, 1975, *Domestic Monetary Management*, p. 136; Howson and Winch, 1977, *Economic Advisory Council*, pp. 146–7.

Index

Munro, Thomas 63
Muslim peasants 204
'mutiny' 78, 119, 175
Myint, Hla 63
Mymensingh 204

Naoroji, Dadabhai 1, 5, 6, 7, 30,
  33n, 55, 57, 58, 62, 63, 71, 72, 73,
  84, 118, 125, 167
    on 'drain of wealth' 123
Napoleonic wars 18
Narainganj Chamber of
  Commerce 185
National income 3, 47, 94
nationalists, Indian
    on 'drain of wealth' 1, 47, 48,
      109, 110, 121–9
    on monetary policy of British
      India 246
Nattukottai Chettiars 28, 35n
Nevill, H.R. 165
New Zealand 260, 261
Niemeyer, Otto 271, 281, 285
Norman, Montagu 16, 269, 270,
  271, 276, 278, 279, 286
North Bengal 181
Northbrook, Lord 114, 117

O'Brien, Patrick 6
O'Conor, J.E. 33n
Opium War 174
Ottawa Conference 259

Paish, G. 134, 136, 144
Palmer, Horsley 56, 62
Pandit, Y.S. 61n, 134, 135, 136,
  144
Paper Currency Reserve (PCR)
  142, 224, 251, 272
peasant(s)
    economy in Bengal 183, 185,
      186, 211

subsistence expenditure 217
uprising and revolts 173,
  204
Permanent Debt 78
Permanent Settlement 173
plantation workers from India 26
Phillips, Frederick 288
'political drain' 119
political reforms 276–7
population growth 187, 206, 211
post-office savings banks 289
poverty 51, 82, 122
Poverty in India 57
Presidency Banks 13, 177n, 224
price(s) 162–3, 166
    domestic 163–5
    and exchange rates 161
    of food grain exports 163–4
    and wages 165
Princely States 58
Proclamation of 1858 83
'productive debt', accumulation of
  111, 128
productive expenditure 108, 109
protection(ism)
    France 53
    Germany 53
public debt 79, 112–14, 175
    'productive debt' 111, 128
    'unproductive debt' 78, 110–11
public works 123
    expenditure on 111–114
    nationalists' views 126
    rate of return on 114

Ragi 164
railways construction 52
    cost 76–8, 89n, 126–8, 179
    and decline in Indian handicrafts
      51
    expansion 159

and irrigation *108, 109*
profitability *126–7*
and trade *11*
railway guarantees *77, 126*
raiyati holdings *218*
transfer of *206–08*
raiyats in Bengal *181, 182–3, 187, 198*
jute and winter rice *200–02*
Ranade, M.G. *72, 79*
Ray, Prithwis Chandra *72*
Raychaudhuri, Tapan *181*
remittances from India *49, 58, 59, 72–3, 75, 100–03, 122, 139, 140*
control over *98–104*
through Council Bills *94, 95, 132–3*
through currency reserve *248, 250*
private remittances *88n, 121, 129*
of tax revenues *124*
Report on Indian Expenditure 118
Reserve Bank of India *258, 294*
Reserve Bank of India Act *258*
Reverse Council Bills (RCBs) *100, 102–03*
Ricardo, David *56*
rice
area under cultivation *215*
costs of cultivation *216–17*
exports *163*
and jute *216–17*
prices *191, 195, 210*
Robertson, J.A. *166*
Rosebury, Lord *117*
Rothschild, Lord *229*
Rothermund, D. *283*
round-table conferences *252, 253, 263n, 276*
Rousseaux, P. *155*

Royal Committee on Indian Currency *see* Herschell Committee
Royal Commission on Indian Currency and Finance *see* Hilton-Yong Commission
Royal Institute of International Affairs *271*
Rupee
demonetization *105*
depreciation *19–20, 104–06*
devaluation *252–4, 260, 277*
and impact on British exporters *278*
exchange rates *74–5, 99, 142, 170–1, 227, 247*
loans *112, 115*
measures to stabilize *105*
revaluation *281*
and silver coinage *20*
stabilization of *75, 234, 235*
sterling link *65–6. 229, 246, 255*
weakness *275–6*
rural indebtedness *189, 290*
ruralization of India *52*
Russian-British rivalry *175*

Samuelson, P.A. *161*
Saul, S.B. *16, 63, 155, 156, 163*
Schuster, George *252, 260, 262n, 291*
Secretary of State, for India *103, 225, 235 see also* India Office
reserve accumulation and money supply *133, 142*
select committees *64, 110, 149n*
Sen, N. *171*
Sen, Sunanda *30, 93*
Sen, S.B. *161*
Settlement Report *182*
Seven Years' War *21*

Notes on Contributors

G. Balachandran is Professor of Economic History at the Delhi School of Economics, University of Delhi, and Professor of International History and Politics at the Graduate Institute of International Studies, Geneva.

K. N. Chaudhuri was formerly Vasco da Gama Professor of the History of European Expansion at the European University Institute, Florence.

John McLane is Professor of History and Director of the Asian Studies programme at Northwestern University, Illinois.

Sunanda Sen retired as Professor, Centre of Economic Studies and Planning, Jawaharlal Nehru University, New Delhi.

Amiya K. Bagchi retired as Professor, Centre for the Study of Social Sciences, Kolkata.

Omkar Goswami is currently Chief Economist at the Confederation of Indian Industry, New Delhi.

Marcello de Cecco is Professor of Monetary Economics, Faculty of Economics, University of Rome 'La Sapienza'.

B. R. Tomlinson is Dean, Faculty of Arts and Humanities, School of Oriental and African Studies, London.